M000049928

Perception

Central Problems of Philosophy

Series Editor: John Shand

This series of books presents concise, clear, and rigorous analyses of the core problems that preoccupy philosophers across all approaches to the discipline. Each book encapsulates the essential arguments and debates, providing an authoritative guide to the subject while also introducing original perspectives. This series of books by an international team of authors aims to cover those fundamental topics that, taken together, constitute the full breadth of philosophy.

Published titles

Forthcoming titles

Perception

Barry Maund

McGill-Queen's University Press
Montreal & Kingston • Ithaca

© Barry Maund 2003

ISBN 0-7735-2465-7 (bound)
ISBN 0-7735-2466-5 (paper)

This book is copyright under the Berne Convention.
No reproduction without permission.
All rights reserved.

Published simultaneously outside North America
by Acumen Publishing Limited

McGill-Queen's University Press acknowledges the financial support of
the Government of Canada through the Book Publishing Development
Program (BPIDP) for its activities.

National Library of Canada Cataloguing in Publication Data

Maund, Barry
    Perception / Barry Maund.

(Central problems of philosophy)
Includes bibliographical references and index.
ISBN 0-7735-2465-7 (bound).—ISBN 0-7735-2466-5 (pbk.)

    1. Perception (Philosophy) I. Title. II. Series.

B828.45.M37 2003   121'.34   C2003-900348-5

Designed and typeset by Kate Williams, Abergavenny.
Printed and bound by Biddles Ltd., Guildford and King's Lynn.

For Gavin, Chris and Jeremy

Contents

Preface

The philosophical issues raised by perception make it one of the central topics in the philosophical tradition. Debate about the nature of perceptual knowledge and the objects of perception comprises a thread that runs through the history of philosophy. In some historical periods the major issues have been predominantly epistemological, and related to scepticism, for example, to doubts raised over whether we have knowledge of the objects that we take ourselves to perceive, and that we ordinarily take to exist independently of us. But an adequate understanding of perception is important more widely, for example, for metaphysics, philosophy of mind, philosophy of language and philosophy of science.

Even for epistemology, there are issues wider than those of sceptical doubt. For example, given that we do have knowledge, we are faced with such questions as: what do we have knowledge of? What grounds for knowledge do we actually apply? How do we acquire this knowledge? And to answer these questions an account of the role of perception is important.

Such issues, moreover, run into those discussed in metaphysics and the philosophy of mind and language. Central are such questions as: are the objects of perception mental or material? Do these objects exist independently of the act of perceiving or are they constructed? What is the nature and role of perceptual experience? What is the role of thought in perception? Of concepts? What role does perception and perceptual experience play in thought? What are sensations and what role do they play in perception?

This set of questions presents a forbidding set of issues. The difficulty and complexity of the problems raised by such questions perhaps explains why it is so hard to get agreement about theories of perception, especially given that discussion of them has continued, on and off, for almost 3000 years. The fact that we are no closer now than we ever were to consensus on the major questions is one of the remarkable features of the current status of the philosophical debate about perception. Another of these features is that for a lengthy period in the twentieth century, the topic of perception and its central issues were largely ignored. What is additionally remarkable is that for most of the first half of that century the topic was of paramount significance.

In this book I intend to develop a philosophical framework that will be helpful in thinking about at least some of these major issues, while also throwing light on the curious history of the philosophy of perception in the twentieth century. I shall argue that there are resources in the longer philosophical tradition that can be reworked to help solve some of the greater problems in this philosophical area.

Some of the material in Chapter 8 has its origins in my article, "Tye on Phenomenal Character and Content", *Philosophical Studies* (forthcoming 2003) and published in an abbreviated form online at http://host.uniroma3.it/progetti/kant/field/tyesymp.htm "A Field Guide to the Philosophy of Mind", pp. 34–47, e-published by the Philosophy Department of Università di Roma III. I am grateful to the editors and publishers for permission to reproduce part of this material.

1 The philosophy of perception

The most natural view to take of perception is that it is a process by which we acquire knowledge of an objective world. We take this world to consist of physical objects and happenings, which exist independently of us and our acts of perceiving, and which are the things we commonly perceive. Problems arise, however, when we reflect on the nature of that process and on how the knowledge is supposed to be acquired. Many of the traditional puzzles of perception arose, for example, when people tried to make sense of the fact that in different circumstances the same things appeared differently, either to different people placed differently, or to the same person on different occasions. Crucial questions that arose were whether we ever know what objects were really like, as opposed to how they appeared, and indeed whether how they appeared had anything to do with what they were really like. Such ancient puzzles were refuelled as the scientific revolution developed, as Galileo, Descartes, Locke and others attempted to make sense of the relationship between perceptual experience and the physical world; and more recently in the philosophy of science, where it has become widely believed that all perception is theory laden and strongly conceptual in nature.

Two different philosophical approaches to perception

Perception is a subject of interest in its own right, from both a philosophical and a scientific point of view. There is little doubt, however, that in philosophy the main interest in perception, historically, has been motivated by the recognition of its pivotal epistemological role. Perception is one of the major sources of our acquisition of knowledge about the world, certainly about the environmental world.[1] There are, however, different kinds of epistemological motivations for developing a theory of perception. One motivation is found in the context of *justificationist epistemology*: we are interested in the justification of general knowledge-claims – for example, those made in everyday life or those made in the natural sciences – and we need to spell out the role of sense perception in the process of justification. At certain historical periods, the motivation has been to find an answer to "the sceptic", who raises, or is taken to raise, doubts about the reliability and validity of the senses. At other times, it concerns the justification of specific knowledge-claims of a specific theory or approach, against those of rival theories and approaches. And at certain times, both concerns may be important. In the seventeenth century, for example, in his *Meditations*, Descartes is driven by the first concern, but other writers, for example, Locke and Descartes himself at other times, are interested in a different project; namely, justifying the claims of the newly emerging sciences against the claims of a set of rival approaches – neo-Aristotelianism, hermetical natural philosophy and scepticism.

In both types of epistemological context, it is important to be clear about the role of sense perception, and of the nature and character of perceptual experiences and perceptual states. We need to keep in mind, however, that there are different major epistemological projects, and that these might well affect our study of perception in different ways. For example, in the epistemological contexts described above, scepticism has a role to play. There is, however, yet another epistemological approach, which takes a different attitude to scepticism. This alternative approach, which goes at least as far back as Aristotle and the Stoic philosophers, and includes more recent philosophers such as Thomas Reid, takes it for granted that we perceive the physical world and its features.[2] For those within this tradition, perception is characterized functionally: in a healthy organism, properly operating sense organs function so as to enable the organism to acquire knowledge of the world.[3] The crucial matter is to understand how perception works; for example, to find out how knowledge is acquired and whether or not it is through having sense impressions or representations or ideas or cognitions, or whatever. It is implicit in this approach that scepticism is not treated as a problem. According to Aristotle, we can safely leave the sceptic "like a bump, sitting on a log".

For philosophers who follow the Aristotelian–Stoic approach, their study of perception falls within what may properly be termed "naturalistic epistemology". This term needs to be understood in a certain way since, after Quine, the term (or its sibling, "epistemology naturalized") is often taken to cover the task of fitting epistemology within the body of science, and more precisely within psychology, where the latter is taken to be a natural science, that is, as relating not so much to cognitive and intentional phenomena as to behaviouristic and neo-behaviouristic phenomena. If "psychology" were interpreted so as to include intentional psychology, social psychology and the social (moral) sciences such as sociology, history, politics and so on, then naturalized epistemology would be more defensible.[4] Even so, there is something seriously misguided about Quine's project of reducing epistemology to psychology. What it overlooks is that psychology, like any of the natural sciences, presupposes an epistemology. The scientist who defends her theories or experimental results is in the business of making knowledge-claims, and even if she doesn't have an explicit epistemology, if she is making knowledge-claims, she is potentially open to epistemological criticism. As a consequence, this scientist, or someone on the scientist's behalf, has to be ready with an epistemological defence for the claims. Because any science is epistemologically sensitive in this way, the project of reducing epistemology to psychology has to be understood as reducing epistemology not to psychology, but to psychology + epistemology. It certainly won't entail the replacement of epistemology by psychology.

This point indicates that there is another way to understand "naturalistic psychology", and that is to interpret it not as applying to a study reducible to a branch of a natural science, but as describing a study for which the natural sciences are relevant. Understood in this way, naturalistic psychology makes a great deal of sense. To pursue it is to acknowledge that the study of certain natural sciences can be extremely helpful in making epistemological progress. (A discussion of the distinction between these two ways of understanding naturalistic psychology can be found in Kornblith 1985.[5])

On the second way of understanding, naturalistic psychology is not an alternative to justificationist epistemology, but is consistent with it.

Naturalistic epistemology in this second, more modest, sense is the study of a field or domain of knowledge, where one of the aims is to show how the knowledge is possible, in the sense of explaining the conditions under which knowledge is acquired, the means whereby it is acquired, and so on. Such a study starts with the assumption that knowledge is acquired, (which does not mean that it ends with that assumption). Its primary aim is not to seek or provide foundations for knowledge, but it does not rule out drawing normative conclusions. It is within this kind of naturalistic epistemology that the Aristotelian–Stoic approach to perception can be found.

This feature of the Aristotelian–Stoic approach marks it off from the dominant philosophical tradition (historically) in the philosophy of perception, where the study of perception is set against the background of justificationist epistemology. There is another important difference. On the justificationist approach, the theorist focuses on our perceptual *experiences*: we know what it is to see a fox, to hear a bell, to taste a wine and so on. We attempt to provide an account of both the nature and structure of these experiences, and of the epistemological role they play. Emerging from this tradition are debates about the nature of perceptual experience, that is, its character, its content and its objects. Within this tradition, the emphasis, standardly, has been on the phenomenology of perception, and on describing perception from the first person point of view. It is within this tradition that we find Descartes, Locke, Berkeley, Hume, Russell, Price, Broad, Ayer and many others.

This approach begins with perceptual experiences and attempts to describe them from the first person point of view, and to give an account of them that will help us determine the extent to which they justify our beliefs in the physical world. The Aristotelian–Stoic approach does not deny a role for the phenomenology of perception or for describing perceptual experience from the first person point of view, but it adopts a different starting point to thinking about perception. It begins with the acknowledgment that perception is a natural process in the world, like breathing and eating. Our first task is to describe the role that it plays, and as a result, to try to solve the problems that arise from attempting to perform that task. It is at a later stage, however, that it becomes important to give an account of perceptual experiences, and here describing the experience from the first person point of view is crucial. But that stage comes after we have set up a framework for describing perception as a natural process. It will still be necessary, following this approach, to provide an account of perceptual experience, for perceptual experience is part of the means whereby the perceiver acquires his or her knowledge of the environment. On either approach then, it will be necessary not only to spell out the epistemological role of perceptual experiences, but to provide the right characterization of them, that is, of their character, their content and their *objects*.

In the remainder of this book I propose to follow the Aristotelian–Stoic approach in trying to deal with the problems of perception. There are several reasons for adopting this approach. The first is that since, as we shall see, it involves giving an account of perception from the first person point of view, it does not rule out taking into account those considerations raised in the first approach. Secondly, as will emerge in later sections of this chapter, the Aristotelian–Stoic approach provides a rationale for treating the first person point of view as important, which is not readily available on the other approach. Finally, it is the most promising as an approach likely to deliver a theory of perception that will provide an integration of the first person and third person points of view. Such integration is a crucial requirement for any adequate theory of perception.

Philosophical theories of perception

There is a small but distinctive range of theories that have fought for dominance among philosophers of perception. These theories may be usefully characterized by where they stand on two of the major questions in the philosophy of perception. These questions arise when we reflect on the nature of perception, especially in response to issues raised in the context of the classical argument from illusion, but in epistemological contexts in general.

One of the questions concerns whether perception is direct or indirect. This question usually arises in contexts in which it is accepted that standardly the perceiver perceives physical objects and their qualities. The issue is whether we perceive them directly or rather by virtue of being aware of certain intermediaries: images, ideas, sense impressions, sensations, sensa or sense-data. The second major question concerns the nature of the perceptual experiences themselves: for example, whether there are different types (or different components) of perceptual experiences, for example, sensations and conceptual states, such as thoughts or beliefs; whether perceptual experiences contain representations and, if they do, what kind of representations they are; how we should characterize the *content* that perceptual experiences carry; and so on. These questions are not unrelated, for how we think of the experiences can affect how we draw the distinction between direct and indirect theories, and indeed makes it difficult to draw the distinction in a non-controversial way.

The classical indirect theory of perception is what is known as the "representative theory of perception". This theory is committed to a theory of indirect realism: we perceive physical objects indirectly, where the physical objects are real entities that exist independently of the act of perceiving. There are, however, difficulties with how we characterize both the representative theory and indirect realism, and this means that things are far more complex than the simple dichotomy between direct realism and indirect realism suggests. The claim that we perceive physical objects indirectly is ambiguous in not distinguishing between saying that we perceive them by virtue of *perceiving* intermediaries, and saying that we perceive them by virtue of *being aware of* the intermediaries or representations. (This point is taken up with other issues in Chapter 4.)

There is a second difficulty. The representative theory of perception is often taken to be committed to a theory of perception that is indirect and inferential. Inferential representational realism implies that we are aware of sensory states or sensory particulars, *as* sensory states, or particulars, and then makes an inference to the hypothetical cause of these states or particulars. Or if we do not actually make the inference, we could if we wished. That is, the perceiver is construed as being aware of some inner item, and inferring from that there is present some physical object or state of affairs causing that inner item. The "classical" representative theory of perception is commonly taken to comprise this form of representationalism. However, this characterization of the theory, it is important to note, comes more from its opponents than from its advocates. It is doubtful that Descartes and Locke, to whom the theory is commonly attributed, actually held it, (see note 9) and C. D. Broad, one of the most important modern defenders of the representative theory, explicitly rejects the inferential component to the theory. He writes that it is false psychologically that we infer existence of physical objects and properties from our sensa, and false logically that we could so infer: "The belief that our sensa are appearances of something more permanent and complex seems to be primitive and to arise inevitably in us with the sensing of the sensa."[6]

On the other hand, not all forms of representationalism (nor theories of perception that involve representations) are indirect. There are many philosophers who cheerfully admit that perception involves representations, but who steadfastly refuse to admit that this commits them to a representative theory. E. J. Lowe, for example, draws a distinction between "representational theories" of perception and the representative theory.[7] The contrast is between theories in which perceptual experiences are representational or intentional states, and theories that involve "indirect realism": the view that we perceive physical objects and their properties indirectly in virtue of being directly aware of some sensory or mental items or states that represent the physical objects and their properties. It has, indeed, become quite common for contemporary philosophers to hold that perception involves representations in the sense that it contains representational states or intentional states – that is, states that carry intentional content – but to deny that they are committed to a representative theory of perception. The contrast is illustrated neatly by Colin McGinn, who, after explicitly repudiating the classical representative theory, maintains that perception works through representations: "My view is that we see objects 'directly' by representing them in visual experience."[8] Indeed, several historians of philosophy argue that Descartes and Locke, who are usually thought of as indirect theorists, held this version of representationalism.[9]

Not all theorists who admit the role of representations would agree with Lowe (and Michael Tye and others) in calling their theory a "representational theory", but they are all agreed that the theory is a form of direct realism: representational states are involved in perception but neither they, nor components of them, are said to be "objects" for the perceiver, nor objects that constitute a veil between perceiver and the world. Let us call this theory "cognitive direct realism". This form of direct realism stands in contrast with "naive realism", which implies that in perception we are directly confronted with the object itself. Myles Burnyeat has characterized a version of the latter theory as "the window model of perception", and attributes it to a number of historical philosophers, including many of the ancient Greek philosophers.[10] Like opening a window and looking out, the act of perceiving reveals the thing, perceived "as it really is".

There is another, important and interesting, form of direct realism that is different from the ones so far considered: that held by the psychologist James J. Gibson, under the title "the ecological theory of perception".[11] It is not easy to pin down precisely what the theory is committed to, but Gibson appears to say, and is often taken to say, that perception is an activity that does not involve representations at all. However, it is not clear whether this is really what he wants to say, or whether it is the doctrine that perception does not involve certain kinds of representation, for example, either the type that figures in Fodor's language of thought hypothesis or the type that is central to the classical representative theory of perception, that is, representations that constitute a "veil" between the perceiver and the world.

Summarizing our discussion so far, we need to distinguish between various forms of representationalism: indirect representationalism (the representative theory of perception) and direct representationalism, where the latter may be thought of as cognitive direct realism (or at least one important form of it). With respect to the representative theory, moreover, we need to distinguish between the "classical" theory and non-inferential forms of the theory.

The debate between direct and indirect theories of perception is, in contemporary terms, usually a debate between forms of realism. Historically, there has been a major rival to these realist theories: idealism/phenomenalism, for example, as defended by Berkeley, by H. H. Price and, more recently, by Howard Robinson.[12] This account of perception is, in part, in agreement with each of the other doctrines, but it rejects an important thesis common to both: the realism with respect to the physical objects perceived. According to idealism/phenomenalism, it is a physical object that normally is perceived, but physical objects are constituted (in some sense) by the same kind of items that are, for the indirect realist, intermediaries between the perceiver and the object. Consequently, while this account of perception is in agreement with indirect realism that in perception these items are sensed or "directly perceived", it rejects the claim that the item sensed is causally related to the physical object in question. On the other hand, it rejects the direct realist's claim that perceiving a physical object does not require sensing the item in question (usually a phenomenal item: sense-data, sensa, sense impressions or whatever).

The general consensus that has emerged is that phenomenalism is highly implausible (see Dancy 1985 for a neat summary of the difficulties) and that it should be accepted only as a last resort, that is, if the chief rivals should be unsupportable.[13] Given this situation, it seems to me that the right approach to follow in the philosophy of perception is to examine the merits of the chief rivals to phenomenalism, and try to decide whether they are so bad as to be indefensible. Robinson's book, *Perception* (1994), provides a strong defence of phenomenalism, but it is aimed at defending a version of the sense-datum theory that can be held in common by phenomenalists and indirect realists. The book does not provide an argument against indirect realism.

I have sympathies with Robinson's project, and admiration for his book. Nevertheless, I believe that the best theory of perception is an indirect realist one. However, just as phenomenalism should be accepted only if its major rivals prove unfounded, so, too, indirect realism should only be held if its major, more plausible, rival proves unacceptable. I think that there is such a rival, a form of what might be called "natural realism", which should be regarded as the default position for the philosophy of perception. It is when we examine this position that we find, so I shall argue, that it needs to be modified. The nature of that modification is that the theory turns into an indirect form of representational realism. This should not be as surprising as it first seems since, I shall argue, there is a version of representational realism that has much in common with natural realism.

This version of representational realism differs from both the indirect and direct versions described above. It might be thought of as a hybrid (mongrel) representational theory that has a mixture of direct and indirect components. Although it has an indirect component, it needs to be distinguished from the "classical" representative theory of perception. It is a major thesis of this book that it is possible to formulate a coherent, viable theory of perception, according to which perception of physical objects is direct and immediate but that nevertheless operates through awareness of intermediaries. It is just such an account that I wish to defend.

The natural view of perception and its rivals

The most natural view to take of perception is that what we are directly aware of are physical objects. In visual perception, for example, we see before us a physical object, a specific chair, one the worse for wear, one with a specific history, and so on. More accurately, we are presented with a range of objects spread out before us, in a configuration. We are confronted visually with a patterned layout or landscape populated with various objects. On any specific occasion, we see a particular object against a patterned background. From the point of view of the perceiver, it is a physical object that the perceiver sees, that the perceiver is visually presented with, that the perceiver is perceptually acquainted with and with which the perceiver can interact.

There is a long tradition within philosophy, perhaps the dominant one, in which this view is challenged. The defenders of the rival views follow the same argumentative strategy. The philosopher usually begins with a statement of what all of us are meant to concede is the "natural view" to take of perception: a form of direct realism. It is then argued that this view faces devastating objections that can only be overcome by adopting a rival view, for example, the representative theory of perception or a form of idealism/ phenomenalism. These objections are presented in the form of one of the variants of the classical "argument from illusion".

The natural realist is taken to hold that in veridical perception we are directly presented with a particular, which is a physical thing, something that exists independently of the act of perceiving. This claim is rejected by the representative realist and the idealist/

phenomenalist, but for different reasons. According to the representative realist, we may perceive the physical thing but only indirectly: the particular that we are directly aware of is presented to us in the act of perceiving, but it is a sensory particular whose occurrence is caused by the physical object or event in question. According to the idealist/phenomenalist, we are aware of a sensory particular, but it is not a physical thing that exists independently of our act of perceiving (nor do we perceive indirectly such a physical thing).

Very crudely, the argument from illusion runs something like this: there is a host of illusory situations in which the particular we are presented with seems to have features that it does not actually possess; and there are hallucinatory cases in which we seem to be presented with a particular that does not exist. The illusory and hallucinatory perceptual experiences are phenomenologically identical to the types of experiences we have in the veridical cases. The only way this can be, it is argued, is that the particular in both veridical and illusory/hallucinatory cases is not a physical thing.

The argument from illusion, in its many variants, has been challenged in a variety of ways. One way is to reject the account offered above of the natural view. For example, we may argue that this characterization is meant to describe typical veridical experiences, but it provides the wrong analysis of perceptual experience. It gives us an analysis that takes an act–object structure, rather than an adverbial structure. With the adverbial analysis in place, the argument from illusion, it is claimed, fails to get off the ground. Another challenge, based on a different account of perceptual experience, is that which is known as "the intentionalist account" (see, for example, Tim Crane[14]). On this account, a perceptual state is a form of intentional state, where it is essential to something's being an intentional state that it has an intentional structure: subject–mode–content. Accordingly, perception involves a relation to what is called an *intentional content*: something that need not actually exist.[15] Just as with the adverbial analysis, the intentionalist analysis of perceptual states is held to undermine the argument from illusion.

I have given a crude and simplistic description of the debate. One way in which the debate is more complex is that even if the natural view is amended in the way(s) just suggested, it is possible also to revise the argument from illusion to take account of those amendments (see, for example, Robinson 1994). In Chapter 6, I discuss the debate in less crude and simplistic terms. In this chapter, for the purpose of constructing a strategy for developing the right philosophical theory of perception, I wish to confine myself to two tasks: to discuss the range of major theories of perception and how best we may characterize their differences; and to highlight the importance of providing the right characterization of the "natural view" of perception.

There is surely something important about the natural view. It is very plausible, to say the least, that in a typical perceptual situation I am presented with, and directly conscious of, a particular object in front of me, seen against a background. Paraphrasing Heidegger, it is a particular chair, one in room 24, one the worse for wear, one which has a certain history, and so on. If I wish to reject the natural view, I need to explain why it seems so intuitively true.

There are two issues here. One is whether there *is* a natural view, one that captures our pre-theoretical understanding of perception, for example, of visual perception; the second concerns how that view is to be characterized. It seems to me that it is obvious that it is important to describe some such natural view, not because it is necessarily right (indeed I shall argue that it needs to be revised) but because, right or wrong, it is significant. In practice, philosophers have always regarded it as significant, either because they thought it misleadingly plausible, or because they thought it to have been misunderstood and unjustly attacked by other philosophers. Examples of the former group are Plato, Descartes, Locke, Hume, Russell, Price and Broad; and examples of the latter are Reid, John Austin and P. F. Strawson.

That it has had a significant role historically in the philosophy of perception is one reason for providing an adequate characterization of the natural view. More importantly, however, there is a rationale that justifies the importance placed on providing this characterization. Those of us who are competent perceivers, for example, those who have good vision, are experts in perceiving. Our expertise, in the case of most of us, is not very theoretical, but we are practical experts, of a high standard. Having said that, the theoretical knowledge, small as it is, is still significant. It may lack the detail of that provided by sophisticated experimental psychologists, but it has a breadth and centrality that these psychologists themselves draw upon. In the next two sections, I shall develop the rationale for this natural realist view, in the context of discussing the psychology of perception, and how it relates to the philosophy of perception.

The philosophy and psychology of perception

Given the epistemological and metaphysical significance of sense perception, it is easy enough to understand the philosophical interest in perception. There is, however, a wealth of experimental and theoretical work on perception that has been done in psychology, the neurosciences and cognitive science. Someone engaged in a philosophical approach to perception needs to say, at least in outline, how we should conceive the relationship between the philosophy of perception and the psychology of (and the more general science of) perception. One obvious connection is that a philosopher ought to be informed, at least in broad terms, of significant results in those scientific areas. (Perhaps this point is too strong: the philosophical debate needs to be connected to the relevant sciences.) There is, however, a need for information to flow in the other direction as well, for there is considerable disagreement between various theories of perception in these scientific areas, and at the heart of the disputes is disagreement about fundamental philosophical issues (but not just about these issues, let me hasten to add).

The theoretical disagreement is clearly brought out in such review books on visual perception as those by Irvin Rock and Ian Gordon. Gordon begins his *Theories of Visual Perception* with the statement that "there are many theories of visual perception. Few psychologists know them all; no teaching department includes more than a small subset in its perception courses; and the theories are often very different from each other."[16] Gordon goes on in the book to discuss a range of different approaches to the study of perception and theories about visual perception, including the Gestalt theory, the empiricist–constructivist theory (Gregory, Rock), direct perception and the ecological optics theory of Gibson, and David Marr's computational approach. Among other things, Gordon highlights the philosophical assumptions and issues that are involved in these different approaches. In the concluding chapter, he describes the problems for the various theories and approaches, and speculates on the future. Interestingly, he predicts in his concluding chapter that "the phenomenological component in theories will grow". His reason for this is that he predicts a swing away from the reductionist, mechanist approach that had dominated Western psychology in the twentieth century.

There is no one issue on which these different theorists in psychology divide. Many of the points of difference are empirical, but it is clear that some of the central issues are at heart philosophical, or largely so. For example, Rock's own philosophical assumptions come out in his account of his own theory. Rock's version of indirect realism, for example, seems close to that defended by classical philosophers and scientists, for example, Descartes, Locke and Helmholtz.[17] In the opening chapter in his book *Perception,* Rock argues for the view that our perceptions are mental constructions rather than direct recordings of reality.[18]

> Knowledge derived from physics informs us that the world from which we obtain sensory information is very different from the world as we experience it. We know that the universe consists of electromagnetic fields, atomic particles, and the empty spaces that separate atomic nuclei from the charged particles that spin around them. The picture the brain creates is limited by the range of stimuli to which our senses are attuned, a range that renders us incapable of perceiving large segments of the electromagnetic spectrum and matter at the atomic scale.[19]

The perceived world we create is said to differ qualitatively from the physicists' descriptions because our experience is mediated by our senses and constructed internally as a representation of the world. Thus, it is argued, we perceive colours, tones, tastes and smells – perceptions that either have no meaning in the world of physical reality or have a different meaning.

> What we perceive as hues of red, blue, or green the physicist describes as surfaces reflecting electromagnetic waves of certain frequencies. Colors, tones, tastes, and smells are mental constructions created out of sensory stimulation. As such they do not exist out of living minds.[20]

However, even though our perceptions are mental constructions rather than direct recordings of reality, Rock claims that they clearly are neither arbitrary nor mostly illusory. As he points out, members of every species must correctly perceive certain aspects of the external world. If they did not, they would never be able to obtain their necessities of life or avoid its dangers, and would die. Human beings are no exception. Within the range of stimuli to which we are attuned, our perceptions of the sizes, shapes, orientations, stabilities and lightnesses of things turn out to be not simply different from the images formed on our retinas but are veridical, where by "veridical" is meant that our perceptions "correspond with the properties of things considered objectively and independent of viewing conditions, such as can be ascertained by measurement". Rock, in this chapter, is at pains to reject the belief that he says philosophers call "naive realism": that the world we perceive is identical with a real world that exists independent of our experience of it.

Gibson's theory, on the other hand, has been endorsed by John Haugeland as presenting a view that is an expression of the ideas of Heidegger and Dreyfus. Haugeland points out how, in his *The Ecological Approach to Visual Perception*, Gibson defends the view that we can only understand animals as perceivers if we consider them as inseparably related to an environment that is itself understood in terms appropriate to that animal.[21] The ecological approach offers a different perspective to understanding visual perception from that offered by physical optics. "A system that sees – a sighted animal – is not responsive, in the first instance, to physically simple properties of light, like color and brightness, but rather to visible features of the environment that matter to it."[22] Gibson calls such features "affordances":

> The affordances of the environment are what it offers the animal, what it provides or furnishes for good or ill . . .
> So for example, a suitably sturdy and flat surface could afford a place to stand or walk to an animal of a certain sort – not to a fish, of course – and what affords standing room to a sparrow might not to a cat.

We can see that Gibson's theory is making certain philosophical claims about what the human being or what particular animals perceive: the affordances. The dispute between Gibson and Rock (and others) reflects the dispute between those in different philosophical traditions.

Not only do philosophical assumptions play a central role in the work of both Gibson and Rock, but common to each is a thesis that is part of the natural realist view that I described in the previous section. Each takes it for granted that perception is a natural process in the world that is a means by which perceivers acquire knowledge about objects in the perceiver's environment. Where they differ is on exactly what that knowledge consists of, and on the character of the processes involved, for example, over whether representations are involved, and if so, of what type.

There is a neat illustration of the philosophical dimension to theoretical disagreements in Psychology, provided by Evan Thompson's discussion of Gibson's ecological approach to visual perception in his book *Colour Vision*.[23] In this book (ch. 5), Thompson contrasts the ecological approach with the computational representational approach of Marr. At the heart of the disagreement is whether perception should be characterized as direct or indirect, and whether the process underlying perception involves representations. Thompson criticizes both Marr and Gibson: Marr for misunderstanding Gibson, in taking him to agree that the retinal stimulation should be regarded as images and in Marr's terms "representations"; and Gibson for not understanding his own approach well enough, for not allowing that there may be action-centred representations. While Thompson sees himself as defending a version of the ecological approach, he takes pains in this chapter to criticize both Gibson and Marr. His theory contains elements of both theories.[24]

In highlighting the philosophical assumptions and presuppositions made in various psychological accounts and disputes, I am not making a trade demarcation point. The issue is not over which discipline is supposed to resolve the problems or answer the questions. The point rather is that there are certain philosophical issues and empirical issues entwined. Just as the philosopher needs to provide an account that allows a role for empirical research, so the psychologist needs to acknowledge the place where certain philosophical issues arise.

Moreover, some of the philosophical issues are very basic ones that relate to issues much broader than those related solely to psychology and cognitive science. I think that progress in resolving some of these basic issues will be achieved by a broadly philosophical approach, one that is cognizant of scientific developments, but is not dominated by them. What is needed, I shall argue, is to set the debate within a certain framework, one that presupposes a very natural view of perception, which I have already identified as "natural realism". It is in this spirit that I propose to set out a certain philosophical framework, one that characterizes natural realism, and examines how and to what extent that account needs to be modified. I do not wish to exaggerate the ambitions of this project. There are crucial empirical issues that divide authors such as Gibson, and those such as Marr and Rock. They will be largely untouched by anything I could say. However, there are also important elements to their disagreement that depend on certain philosophical assumptions. Progress on perception, I believe, will depend on cooperation between different approaches.

Natural realism in philosophy and psychology

I have attempted to outline a philosophical approach to perception that coheres with psychological approaches. I see the two approaches as intimately connected. To illustrate how we should understand this connection, it will be helpful to refer to the influential book by Marr, *Vision*, especially its introductory chapter.[25] This book, an exposition and defence of a computational theory of vision, was very significant both for those it inspired and for those critics who saw it as providing such formidable opposition. My purpose in referring here to this book, however, is not to discuss its arguments or its point of view, but to use it to explain the philosophical project that I am engaged upon.

The introductory chapter to the book opens with the question "What does it mean, to see?", and continues "the plain man's answer (and Aristotle's too) would be: to know what is where, by looking". This statement is perhaps not controversial, although it certainly hasn't always been obvious. What is more remarkable is how Marr proceeds. "In other words", he writes, "vision is the process of discovering from images what is present in the world, and where it is". This surely does not capture the plain man's view, nor does it recognizably belong to Aristotle. It is, of course, Marr's own view, one that is challenged by many other thinkers on vision, for example, J. J. Gibson, John Haugeland and Evan Thompson.

I do not think that Marr gets the plain man right. Still, there is an important insight in this passage. It is repeated a page later, when he identifies the range of perspectives that must be satisfied before we can be said, from a human and scientific point of view, to have understood visual perception.

> First and I think foremost, there is the perspective of the plain man. He knows what it is like to see, and unless the bones of one's arguments and theories roughly correspond to what this person knows to be true at first hand, one will probably be wrong (a point made with force and elegance by Austin 1962).[26]

This remark is interesting both in its reference to the plain man, and to the philosopher, John Austin. Other remarks in the book show that Austin has a lasting, if small, influence on Marr, an influence, I shall argue, that should be resisted.

The reference to the plain man expresses an important insight, one that is not only easy to overlook, but one that can be strengthened. The plain man (and the plain woman too, dare I say) is an expert on vision. He knows what it is to see, and to hear, and to touch and feel, and so on. It is true that he sometimes makes mistakes, for example, claims to see a barn when it is a church, but all experts make some mistakes. Napoleon did not win every battle, and Michael Jordan did not score every basket. The plain man is an expert. He is not infallible: not the final authority or the ultimate one.

The viewer's expertise is not simply knowledge-how: it does not consist simply in having a capacity to see. The plain man knows what it is to exercise the ability. In part this exercise involves knowing-that: knowing that he sees a fox, an apple, a church and so on. I am not making a claim about subjective experiences or about qualia, or about "what it is like", and so on. What is known is not just knowing what it is like to have visual or auditory experiences: it is knowing what it is like to *see a fox*, to *see an apple*, to *see a bird* in the tree and so on, and part of what this involves is to know what it is to see successfully: to know that it is a fox that you see. But there is further theoretical knowledge contained in the plain man's expertise: knowledge of *another*, of what it is for it to be true of someone else that she is seeing (perceiving) a fox, seeing a rabbit and so on. One of the points about this expertise, moreover, is that you know of yourself and of another what kind of conditions make it easier or more difficult to see. You know that vision is improved under certain conditions, for example, by examining things up close, by seeing certain things by standing back, by taking the object out into the daylight, or by looking at something with your eyes screwed up, or shaded, or with one eye closed and so on. To talk of knowledge of your own capacities to see and of knowing of another's may be misleading. Part of the knowledge about yourself is knowledge about anyone, that is, anyone who has these capacities.

So, given the status of expert perceivers, it is clear why the natural view is significant, even if it should turn out that there are good reasons for revising it, for example, if there are reasons for thinking that expert perceivers are misled about their capacities, or about the structure of their perceptual experiences. Given this rationale, therefore, we can also see how important it is to get the characterization of the natural view right. We can see, for example, that the characterization of the natural view that I gave earlier (in the third section, p. 10) is incomplete. There I introduced the view by saying that it is very natural to take it that in visual perception I am presented with a range of objects spread out before me, in a configuration. I am confronted visually with a patterned layout or landscape populated with various objects. That is a characterization of what it was to perceive, as described from the point of view of the perceiver. What needs to be added is something that reflects the third person point of view.

It is also part of the natural view to treat perception as a natural process or activity: It is a process or activity whereby the perceiver comes, in the first place, to acquire knowledge of things in the world in which the perceiver is situated, and secondly, is enabled to act selectively with respect to those objects. It is this aspect to perception that is emphasized in the Aristotelian–Stoic approach to perception that I discussed in an earlier section. According to this view, perception is a process or activity whereby the perceiver comes to acquire, primarily, knowledge of things in the world in which the perceiver is situated. *Seeing* is a way of knowing, or acquiring knowledge, by using your eyes; *hearing* a way of knowing by using your ears; *feeling* a way of knowing by using your body, and so on. It is by these perceptual processes that the perceiver may also acquire many beliefs that do not amount to knowledge, but unless the perceiver acquired some knowledge, he or she would not acquire any perceptual beliefs.

Perception, in other words, is taken to be a process or activity whereby the perceiver comes to acquire knowledge of things in the world in which the perceiver is situated. On this view, it is taken for granted that we perceive the physical world and its features. We take this world to consist of physical objects and happenings, which exist independently of us and our acts of perceiving, and which are the things we commonly perceive.

Given the importance of this view, it is an important philosophical task to spell out what is involved in these perceptual activities and processes. The crucial matter is to understand how perception works; for example, to find out how knowledge is acquired and whether or not it is through sense impressions or representations or ideas or cognitions, or whatever; to find out whether there are assumptions built into the view that are open to criticism or revision.

Natural realism and folk psychology

The relationship of plain man/expert to the psychologist is not just as a subject for the scientist of perception to study. He or she is an expert in seeing in the same way as the psychologist is an expert (or in one of the ways that the psychologist is an expert; in other ways, of course, he or she does not share the expertise). In stressing as I have, the expertise of the ordinary perceiver and the fact that perception involves the acquisition of knowledge, I need to guard against the possibility of a serious misunderstanding arising. In philosophy there has recently developed something of a fashion to speak of "folk psychology".

Given this practice, it is tempting to think of the natural view as a "folk theory" of perception. I am happy to conform to this practice of using this term, but we need to acknowledge the dangers implicit in this use. Not the least is the danger of treating folk psychology as a scientific theory of perception: only a primitive one, and a second rate one at best. Perception, and vision in particular, are subjects for study by sciences such as experimental psychology and cognitive sciences. Because this is so, there is a tendency to think that folk theories of perception, falling within folk psychology, should be seen as trying to perform the same tasks that these sciences perform, only in a more naive or primitive form. This way of looking at things is grossly misleading. At the very least, it is not mandatory. The natural view is more important than this picture suggests. It is much more important, even if, as I shall later argue, there are important respects in which it needs to be modified.

There is a role for picking out and describing folk psychology and with it a folk theory of perception, and for that matter a folk physics. While we can use the term "theory" in these contexts, the use of the term is misleading. First of all, folk psychology and folk physics can be described at different levels of abstraction. Secondly, they can be thought of (in part) as embedded in a set of practices, both discursive and non-discursive. That is to say, the principles may be expressed in people's *doing things*, as well as saying things. Folk physics is concerned with opening a door, fighting with an opponent, chopping a tree down, sailing a boat, lifting a weight, throwing a ball and so on. While some of folk physics has been affected by the growth of Newtonian mechanics, and its more recent successors, it is important to remember that much of folk physics has been relatively untouched or has been only refined.

The view that I am defending, that folk physics is not a primitive competitor to more recent physics, is supported by the view of science and, more particularly, the causal/entity realism defended by Ian Hacking.[27] On Hacking's account, one of the predominant features of science is its capacity to build on, extend and develop our causal knowledge of things. Central to this causal knowledge is practical knowledge: the capacity to build and use instruments and devices. Theories will have an important role in the development of this capacity but, if Hacking is right, the theories may largely be false. Hacking gives the scientific example to illustrate his claim that scientists typically believe in the reality of particles – X-rays, electrons, charges and so on – when they can manipulate them, when they can control them causally. They can acquire this causal knowledge, of their causal powers, even though their theoretical knowledge of these particles might be quite deficient, and even though different experimenters may disagree about what they think the nature to be. One of the important implications of this account is that there is a realist attitude (entity-realist) intrinsic to science that is on a par with the realist attitude of common sense. Another is that progress in science can be measured by: (a) widening the category of entities that are known to be real, for example, to include (previously) theoretical entities (e.g. germs, bacteria, genes, proteins, atoms, electrons, X-rays); (b) increasing *causal knowledge* about entities already known (wind, boats, canoes, ships, trains, planes, wheels, carts, knives, swords, projectiles, guns, clocks, shovels, bridges, roads, buildings, dyes, acids, bleaches, gases, iron, copper, lead, aluminium, water, etc.). This causal knowledge is in part *practical knowledge* (know-how), in part representational knowledge.

There is an added reason for worrying about the implications of the term "folk theory of perception". The theory is of a piece with a wide range of bodies of scientific knowledge, that is, it is presupposed in natural sciences such as physics, chemistry, biology, geology, ecology and so on, as well as geography, history and psychology itself. One of the things that is characteristic of human beings, and of the institutions in which they participate, is that they are regularly and consistently making knowledge-claims not only in fields such as the law, business and in family life, but as well within sciences where bodies of knowledge are built up and revised. In making such claims, the person is open to questions such as "How do you know?" That is, we are called upon, or should be ready to be called upon, to justify our knowledge claims. Central to the practices of justification are claims such as "I saw it happen", "I saw that it was true" and so on.

In so far as a science such as physics or biology makes knowledge-claims, or in so far as we make such claims within everyday life, then we are dependent on a theory of perception and of visual perception, in particular. We employ a concept of perception and it is central to our justificatory practices. Now, the scientists doing physics or biology who employ the concept of seeing may to a certain extent be affected by results from experimental psychology, but the concept of visual perception that they standardly use is that of folk psychology. The way that experimental psychology will affect their practice is by affecting the folk psychological concept. It is the folk psychological concept that will be modified, that is, revised, and not eliminated or replaced.

It is important to acknowledge that vision has played an important role in the history of science. I do not mean merely that scientists have developed theories of optics and light, which are obviously related to theories of vision. Rather, the way vision has made its significant contribution to the development of science is through the relevant scientists drawing upon what is called the "folk theory of vision": they are drawing upon, and in certain cases refining, the expertise that they share with fellow visual experts. It is important to make the point since critics of folk psychology, for example, the Churchlands and their sympathizers, is that folk psychology is something out of the dark ages, a primitive form of scientific theorizing, and a poor one at that, to more sophisticated theories of psychology. My claim is that this view is based on serious misunderstanding of the place of folk psychology in experimental psychology and, more generally, in science.

Finally, there is an important methodological point to make. Specifying the natural view means in part making explicit what is implicit in the understanding of competent perceivers. The exercise is performed in two ways: by studying and thinking about how perceivers actually operate in the world; and by reflecting on one's own abilities as an expert perceiver. This second kind of practice is very important. Although it includes reflecting on perceiving as it occurs in one's own case, for example, on what it is to see a bird, to see an apple, to hear a fire siren and so on, it involves much more. It involves thinking about the practices in which one engages and interacts with other perceivers, for example, in justifying and challenging knowledge-claims.

Conclusion

In this chapter I have attempted to set up a broad framework for thinking about the philosophy of perception. I described several contrasting epistemological motivations for developing a theory of perception, arguing that the most fruitful approach to follow is one in keeping with the Aristotelian approach to perception, according to which perception is a natural process or activity whereby the perceiver comes to acquire knowledge of things in the world in which the perceiver is situated. On this view, it is taken for granted that we perceive the physical world and its features. We take this world to consist of physical objects and happenings, which exist independently of us and our acts of perceiving, and which are the things we commonly perceive.

Given the importance of this view, it is an important philosophical task to spell out what is involved in these perceptual activities and processes. The crucial matter is to understand how perception works: for example, to find out how knowledge is acquired and whether or not it is through sense impressions or representations or ideas or cognitions, or whatever; to find out whether there are assumptions built into the view that are open to criticism or revision.

I then set out a strategy for developing a correct philosophical theory of perception. The strategy consists in starting with an accurate characterization of natural realism, the natural view to take of perception, and then to see in what respects, and how, it needs to be modified, if at all. I also argued that the philosophical study is complementary to psychological and other scientific studies of perception, since those approaches presuppose (something very like) natural realism. In the following chapters, I attempt to specify natural realism before going on to follow the strategy advocated above.

I also identified various theories of perception contrasting direct and indirect realist theories, first against each other and then, together, against idealism/phenomenalism. As well, I distinguished between indirect and direct versions of representationalism, where the latter can be thought of as committed to cognitive direct realism. I described the possibility of accepting a third version of representationalism, one that is a hybrid (mongrel) representational theory, which is a hybrid of direct and indirect components. It is this theory that I shall defend in this book.

I should acknowledge, before proceeding, a point that may be only too obvious. Although presenting a theory of perception, my discussion concentrates on visual perception. There are several reasons, some practical, for adopting this strategy. However, let me say that, while some philosophically significant features of visual perception will readily generalize, we should not assume that all will. I make no such assumption (and I do not totally ignore other sense-modalities). The extent to which the points do generalize will, I hope, be obvious enough.

2 A theory of natural realism

In Chapter 1 I argued for the importance of giving an account of what might be called the "natural view" of perception, even if only as the initial step in leading to a theory that revises that view. This natural view is often explained in terms of a description of what it is to perceive, from the first person point of view, that is, from the view of the perceiver. I argued that while this point of view is of great importance, considerations of the natural view need to be set within a wider context, one that takes into account both a third person and first person point of view. Such a context, I also argued, can be found in the Aristotelian–Stoic approach to perception.

For those within this tradition, perception is a process or activity whereby the perceiver comes to acquire knowledge of things in the world in which the perceiver is situated. Perception is characterized functionally: in a healthy organism, properly operating sense organs function so as to enable the organism to acquire knowledge of the world. Adopting this approach, it is possible to spell out the natural view of perception as a form of "natural realism".

There are two sides to this view: an objective side and a subjective side. By adopting the third person point of view, we can describe the role and function of perception as a means by which someone navigates their way through their environment. It is clear, from what has been said, how central to the account is the role of the third person point of view (the objective side). There is, however, a subjective side to the natural view. We can reflect on what it is to perceive, from the first person point of view. This view is also important for those of us, that is, most of us, who are competent, expert perceivers. Since we are expert perceivers, it is surely the case that what we take to be natural, when expressed from the first person point of view, is of some relevance. Our view is not going to be complete if we ignore the third person point of view, but the same thing can be said if we neglect the first person point of view. In this chapter, I attempt to spell out the details of natural realism, trying to show in particular how the subjective and objective sides are connected.

Natural realism: the objective side

The Aristotelian–Stoic approach to the philosophy of perception lends itself easily to spelling out clearly the details of the natural view of perception, described from the objective, third person point of view. According to this view, perception is a process or activity whereby the perceiver comes to acquire, primarily, knowledge of things in the world in which the perceiver is situated. *Seeing* is a way of knowing, or acquiring knowledge, by using your eyes; *hearing* is a way of knowing by using your ears; *feeling* is a way of knowing by using your body and so on. It is by these perceptual processes that the perceiver may also acquire many beliefs that do not amount to knowledge, but unless the perceiver acquired some knowledge, he or she would not acquire any perceptual beliefs. This view takes it for granted that we perceive the physical world and its features. We take this world to consist of physical objects and happenings, which exist independently of us and our acts of perceiving, and which are the things we commonly perceive. (To foreshadow: illusions and false beliefs may not only be present, but can play a significant role, for example, by being advantageous.)

According to this "natural realist" view, perception is a process or activity whereby the perceiver comes to acquire, in the first place, knowledge of things in the world in which the perceiver is situated. There are, however, two kinds of knowledge involved, a practical form of knowledge, and a more theoretical, propositional form of knowledge, corresponding to two levels at which perception operates. Most philosophical discussions of perception concentrate on the more theoretical reflective kind of knowledge. There is, however, a more primary level at which perception operates. At this level, perception is a process whereby the perceiver comes to identify and recognize objects in the environment. Through perceiving at this level, the perceiver discriminates objects, that is, picks them out from their background, in such a way that he or she can exercise one or more of a range of abilities:

- locate the object in space;
- track it while either the object or the perceiver, or both, move through space;
- act with respect to that object: grasp it, gaze at it, approach it, avoid it, throw something at it, charge at it and so on.

In so doing, the human perceiver exercises much the same abilities as do other animals, particularly primates. At this level, the perceiver requires no language, either to perceive or to have the relevant abilities. These abilities are expressed in non-linguistic actions. It is an entirely different matter whether the perceiver needs to have concepts. What is true is that he or she does not have discursive concepts, concepts that require language for their expression, but it is at least an open question whether the animal has concepts at all. It seems to me obvious, however, that the perceiving animal has what might be called "practical concepts", ones expressed in bodily actions, and that some of these are concepts that might eventually come to be expressed in language. (It also seems possible to me that there are at least certain concepts whose possession can only be shown and not expressed in language, but I do not need to explore that possibility here.)

There is a second level at which perception operates, at least for more sophisticated perceivers. Perception is a process that enables a sophisticated perceiver to form judgements and thoughts about objects that he or she perceives. The perceiver comes to form a judgement about a certain object before him or her: *that fox* is very cheeky, *that cup* is cracked, *that plant* is wilting and so on. It is at this level that we the perceivers acquire theoretical perceptual knowledge, which forms the basis of our theoretical knowledge of ourselves and of the world, including our sophisticated scientific knowledge. Clearly one of the functions of perception is to provide this kind of propositional knowledge.

It is important that we be clear about the form of this propositional knowledge. The primary cases are ones in which the perceiver makes judgements that employ demonstrative concepts, for example, *that ball*, *that church*, *this golf-club* and so on. The point is that the perceiver is not in a position merely to make the judgement that "there is a ball in front of me" or "there is a church in front of me", but rather to make a more specific judgement, about a particular ball, a particular church and so on. In the words of Heidegger, "it is the chair itself, a particular chair, one in Room 24, one much the worse for wear, etc.", that is presented in a natural perception.

It is also important to recognize that, at this stage of the analysis, that is, of the objective side of natural realism, nothing has been said yet about perceptual experiences. It is not that they have been denied; it is just that before we try to describe the role of perceptual experiences, it is possible for us to identify the various perceptual processes and identify their various functions. It is at a later stage when we try to explain how these functions operate and also how they can come unstuck, that it will be important to give an account of perceptual experiences.

I have identified two roles for perceptual activities, such as seeing, hearing, touching and so on, related to the acquisition of practical and theoretical forms of knowledge, respectively. There is a third role that perceptual activities have to play: they serve a justificatory function. Claims to knowledge are backed by claims such as "I saw him take the cake", "I could hear her talking to her husband" and so on. The reason that this role is distinct from the second is that it could be that perception was part of a reliable mechanism whereby perceivers acquired beliefs that amounted to knowledge, without there arising an epistemological practice in which perceivers justified to each other their knowledge-claims through appeal to perception. Perhaps this is unlikely but it is possible.

If we reflect on these various roles and how perception serves them, we can identify certain conditions that are involved in, or presupposed by, those roles (or by serving them). For example, the fact that perception is a means for acquiring the relevant practical knowledge requires, first, that there exist certain objects that the perceiver interacts with, for example, a tool, a ball, a hammer, and, secondly, that the perceiver has a body that he or she controls. The fact that perceivers can make demonstrative judgements about *that cup* or *that fox* or *that church* presupposes that the cup or the fox or the church is something that exists. There is, moreover, a crucial implication that flows from this account; namely, that there is a link between the acquisition of the practical and theoretical forms of knowledge. In the section after the next (p. 31), I shall explore this link.

To summarize this section, adopting the Aristotelian–Stoic approach to the examination of perception it is possible, I have argued, to describe what we may call a "natural realist view of perception". It is a general, minimal account of perception that describes perception as a natural process involving the perceiver and the world in which the perceiver is situated, such that it reflects the fact that perception serves (at least) three roles, as:

- the means of acquisition of practical knowledge
- the means of acquisition of more theoretical knowledge: ordinary knowledge; scientific knowledge
- an important means of justifying knowledge-claims.

Practical concepts and embodied thoughts

I have claimed that the practical knowledge, acquired standardly in perceiving, involves practical concepts. These concepts are expressed in actions that may be thought of as "embodied thoughts". An insight into the nature and role of such practical concepts has been provided by John Campbell.[1] (Similar concepts are discussed by Aristotle and Heidegger.) Campbell describes what he calls a "primitive physics", reflecting on the character of our most primitive physical thinking: our sense of the physics of our environment that we exercise in everyday interaction with it, such as lighting a fire, throwing a rock or putting up an umbrella.[2] Campbell describes a set of practical concepts whose application reflects a practical understanding of things rather than a theoretical one. Central to this framework are what are called "indexical notions" and "working concepts". These practical concepts, Campbell is at pains to point out, are ones that we can share with animals. At least, some of them are. Campbell's exposition of these concepts demonstrates quite convincingly his claim that we need to leave behind Ryle's dichotomy between knowing how and knowing that as being too simplistic.

The notion of "working concepts" is borrowed from Aristotle.[3] Typical of these are terms whose reference need not depend on the causal powers of the speaker, but a grasp of whose causal significance does involve the causal powers of the speaker. There are cases in which our grasp of the causal significance of a notion does not have to do with adopting any detached posture, but rather consists in our practical grasp of its implications for our own actions. Aristotle's examples concern working with wood or metals. We can contrast a theoretical understanding of the causal properties of particular types of wood or different metals such as iron or silver, with the understanding possessed by the carpenter or metalworker. The artisan's grasp of causal properties is not a matter of having a detached picture of them. It has to do with the structure of his practical skills: the particular way in which he deals with various types of wood or how he uses different metals.

Some of the working concepts take their place among linguistic terms. There are some terms that are causally indexical, in that their reference depends upon the causal powers of the speaker, on just what the speaker is capable of doing: *hot*, *heavy*, *being within reach*. Even a creature that did not grasp the first person use could use causally indexical representations. A creature could use representation of things as within reach, or out of reach, without having the ability to think using the first person.

> An animal may reliably perform a task even though we vary a number of parameters, but then it may give up at some point. The ball has been thrown too far for the dog to recover it, the stick is too heavy for it to lift. In such cases we can test for just why the animal is not attempting the task and we have to be able to say, for example, that it is because the ball seems to have been thrown too far, or the stick seems too heavy.[4]

Campbell emphasizes that the grasp of the relevant term requires not just the ability to register when it applies, but it is shown in the way one behaves, for example, by the difference in ways when we prepare to lift something heavy or to touch something hot.[5]

Once we allow for practical concepts of this kind, and for the associated embodied thoughts, as being characteristic of perceptual situations, certain implications emerge. The first is that we can identify a primary kind of seeing, an object-based seeing, that is a form of conceptual seeing: seeing-as. For, given that the primary kind of seeing, object-based seeing, which targets objects as well as being caused by them, involves practical concepts, it is possible to recognize that this kind of seeing is conceptual, that is to say, that it involves *seeing-as*. As well as being conceptual, this kind of seeing is extensional in that it involves seeing a certain object as being a certain way, and implies that the object exists. In the second place, once we extend natural realism beyond the kind of perception we share with other animals, not only can we see how the two kinds of perception are linked but, by appealing to the phenomenology of perception, the first person point of view, we can see the role of perceptual experience. This point will come up later.

The link between practical and theoretical knowledge

The dominant feature of the natural realist account of perception that I have described is that perception is object-based. Perception is a natural process involving causal "commerce" (causal interchange) between object perceived and perceiver. At least, this is true of central primary cases of perception. Perception is a complex activity that involves causal contact between object perceived and perceiver, such that it allows the perceiver to act and to have thoughts of a certain kind: ones focused on specific objects. Central and paradigm instances of such activities are those of *object perception*: seeing a church, seeing a rabbit, seeing a cup and so on. Perception, that is to say, is a process that allows us to acquire both practical knowledge and theoretical knowledge.

It is important that we understand how the perceptual process incorporates both forms of knowledge, and how these forms of knowledge are intimately linked. The causal contact between object and perceiver is of such a kind that it involves identification of the object (discrimination from its surroundings) and it is this act of discrimination that enables the perceiver both to act with respect to that object, target the object in his or her actions and acquire knowledge about the object.

To clarify what is involved, let us concentrate on visual perception. It is clear that seeing is a natural process involving causal contact between the perceiver and objects in the world, whereby the perceiver comes to detect and discriminate those objects. The perceiver, more strictly, is a perceiver-agent. Through causal contact with a specific object, say a peach or a lemon tree, he or she not only acquires but can exercise a range of capacities, ones that are connected with the agent's occupying some spatial location. The perceiver is in causal contact, via his or her perceptual systems, with physical objects in such a way that the perceiver is able to locate the object in space, and track it with the eyes (for visual perception) and to act with respect to it. In causally interacting with the object, the perceiver acquires perceptual states (whether they are experienced or not) that enable the possessor of these states, the *perceiving agent*, to exercise certain important capacities. Central to these are certain spatially related capacities: to locate himself or herself in space; to locate things in space; to move within that space.

In addition, there are other capacities that depend upon these space-centred capacities and that depend upon the agent's control over his or her body and bodily actions, and upon the knowledge he or she possesses of his or her body. Such capacities include the capacities:

- to grasp, to hold, to touch, to push, . . .
- to move towards, to avoid, to go around, . . .
- to watch, to attend to, to stare at, to keep track of, . . .
- to throw at, . . .

In exercising these capacities, that is, in performing these kinds of actions, the perceiving agent may be construed as engaging in a special kind of thought – embodied thoughts – and as employing a special kind of concept – *practical concepts*. These abilities, which are ones we share with animals and which do not require language, constitute a form of practical knowledge, which can be contrasted with reflective or theoretical knowledge.

There is a link between the theoretical knowledge and the practical knowledge. Our primary perceptual judgements, as we have seen, are expressed in terms of demonstrative concepts, for example, *this peach* is tempting, *that cup* is Grandma's and so on. Our understanding the demonstrative concept that *this peach*, *that cup* and so on requires having the practical knowledge in question, that is, in being affected by the object so that we can locate it in space and target it, for example, we can grasp it or move towards it. The link between the two forms of knowledge, practical and theoretical, is as follows: exercising the demonstrative concept requires exercising the practical capacity of discriminating and locating the object in space, and thereby having the capacity to grasp the object and to make a judgement about it, for example, that *that peach* is worth biting.

The point is that understanding the use of demonstrative concepts in these perceptual contexts requires special individuating knowledge about the object. It is the practical, perceptual abilities to discriminate the object from its background, to locate it in space relative to the perceiver, to causally intervene with respect to the object, that provide this individuating knowledge. These primary cases of perceptual knowledge are at the interface between practical knowledge and theoretical knowledge, having elements of each.

Seeing and seeing-that

The natural realist view of perception, as I have just argued, needs to be extended to language-using perceivers and, as a consequence, needs to provide an account of perception that is relevant to the acquisition of reflective knowledge. Once we extend our account to such contexts, we need to take into account the fact that perceivers not only use perceptual-claims such as "I saw . . ." and "I heard . . ." to justify knowledge claims, but they also frame their perceptual-claims in certain characteristic ways, when speaking both of themselves and of others.

Perceptual-claims, it is important to note, are expressed in two very different ways, sometimes as in A below, sometimes as in B:

A. Robert saw the bird;
   Robert saw the sun rising;
   Robert saw the boar coming towards him.

B. Percy saw that the horse had bolted
   Percy saw that the window was shut;
   Percy saw that the wound was dripping blood.

The sense of "sees that" contained in B is the perceptual sense. There is a different use of "sees-that", which is non-perceptual, that is, "sees-that" is a synonym for "knows that". Someone can claim to see that the government will lose the next election or to see that a certain mathematical problem has a solution. These uses are very different from the perceptual uses.

That there are these two perceptual uses of "sees", "seeing-X" and "seeing-that X is . . ." raises the question of whether there are two kinds of seeing and, more generally, two kinds of perceiving. Some philosophers, for example, G. Warnock, F. Dretske, C. Landesman and K. Mulligan, have argued that it is vital to recognize a form of perception, for example, *simple-seeing* or *non-epistemic seeing*, that can be contrasted with conceptualized seeing, *seeing-as* (in the conceptualized sense) and *seeing-that*.[6] Simple seeing, or non-epistemic seeing, is held to be a *sui generis* mental activity whose objects are particulars, for example, physical objects, events, or processes. What is true of seeing holds more generally of perceiving.

Dretske provides the most detailed and plausible account of the distinction between seeing and seeing-that. For him, *non-epistemic seeing* stands in contrast to *seeing-that*, which is judgement-like, epistemic, propositional and conceptual. To see a cabbage, in the non-epistemic sense, is to differentiate visually the cabbage from its background but, holds Dretske, it does not require forming any judgements or beliefs about the cabbage. In particular, it does not require seeing it as anything, either as a cabbage, or as a green thing, or as cabbage-shaped and so on, where this requires exercising concepts of a cabbage, or a green thing, and so on. The phrase "visual differentiation", so it is held, functions as a pre-intellectual, pre-discursive sort of capacity that a wide variety of beings possess:

> It is an endowment which is largely immune to the caprices of our intellectual life. Whatever judgements, interpretations, beliefs, inferences, anticipations, regrets, memories, or thoughts may be aroused by the visual differentiation of D, the visual differentiation of D is, itself, quite independent of these accompaniments.[7]

Seeing in the non-epistemic sense, seeing$_n$, does not require identification, recognition or knowledge, with respect to the object in question. Although this type of seeing is the basis for identification and recognition, and is normally accompanied by such cognitive acts, nevertheless, so Dretske argues, seeing$_n$ is distinct from all of these acts.

This view raises a natural question: can someone see anything without seeing it as having some features? Can someone discriminate any object from its background without conceptualizing it at all? Indeed, can one differentiate it without identifying it under some aspect? To see a bear need not require identifying it as a bear, but it is less plausible that it does not require identifying it at all, for example, as a huge shaggy thing or even as a figure near a tree. It is plausible, for example, that a fox doesn't just see something, but sees something as edible, plump and ready-to-paw (so to speak).

In arguing for the claim that we identify cases in which people see something without having beliefs about that thing, Dretske claims that there is no general classification that the perceiver must bring that particular under.[8] He does not show, however, that there is no classification that the perceiver employs. For example, it may be, as Dretske says, that you perceive a face in the window without taking it to be a face, or even as a physical object: you may take it to be an image or something imaginary. But that very example attributes to the perceiver a classification of the object. Furthermore, Dretske does not argue against the view that even when you see something imaginary or hallucinatory, and whether you take it to be real or not, you are still able to locate the object, imaginary or real, as being in a certain position in space.

We can grant to Dretske and others, for example, Landesman, that we can contrast the two uses, "sees X" and "sees-that", but this fact does not in itself show that there are two kinds of seeing. Nor does it show that seeing X is non-epistemic, and much less that it is non-propositional and non-conceptual. What it might reflect instead is a difference in the kinds of proposition or kinds of concepts (and knowledge) involved. For example, there does seem to be an important difference between the two sorts of perceptual-claims in A and B above. It can be true that Percy saw that the window was shut or that the horse was ill without Percy actually seeing the window or the horse, and without the window or horse having any perceptual or causal contact with Percy at all. It could be that Percy saw from the look on Linda's face that the horse was ill (and she may have heard it on the telephone). On the other hand, if Robert saw the bird, he was causally affected by that bird, and in such a way as to discriminate the bird from its background.

But we can make this kind of distinction without agreeing that seeing X does not involve seeing-as (or seeing-that), for we can make a distinction between two kinds of seeing-that, one of which is object-based, the other not, and only the latter should be contrasted with seeing X. That is to say, it is possible to hold that seeing X always involves discriminating X from its background, and locating it in an egocentric space, and that these activities involve conceptualization and some knowledge, for example, a form of knowledge by acquaintance, which includes some theoretical knowledge.

We can identify a primary form of seeing, a form of object-based seeing, without making the stark contrasts employed by Dretske, Landesman and others. On the natural realist view, as described at the start of this chapter, there is a primary kind of perceiving that humans share with other animals. Here the perceiver causally interacts with an object by visual means, looks in a certain direction, uses the eyes, fixes the gaze, tracks the object and so on, so as to act in a non-discursive manner with respect to this object: the perceiver sees a specific fox, church, tree, shadow, fire and so on. Perceiving in this sense is object-based: it involves causal commerce with objects. The perceiver causally interacts with specific objects being affected in characteristic ways, and targeting specific objects in its behaviour.

It is true that, in the case of language-users, perceiving works at another level: the perceiver uses the eyes in the same manner but can form explicit judgements about that object, judgements that can be expressed linguistically:

> "*that fox* is looking for the hen";
> "*that church* has just been painted";
> "*that fire* needs stoking".

But this kind of perceiving is also object-based. The perceiver is in causal commerce with the object so that he or she can both locate the object in space and make demonstrative judgements about that object. Indeed, the capacity to make the demonstrative judgements is tied up with the capacity to locate the object in space, to track it with the eyes and so on.

This perceiving is certainly a type of *seeing-that*, but in saying this we need to distinguish it from the weaker type of *seeing-that*, in which Percy saw that the window was shut from the look on Linda's face. The stronger type of seeing-that is one in which the perceiver is visually affected by an object in such a way that he or she sees, say, "that *it* is looking for a hen", "that *it* has been painted" and so on. In this second case, we should mark it by some such device as

> "Mary saw that *that fox* was looking for the hen";
> "Mary saw *of that fox* that it was looking for the hen".

The point of using this device is to indicate that the capacity to make the judgement about the fox is linked with the fact that the perceiver and fox are in causal commerce: the fox causally affects the perceiver in such a way that the perceiver has the capacity to discriminate the fox from its environment, to locate it in space, to track it with the eyes and to make judgements. This type of seeing-that, far from standing in contrast to seeing-X, involves the latter. This type of seeing-that, moreover, stands in contrast to the other type of seeing-that, in the same way as seeing-X does.

What I have argued is that the distinction made in natural language between seeing the window and seeing that the window was F, should be understood as a distinction between two types of seeing-that. It is easy enough, moreover, to understand the point of making this distinction in the way that we do. It is that the report "Percy saw that the window was shut" states precisely the content of Percy's perceptual thought (belief), whereas "Percy saw the window" or "Freda heard the car crash" leaves open whether Percy identified the window as a window or Freda the car crash as a car crash and, perhaps even more importantly, leaves open whether Percy or Freda had false beliefs about the perceived object or event. If it is true that all perceiving is conceptualized, for example, all seeing-X is seeing X-as . . ., then, given that the same thing, the window or the horse or the car crash, can be seen under a range of different aspects, and given that it is always seen under some of these aspects and not all, then it makes good sense to be able to distinguish between those cases in which the perceiver sees the thing (X) under some aspect or other, and those cases in which we want to say precisely which aspect it was.

One of the main reasons for thinking that there is a form of seeing that does not involve concepts is that there is a primary kind of seeing that we share with animals, and it is doubtful that they have the same concepts as us. Now, if by "concepts" we mean linguistically expressed concepts then, clearly, animal perceiving will not involve this kind of concept. However, once we attribute to the animals the practical concepts described earlier in this chapter, then it is far more plausible that all perceiving involves perceiving-as, in the conceptual sense. We should note, moreover, that the primary evidence that we have that the animal sees something is evidence at the same time that the animal sees that something as being a certain way, for example, as watching it, as standing before it, as being edible, as being ready to paw and so on. Our evidence for such claims is the behaviour the animal engages in. For example, the ability of a gazelle to track with its eyes the movements of a lion indicates its ability to locate it in space, that is, to see the lion as occupying a certain place. There is a further important point to make in this context. To say that all perceiving involves perceiving-as and therefore involves conceptualization is not to deny that perceiving also involves non-conceptual elements. Indeed, as I shall argue later in the book, there is good reason to think that an adequate theory of perception requires an integration of non-conceptual and conceptual elements.

Whatever the case with animal perception, there is, as I have argued, good reason for thinking that for sophisticated language-users there is a primary kind of seeing that is both object-based and is a type of *seeing-that* (and hence *seeing-as*, in the conceptualized sense). There are additional reasons, however. These reasons depend on the important fact that language-users can describe their experiences of seeing; that is to say, they can appeal to the description of seeing from the first person point of view. I don't just see a bird or the sun: I see a bird before me or facing me or facing away. Similarly I see the sun rising or setting or (very occasionally) standing still, or shining brightly. That is to say, I ordinarily see objects – apples, foxes, trees, people – but objects under an aspect. I see an apple before me, standing out against a background, as presenting a certain face, as resting and so on. It need not be true that I see *that* an apple is before me, *see that* an apple is standing out and so on. I see a particular apple, but not necessarily as an apple. What is true is that the perceiver sees *of that apple* that *it* is before him or her, that *it* is standing out against its background, that *it* is presenting a certain face and so on.

In addition, to claim that Percy saw a boar coming towards him implies that Percy acquired certain beliefs, for example, that something (yet to be specified) was coming towards him. It is not necessary that Percy believed that it was a boar; he may have taken it for a warthog, or a jackal, or he may simply have been unsure what it was. What we can say is:

Percy saw of *that boar* that it was coming towards him.

What is necessary is that Percy discriminated visually the boar from its surroundings. He must have some true belief about the boar, although what exactly is left undetermined. For Percy to see the boar coming towards him requires that Percy believe that something was coming and that belief to be true.

We can now say the following: perceptual reports of the form "Percy saw that X was F-ing", have two different uses, depending on the context. In one, it is implied that Percy saw X; in the other, it does not. In this second case, it is implied that there was something that Percy saw, but not necessarily X. This means that central to both cases is a primary sense of seeing, *seeing an object*: Percy's seeing a bird, seeing a church and so on. This kind of seeing is extensional: to correctly say that Percy saw a bird implies that there existed a bird that was seen. It does not mean, however, that Percy's seeing a bird is non-conceptual. We can capture a conceptual, extensional sense of seeing X as follows:

Percy saw of *that bird* that it was jumping.

Percy need not conceptualize the bird as a bird, but he would need to conceptualize it in some way, for example, as an object that is located at a certain place and that stands out from its background.

We may summarize the result of this discussion as follows: there is a primary kind of seeing, object-based seeing, which is usually described in the form "the cat saw the bird" or "the cat saw the bird on the ground". This primary kind of seeing is both object-based and conceptualized. For the cat to see the bird requires seeing the bird as being a certain way, or as being in a certain place. We can characterize this kind of seeing as follows:

1. Percy sees a bird:
   For some bird, and for some property F, Percy sees of that bird that it is F.
2. Percy sees of a bird that it is F:
   There is a bird in causal contact, of a visual kind, with Percy. Percy is causally affected so as to acquire a perceptual state that enables Percy to locate the bird, and to know that it is F.

Natural realism: the importance of the first person point of view

The task I have embarked upon in this chapter is to spell out the details of the "natural realist" view of perception. There are two sides to this task: to describe it from both the subjective, first person point of view and the objective, third person point of view. One side expresses the view of an expert perceiver who reflects on what is very familiar to them, on what it is to perceive an object. The second side expresses the view of someone who reflects on what it is for another to perceive. This point of view is the third person point of view. These two points of view are connected. As P. F. Strawson, Wittgenstein and others have argued, it is unlikely that I would be in a position to reflect on, and describe, what it is for me to perceive unless I had already become aware that I perceive, through being a member of a community, one that described perceivers and perception from the third person point of view. We need, therefore, to demonstrate how the two approaches are actually linked.

That the first person point of view is significant in giving an adequate account of perception is clear from what has already been argued in this chapter; namely, that perception serves the function implicit in its having those roles with respect to the acquisition of knowledge. It is the means of: the acquisition of practical knowledge; the acquisition of theoretical knowledge; and the justification of knowledge-claims. In gaining an understanding of how perception serves these roles, it is clearly of importance to take into account what can be described from the first person point of view. Furthermore, as was argued in the previous section, the first person point of view has a role to play in developing an adequate account of *seeing* and *seeing-that*. In these cases the role of the first person point of view is understood against the background of an account of the natural realist view, described from the third person point of view.

That discussion, moreover, brought out something more important. At least certain of the aspects that we recognize as essential to seeing are such that their recognition depends on appeal to phenomenology, that is, appeal to the first person point of view. If we restrict ourselves to describing from the third person point of view, then we can give an account of perception as involving the perceiver as: (a) identifying objects; (b) responding to the object; and (c) acting in response to various qualities possessed by the object, for example, its shape, colour, contour, texture and so on. However, there are aspects to perception that seem to require understanding what it is to perceive an object, that is, require an appeal to the first person point of view. For example, perceptual experience of, say, a watch or a cup in my hand is often a continuous experience over an extended period of time. I see the watch or the cup as a unified, three-dimensional whole. It is hard to see how we can understand this aspect to perceiving, except through knowing what it is like to have such experiences. Another important aspect to perceiving concerns picking out an object from its background, that is, as having a contour whereby it stands out against the background. This aspect is crucial for locating the object in space and in targeting the object in action. But what it is to visually discriminate the object from its background is something that we need to be able to identify from the first person point of view. From the third person point of view, we know that someone has discriminated something because they act, but it is necessary for the perceiver to discriminate in order for them to act. It thus appears that the claim that seeing is seeing under an aspect, at least for certain crucial and central aspects, requires reliance on the first person point of view.

In emphasizing, as I have, the importance of the first person point of view, I am, at the same time, emphasizing the importance of perceptual experiences. The question of how perceptual experiences are best characterized is a vexed one, with a variety of important rival theories on offer. One of the difficulties is that the term "perceptual experience" can be used either in a philosophically charged way, as involving certain assumptions, or in a neutral way. There is, for example, a long philosophical tradition in which perceptual experiences are thought of as some kind of inner conscious state, which is both caused by sensory stimulation and capable of influencing the perceiver's actions. There is, however, another philosophical tradition that rejects this view, proponents of which are, for example, Wittgenstein, Gilbert Ryle and P. M. S. Hacker. Moreover, among those who do think of experiences as some kind of inner state, there is widespread dispute about what kind of states they are, for example, concerning the phenomenal character of such states, the type of content they carry and so on.

In Chapter 3, I examine this question but, for the moment, I want to argue that we can accept the importance of the first person point of view without troubling ourselves about the precise role of perceptual experiences. The point of acknowledging the subjective side to the natural realist view is a simple one. It is that this theory of perception is one formulated by those who themselves are competent perceptually, that is, they are experts with respect to the simple abilities specified above. Success in perception, perceptual achievement, is something that each of us experiences and knows through experience. Another way of putting this point is to say that the theorist knows from the inside what it is to see a peach, a blue sky and so on. Moreover, the theorist depends for checking his or her theory on assuming that the subjects being studied are such experts. This is so even if there are occasions on which the theorist corrects the subject. There is a temptation to dismiss this kind of knowledge on the grounds that it is "know-how". It may involve *know-how*, but we need to be alert to the fact that there are different kinds of know-how. As far as these perceptual capacities are concerned, the perceiver knows not only how to do things, but what it is to exercise the abilities in question. That is, he or she knows what successful achievement is. In order to know what is involved in exercising these abilities, he or she knows, among other things, what it is like to formulate the knowledge/beliefs gained.

In stressing the importance of first person experience, I am not claiming that the first person access is incorrigible, that it is always productive of indubitable, certain pieces of knowledge. Nor am I claiming that the person is the final or ultimate authority. The claim is that from the first person point of view, the person is an authority, that his or her reports not only have weight, but have considerable weight, and that while the person's report can be rejected or revised, and the person can be asked to "try again", the reports ought not be lightly dismissed.

Another way of making the point is as follows. Those of us who can see are competent at vision. For those of us who are competent in this way, it is possible to reflect on our capacities and skills, and to describe what it is that happens when we see things. There is no need to hold that such descriptions are infallible. Some people will describe better than others; any of us might make mistakes. Notwithstanding these concerns, there is no reason why first person descriptions of "what it is to see" should not provide important data for any adequate theory of vision. It is important to acknowledge that, while adopting the Aristotelian–Stoic approach to the philosophy of perception leads one to emphasize the description of perception from the third person point of view, this emphasis is not exclusive. There is, on this approach, an important place for the first person point of view. In the rest of this chapter I shall try to show how we can, on this approach, integrate the two points of view.

Direct perceptual acquaintance

On the face of it, the subjective side to the natural realist view coheres neatly with the objective side. From the first person point of view, the most natural view to take of perception is that what we are directly aware of are physical objects. In visual perception, for example, we see before us a physical object, a specific watch, one that is silver, slightly battered, one that has a history and so on. According to the objective side to natural realism, that is, the account from the third person point of view, it seems non-controversial that what we perceive are physical objects and processes. It is objects such as these that causally affect the perceptual systems, in such a way as to enable the perceiver to act selectively with respect to them.

Before we can conclude, however, that everything is in order, we need to explore more fully the description of natural realism from the first person point of view. It would be more accurate, for example, to say not just that I see a physical object, but that I am presented with a range of objects spread out before me, in a configuration. I am confronted visually with a patterned layout or landscape populated with various objects. On any specific occasion, I see a particular object against a patterned background.

Furthermore, perception does not consist in an instantaneous act of perception, a perceptual experience at a given time, t. It consists of a series of perceptual experiences integrated into a coherent sequence. That integrated sequence of perceptual experiences takes place within a situation in which the perceiver engages with things in the environment. In visual perception, one moves the eyes, and changes the focus of one's gaze, one moves the head, the direction in which one looks and so on. Visual perception takes place, moreover, within a context in which we use our other senses to engage with things in the world, and we are poised to act within that world.

More generally, the following components to the natural view are crucial:

I am presented with a specific particular object:
(a) It is a specific object, for example, a particular chair, with specific detailed characteristics. It is not just blue, but a highly specific shade of blue, say Prussian blue. It is not just long but has a specific length; it has not just an elliptical seat, but one that has a certain degree of ellipticity.
(b) It can exist independently of the act of perception, that is, of that perceptual experience;
(c) It is seen against a patterned background, as having borders that demarcate it from that background;
(d) When it is not perceived, the object has those properties that it is presented as having in the act of perception, and in just the same form.

In perception, I am perceptually acquainted with a specific particular, discriminated from its background, having a high degree of specificity, where that particular can exist independently of the act of perception. There may be some doubt about item (d), about whether it is plausible to think of this as part of a "natural view". There is of course a danger that I am over-intellectualizing the natural view.

However, it seems to me that this thesis is at least a tacit belief presupposed by the natural view that informs the view of perception that we ordinarily and naturally assume. This point may be expressed as follows. Perceptual acquaintance is thought of as a two-term relation between the individual perceived object and the perceiver. This is an extensional relation, that is to say, Elaine's seeing a peach is similar to Arthur's touching a football, Tom's standing on a horse, Freda's being two miles from the city centre and so on. In these cases both objects have a distinct character that remains the same whether they stand in that particular relation or not.

The natural view that I am describing has affinities with the "common-sense theory of vision" that Landesman describes in his book, *The Eye and Mind*. In this book, he argues that, prior to scientific and philosophical reflection, we have a general understanding of vision and how it relates to the world that it discloses.[9] It includes, he says, a primitive and undeveloped psychology of vision:

> This common sense theory is part of our wider pre-scientific conceptual scheme that incorporates our basic concepts of interpretation as well as generalisations and information that we use in applying our concepts . . . It is implicit in and implicated in our response to the world, in both our actions and thoughts.[10]

Making explicit what this understanding consists in, for example, in expressing it in the form of certain central theses or principles, is an important philosophical task. In performing this task, we rely in part on reflecting on our participation in such practices. We are, after all, experts in using perceptual-claims. In part we rely on standing back from the practices and reflecting on them.

Landesman sets out a list of main tenets (principles) that he takes to belong to the common-sense theory, and to each of which he gives a label.[11] Some of the principles are obvious: (a) that we take for granted that things we see exist independently of our seeing them (*the principle of independent existence*); (b) that it is not only the objects that have independent existence but also their features (*the principle of feature objectivity*). Other principles are not so obvious, until pointed out to us: for example, (c) visual perception is a certain function or activity of humans and animals that can be divided into various phases: conducting a search with one's eyes; seeing or catching sight of what I was searching for; the acquisition and knowledge based on the seeing. There are other principles that Landesman claims are central. These principles are components of the accounts of common-sense realism, or naive realism, that earlier generations of philosophers, Broad, Price and later Mundle, drew attention to, even if only to oppose. One is *the principle of direct acquaintance*: we take seeing things to be a direct apprehension of them. By way of elaborating the principle of direct acquaintance, Landesman writes:

> Sometimes we acquire information indirectly, from what others tell us, for example, or by means of signs and evidence. Often we discover what must have happened by an inference from data taken as premises. In contrast, seeing something is non-inferential. When you see something, it is right before your eyes. When I see, for example, a yellow pencil, I do not infer its existence from signs; I am inspecting the pencil itself. The belief that I acquire that there is a yellow pencil lying upon my desk is not based on evidence; you don't need evidence when you have the very thing itself.[12]

All inferences must, sooner or later, it is argued, be traced back to a direct acquaintance with objects. This notion of *direct acquaintance* is a notion expressing a relationship between the perceiver and an object. The acquaintance presupposes the existence of the object. There is a further controversial question about the status of the acquaintance involved. On the face of it, direct acquaintance is a special form of knowledge, knowledge by acquaintance, as opposed to knowledge by description, *knowledge-that*.

Given this (incomplete) characterization of the natural view of perception, there are a number of components that are of greatest relevance for our enquiries. Describing these components by reference to the point of view of the perceiver, we can say:

(a) The natural view is *realist*. I am presented with a particular that exists independently of the act of perception.
(b) The relation of perceptual acquaintance is *epistemic*, although

of a special sort. It is an occurrent state of perceptual awareness: I am aware of (conscious of) the particular.

(c) The view is a *direct realist* one. It is a certain particular, a physical
object that is presented to me, and of which I am aware. There
is no intermediary between the physical object and the perceiving subject, which is either presented or that I am aware of.

There is a question about how this notion of *being aware of* is to be
understood. It is an epistemic notion. The subject is aware of, or
conscious of, the particular. However, it seems that this perceptual
awareness is a *sui generis* state of awareness. It seems quite unlike
other epistemic states, for example, beliefs, or judgements and
thoughts, which have propositional content: Tracey believes that
Martha is angry; Jay believes that the shed is rusty and so on.

These notions of *perceptual acquaintance* and *perceptual awareness* have been of crucial importance historically in the philosophy
of perception. It is important that we get as clear as possible about
them, in order to make progress in the subject. One possible way to
understand the notions is to treat them as equivalent to (the gener-
alized perceptual forms of) seeing X, rather than seeing-that X has
certain features, where the object of seeing is taken to be some
particular, either an object or an event, and is not propositional. As
I argued in an earlier section (pp. 34–7), there are problems with
this distinction, expressed in the sharp form defended by Dretske,
Landesman and others. We can, I argued, defend an account of
perceptual acquaintance that treats it as involving a special form of
descriptive knowledge. The argument on this point, which I began
in this chapter, will be continued in Chapter 4, where I lay out a
theory of perception that modifies the account of knowledge-by-
acquaintance, defended by Gareth Evans and John McDowell.

Perceptual experiences and natural realism

The discussion in the previous section has underlined the importance of the first person point of view in making clear the natural
realist view of perception. Its role has been to enable us to flesh out
the view as described from the third person point of view. In the
chapters to follow, I shall examine a range of theories that attempt
to give a more complete account of perceptual experience. For the

time being, let me state in summary form what I take to be a non-controversial account of perceptual experiences in perception, as described from the first person point of view. If we concentrate on the phenomenology of perceptual experiences, that is, on the first person point of view, then it seems plausible to hold that in a typical veridical perception, for example, I perceive a bird bath in the garden with the occasional bird landing and then removing itself, then I enjoy a perceptual experience, or sequence of experiences, such that the perceptual experience:

(a) involves the discrimination of a bird bath, a three-dimensional object with contours and hard edges, from background;
(b) provides the basis for actions *vis-à-vis* that object, that is, focusing on it, staring at it, moving towards it and so on;
(c) provides the basis for explicit judgement:
  • the bird bath contains the same bird as yesterday;
  • it contains little water
(d) involves (is associated with) thoughts/beliefs:
  • there is a three-dimensional unified-whole before me;
  • *that object* has a reverse side.
(e) provides the basis for having thoughts about the perceived objects, for example, thoughts that:
  • *that table* used to belong to mother;
  • *that grass* should be cut.
(f) provides the basis to make judgements in relation to my perceptual capacities:
  • I can see a green bird in *that tree*
  • *that plate* looks very old to me

Having set out the natural view of perception, natural realism, in this way, it is important to emphasize that to describe the "natural view" is not necessarily to endorse it. I am claiming that this view is natural to adopt for someone who is a competent perceiver and who attempts to describe how it is, typically, with him or her, when he or she perceives. The natural view reflects the phenomenology of perception.

I propose to argue that once we take into account other perceptual phenomena, there is reason to think that this natural realist view cannot be sustained, at least in its entirety. We need to amend it so that it can accommodate the other phenomena. Of course, this does not mean that we have to reject everything in the natural realist view. After all, if the natural view seems to reflect the phenomenology of the situation, we need to account for that fact. If this view represents the best attempt of those who are experts in perception, that is, expert perceivers, then we need to accommodate, *as best we can*, their attempts to describe that phenomenology. That is to say, if we reject the natural view, we need to explain why it is so plausible. That explanation, we might note, is likely to be easier to achieve the less we have to deviate from the natural view. It is, I suggest, a good strategy, in choosing rival theories, to choose that one which requires the least changes, other things being equal.

Conclusion

My aim in this chapter was to set out a framework for thinking about perception, a "natural realist view of perception", one that will provide an account of the roles perception plays and will provide a motivation for the discussion of perceptual experiences. Adopting the Aristotelian–Stoic approach to the examination of perception it is possible, I have argued, to describe what we may call a "natural realist view of perception". It is a minimal account, describing in general terms the processes and activities of perception that perceivers engage in. It is a general, minimal account of perception that describes perception as a natural process involving the perceiver and the world in which the perceiver is situated, such that it reflects the fact that perception serves (at least) three roles:

- the means of acquisition of practical knowledge;
- the means of acquisition of more theoretical knowledge
  - ordinary knowledge
  - scientific knowledge;
- an important means of justifying knowledge claims.

While it is important to emphasize the role of perception in the acquisition of knowledge, it is just as important to recognize the ways in which the perceiver can acquire perceptual states that do not amount to knowledge. Some of these states are illusions and hallucinations, and some are variations in the way objects appear, but some are perceptual thoughts. I can, for example, have a thought about a perceived object, about how I might make plans to use that object, for example, to mow the grass, to paint the chair, to throw away the cup and so on.

An adequate theory of perception has to accommodate both features of the perceptual process. These features play a part in our extending a minimalist version of natural realism to include perceptual experiences. More generally, however, it is reflection on perceptual situations, from the first person point of view, that leads us to see that the minimalist version needs extending. Once that extended version is in place, it is possible to see clearly why an adequate account of human perception requires an account of the role perceptual experiences play.

Summarizing, perceptual experiences, it would seem, serve the following functions:

- they are the means for discriminating objects and locating them in space;
- they are guides to action;
- they are connected with perceptual thoughts and beliefs.
- they form the basis for judgements.

The perceptual experience is a conscious experience, one that I am reporting on from the first person point of view. That is to say, the description given is meant to reflect the phenomenology of the situation. So far it is meant to be neutral with respect to the many theories of perceptual experience, although accepting some of the claims above as descriptions of experience would seem to rule out certain of the theories. At the very least, they place an onus on defenders of these theories to provide suitable reconstructions of the descriptive claims.

Theories of perceptual
3 experiences

Two crucial elements emerge from my elaboration of the natural realist account of perception. The first is that perception is a process involving the acquisition of perceptual knowledge, both practical and reflective. The second is that an adequate description of the natural realist account requires the minimalist account to be extended so as to include an account of perceptual experiences and their role in the acquisition of this knowledge.

In arguing about the role of perceptual experiences we need to be careful since, as was argued in Chapter 2, we can draw a contrast between a neutral sense of "perceptual experience", and one that is philosophically charged. The term "perceptual experience" is often used in philosophical discussions with certain philosophical commitments built into it, for example, it is thought of as involving sensations, or sense impressions, or phenomenal elements or qualia and so on. Understood in these ways, the existence of perceptual experiences is controversial and needs to be argued for. However, it is also possible to use the term in a neutral sense. In the most neutral sense, examples of perceptual experiences are instances of *seeing things*, *hearing things* and so on. More specifically they are, for example: seeing a jacaranda tree in full bloom, hearing a flute played, touching soft velvet and so on. The class of perceptual experiences can be widened to include cases that aren't veridical perceptions: "I am seeing stars"; "that wine tastes sour to me"; "that cloud looks like a ship on fire to me"; "her face looks unfriendly to me"; "it seems to me as if that glass has a film over its top"; "it seems to me as if there is a noise inside my head" and so on. That these are examples of experiences, few would dispute. What stirs controversy are questions of how we should think of these experiences: how we should analyse them, what their structure is and so on. Any account of perceptual experiences will have to include cases such as these, and any adequate theory of perception will need to give an account of the role of perceptual experiences.

Before proceeding, I should clarify the claim that it is a central requirement for a philosophical theory of perception that it should give us a clear and viable account of perceptual experiences, that is, conscious states. This claim might be questioned since it would appear that there are forms of perception that are non-conscious. Whether there are or are not such forms, there is certainly conscious perception. This is the kind of perception that I wish to discuss. This is not an idle whim. One of the prominent features of human beings who learn about their environment and intervene in it is that they are conscious perceivers. Whatever perceptual mechanisms are involved, perception is a process whereby such perceivers become aware of the world and, on the basis of that, act in the world, make judgements about the objects perceived and have thoughts about those objects. Whatever non-conscious tasks are achieved, there is a conscious achievement, of seeing, hearing and so on, which is central to perceiving.[1]

In this chapter, I shall describe what I take to be the major competing theories of perceptual experience, finishing with an outline of a theory that presents a natural-sign view of perceptual experience. I shall begin, however, by considering the views of those philosophers who seem to deny the reality of perceptual experiences, arguing that their view is in effect not the denial of perceptual experiences but a view about the character of perceptual experiences.

Conscious perceptual experiences: their reality

Even if we take the term "perceptual experience" in the neutral sense just outlined, an ambiguity remains. On the one hand, it may be understood as describing a complex process, or activity, one of using our sensory organs, for example, the eyes, or ears and so on, in the performance of a task. The task, when successful, has a certain upshot, the achievement of a certain kind (e.g. discriminating a bird from the background foliage) or a quasi-achievement (e.g. seeming to see a bird). On the other hand, the perceptual experience can be taken to comprise not so much the whole process but rather the upshot of that process: the end-state(s) that comprises the achievement of the task. It is perceptual experiences of the latter kind that comprise the target for standard theories of perceptual experience. An account of such perceptual experiences is of crucial importance, but it needs to be set against a background in which an account of the perceptual experiences, in the more general sense, is provided.

There are, however, some philosophers who seem to deny that there are perceptual experiences of this second kind. Ryle is famous for arguing that verbs such as "see" and "hear" do not denote "special experiences or mental happenings, they denote achievements of tasks, or successes in undertakings".[2] But if we take the special perceptual experiences to be part of what the successes in undertakings involve, and also of the failures, then again Ryle's positive remarks can be accommodated by a philosopher who does insist on the existence of special experiences.

Hacker, for another example, concedes that there is a viable notion of *perceptual experience*, but he denies that this notion fits any notion of "perceptual experience" as used by so many philosophers of perception.[3] He writes that the term "perceptual experience" is legitimately introduced into philosophical discussion "only as a general term to avoid the circumlocutory forms 'seeing, hearing, tasting, smelling, or feeling' (these being ways of learning how things are 'by experience')". Perception is the acquisition of knowledge, by virtue of the exercise of faculties of sense, and of the performance of certain activities:

> The perceptual senses are faculties for acquisition of knowledge about what is in one's environment. To perceive is to apprehend, discern, observe, recognise or distinguish some current feature of one's environment by the use of one's sensory organs.[4]

The perceptual organs are used in the exercise of the corresponding perceptual faculty. Hence "the concept of the sense of sight is essentially connected with the concept of looking (and watching, observing, scanning, surveying, glancing and peeping)".[5] Furthermore, the use of expressions such as "it looks to me as if . . ." is not to describe anything at all, let alone to provide descriptions of perceptual experience: "To a first approximation, such sentences, in the first-person present tense, are used as expressions of what one takes oneself to be observing".[6]

Much of what Hacker has to say here may be perfectly acceptable. It leaves entirely open, however, the question of whether there is a need for a further notion of "perceptual experience", in addition to the one admitted by Hacker. As well, he leaves open the further question of whether such a concept is necessary to fill the gaps in an adequate account of perception, especially the gaps left untouched by the positive things that he has to say. A possible argument would be that when the use of one's perceptual organs in the activities of looking, tasting and so on leads to a successful upshot, then that upshot involves perceptual experiences. Nothing he has said above rules that out.

When philosophers such as Hacker and Ryle deny that there are visual experiences what they are really rejecting, I suggest, is that there are sensory experiences, or sensory, sensuous, phenomenal components to perceptual experience. In other words, they are denying that, when one exercises one's perceptual capacities, in making perceptual judgements, there are sensory experiences that are, or could be, the ground of the judgements. That is, they should be interpreted, not so much as denying perceptual experiences, but rather as rejecting a very specific view of what perceptual experiences consist in.

We may concede to Ryle and Hacker that the term "experience" is ambiguous. In one sense it describes an activity, for example, the experience of travelling through Siberia, or living for six months in the Arctic region. Seeing, hearing, smelling and so on, it is suggested, are experiences like that. We can, however, accept this suggestion while claiming that the activity involves perceptual experiences in a stronger sense. Indeed, the account of minimal natural realism allows just that. Seeing a fox or a tree, it is claimed, consists of a complex activity or process, in which: (a) there is causal contact, through the use of one's eyes, between the fox (tree) and the perceiver; (b) the fox (tree) catches the attention of the perceiver. Perceiving is an activity that culminates in successful completion of the activity. There is a dateable episode or event that constitutes the achievement. On the face of it, this episode or event is an experience. It is an experience of "seeing a fox", and what it consists of exactly will depend on the theory involved. It may be the having of a sensory experience by which one discriminates the fox from its background, an experience that carries non-conceptual content, and that gives rise to conceptual states, for example, "that fox is turning away". Or it may be, as others would have it, an experience with conceptual content, an experience that can be analysed into different components. However hard it is to decide on the character of these experiences, it seems undeniable that there are experiences.

When, therefore, philosophers are (usually) providing theories of perceptual experiences, it is perceptual experiences, in the narrow sense, that they are aiming at. There should be no doubt that there are such experiences and that, for them, a theory is required. It seems to me that there is little difficulty in giving examples of such experiences.

One can start with a number of simple cases. I close my eyes, and then place my hands over my eyes as well. I then turn my head in different directions. I will have a range of visual experiences, mostly mottled grey, with some patterns emerging after a while. When I face the window, the experiences are lighter. Secondly, while looking at the range of objects on my desk, a computer, a pad, a cup, a lamp, wires to the modem and the plug socket, stapler and so on, I place one finger on my left eyeball, and then roll it around. I have a distinctive visual experience, which in part is quite unlike any ordinary case of "seeing", and in part is very like. I have two extended visual images: one that moves as the eye-ball rolls, and another that remains stable. Thirdly, after reading Reid, I pay more attention to what goes on when I change my gaze around my room, when I look at objects at different distances, and in different states of juxtaposition. When I focus on my computer screen, I now notice that there is a double image of a pen-holder behind it. As I change my gaze to the pen-holder, I notice the two images move together and merge. At the same time I now notice the screen to form duplicate images. I am seeing the same objects, I am having the same beliefs about those objects, but I am noticing aspects of my visual experiences. (Possibly, a rival philosopher may give an account that shows that these are not experiences but only "experiences" but that will need to be argued, and extremely convincingly. My immediate purpose is to indicate that there is a notion of visual experience that is prima facie legitimate.) Fourthly, in the wheat-belt, I look over an extensive wheat field. I now notice different aspects to my visual experience: I notice that the wheat looks very different close up from the wheat at a distance. Up close I can distinguish the various stalks, but at a distance, the stalks "fuse" together. There is a different character to my experience of objects at a distance. The mountains look blue, but it is a special kind of blue: it has more in common with the blue of skies and of rainbows, which is quite different from the blue of paper and dresses. Fifthly, I look at a lit lamp for 20 seconds and then gaze at the white wall across the room. As my gaze moves, I have a visual experience of a moving coloured patch that gradually fades.

There seems to me that there is no question that there are visual experiences, or at least that there is a viable notion of *visual experience* that might be introduced in philosophers' discussions, but that would be easily understood more widely. The real matter is to give an adequate account of them, to show how they are involved in perception, and how the various types of visual experience are similar to and different from each other, and what kind of content they carry.

On the face of it, there are two characteristic features of perceptual experiences: they have a sensuous, phenomenal character and they are intentional. The taste of a ripe juicy peach, the smell of newly mown grass and the feel of soft velvet each has a rich sensuous character. The experiences are intentional in that they represent the world as being a certain way: as containing a robin before me, of there being a car crash in the neighbourhood and so on. There are some visual experiences that lack intentionality. If I close my eyes then I have a mottled darkish blue-grey visual experience. It is shapeless and without depth, but it does have a sensuous character. If I face towards a direct light, then my visual experience lightens. If I hold my arm across my closed eyelids, the experience darkens.

These two features of perceptual experiences, their sensuous, phenomenal character and their intentional content are "phenomenological" features. That is to say, they are features that the experiences appear to have. There is another possible phenomenological feature of experiences: the issue of whether they have a "feel". This concerns the issue of whether there is "something it is like to have the experience". Before proceeding, it is necessary to say something about the expression "what it is like". The term is used predominantly in discussions of qualia, that is, of subjective, qualitative, intrinsic qualities of experiences, but often not very clearly. It is sometimes assumed that to speak of the "what it is like" aspect of experiences is automatically to speak of the qualitative, intrinsic features of experiences, and to think of experiences in this way is to think of the phenomenal character of experiences. This seems to me to be unfortunate for a number of reasons:

(a) Some intrinsic features of experiences are quantitative, or at least numerical.

(b) It seems possible, for example, that there could be intellectual experiences, such as thoughts of certain kinds, without sensuous or qualitative character. It seems that they may have a feel to them, but a non-sensuous one. One possible example is provided by kinaesthetic perceptions that involve acquiring knowledge of where one's limbs are, without involving sensations. Perhaps, though, the point here is that the experiences have some feel, but a slight one and not one characteristic of specific perceptions. That is to say, perhaps a wide range of different perceptions share the same feel, a slight, vague, nondescript feel. Perhaps there is a spectrum of experiences with the least sensuous and most intellectualist on one end, and the most sensuous, least intellectual at the other.

(c) To talk of the "what it is like" aspect of experience is to talk of what it is like to be a subject of a certain type of experience. It may be that given that one knows what it is like to be a subject of a certain type of experience, for example, of seeing something blue, one is in a position to refer to the intrinsic qualities of those experiences – but sometimes one is not in such a position. There are certain experiences where I know what it is to be a subject of the experience, but I am in no position to describe the intrinsic qualities. For example, many acts of understanding: I can understand what you said when you said

"Would you like some more tea?", but there need be no distinctive intrinsic qualitative features to that experience.

Indeed it has been argued, with respect to all perceptual experiences, that when one knows what it is like to be the subject of a perceptual experience, what one knows is what it is like to have an experience with a certain content, that is, with a certain intentional or representational content. (See Tye, Dretske and R. Millikan, for example.) According to this line of thinking, all that one knows is the content of the experience (or that one has an experience with that content); one is not aware of the intrinsic qualities of the experience. In Chapter 9 I shall argue against this position. For the moment we need to acknowledge that some argument is required to dispose of the sort of dissenting view just described. We cannot exclude such views simply by fiat, or by definition.

Varieties of accounts of perceptual experiences

There is a range of different philosophical theories about perceptual experiences. These theories agree that there are perceptual experiences in the neutral sense described previously. The experiences are dateable episodes or events that are culminating stages in a physical process, which in cases of vision involves causal contact between object and the perceiver's eyes. The experiences have a role in the acquisition of perceptual knowledge, although the nature of that role is controversial. It is usually agreed as well that perceptual experiences have intentional content – they represent the world as being a certain way – and they have a phenomenal character. Where the accounts differ is over the nature of that content, and the phenomenal character, and how the two are related.

One important controversy concerns the issue of whether we need to allow for both perceptual experiences and sensory experiences (sensations). There is one tradition in which it is believed that there are two kinds of experience, or at least acts of the mind. This tradition goes back at least to Reid, who distinguished sensations from perceptions, treating them as distinct but related acts of the mind. The chief differences between the acts (or states), for Reid,

are that sensations have no objects and perceptions do, and that
sensations are non-conceptual whereas perceptions are conceptual.
Reid expresses his position as follows:

> Sensation, by itself, implies neither the conception nor belief of
> any external object. It supposes a sentient being, and a certain
> manner in which that being is affected; but it supposes no more.
> Perception implies a conviction and belief of something external
> – something different from both the mind that perceives and the
> act of perception. Things so different in their nature ought to be
> distinguished.[7]

Thinkers who have followed Reid closely in this are C, Ducasse, R.
Chisholm and, more recently, Evans, Dretske, Lowe and Alan
Millar. For those who adopt this approach, it is common to treat
sentences that refer to ways of tasting, looking, sounding and so on
as ambiguous. It is argued that, with respect to expressions such as
"tastes", "looks", "sounds" and so on, we need to distinguish between a conceptual sense and a phenomenal, non-conceptual sense.

There is another tradition that also makes a distinction between
sensory experience and perceptual experience, but draws it in a
conceptual way. Sensory experiences are thought of as components
of perceptual experience rather than as separate acts. On this view,
we should think of a perceptual experience as containing a sensory
experience with additional components, usually epistemological.
Broad, for example, took the perception of a bell to consist in a
complex act made up of being presented with a sensory presentation, combined with a belief (or thought) in the existence of a
physical object, a bell. The state of "being presented with a sensory
presentation" is thought of as comprising intuitive knowledge by
acquaintance.

Philosophers within this tradition included, besides Broad,
Price and G. E. Moore. Price is especially important. For Price,
there are typical perceptual experiences (acts), such as seeing a
tomato, seeing the blue sky and seeing pink rats, each of which
contains at least two elements: (a) the sensing of a sensory
constituent (being acquainted with sense-data); and (b) being *perceptually conscious* of a material object such as a tomato, a blue
vault or a pink rat. Being "perceptually conscious" he explains as

"taking its existence for granted", although in cases such as the blue sky or the pink rat, where the perceiver may know that the object does not exist, then presumably the "taking for granted" must be bracketed (in Husserl's or Dennett's sense). For Price, the two components, the act of sensing and the act of perceptual consciousness not only coexist in the single act, but are linked. It is not altogether clear how they are linked, but they are integrated into a unitary complex act. The perceptually conscious subject takes for granted not merely that the material object exists, but that "there exists a material object to which the sense-datum belongs".[8] There is, he writes, "no passage from sense-datum to the taken-for-granted, both coming before the mind at once as one single complex".[9]

This view is similar to that expressed by Broad. In all perceptual situations, Broad points out, there is, besides the subject, an objective constituent, some existing thing that the subject is aware of (and acquainted with) and, as well, a certain practical conviction (belief or thought): that this constituent is part of a large spatiotemporal continuous whole (a physical object).[10] That is to say, in all perceptual situations there is an external reference beyond the objective constituent. (The objective constituent is a sensum or group of sensa.) Broad calls the belief a "practical conviction", to indicate that it is not intellectual: it is possessed by animals and small children. To have this kind of practical conviction is "to act as it would be reasonable to act if one believed so and so, and to be surprised if the action turns out to be a failure".[11]

Part of this debate between the two camps is verbal and can be fixed quite easily. Both sides are agreed that there are different acts (or states): one a sensing and the other the acquisition of a belief, or the having of a thought. Both sides, moreover, distinguish these two acts from a further act: the making of an explicit judgement. They agree that if I see through my window a tree in leaf in the garden, then normally I form a belief about the tree, but it is another matter to go on and express the judgement "there is a tree in leaf in the garden", or the more complex judgement "I see in the garden the tree in leaf". This type of explicit judgement might be made overtly in conversation or sometimes in "inner speech". Either way it is distinct from the forming of the corresponding belief. We thus can have, on some occasions at least, three things: a sensory experience, a perceptual thought or belief and an explicit judgement. Mostly, we have only the first two.

There is a substantial dispute, however, both on the nature of sensory experiences and on their relation to perceptual experiences. With respect to the first issue, there is the question of whether sensory experience should be given an act–object analysis, as the Broad–Price group held, or whether it requires an adverbial analysis. According to Broad and Price, sensing is a form of knowledge by acquaintance that is directed at an object, a sensory presentation, or at a group of such objects. On the adverbial analysis of sensory experience, on the other hand, to taste a bitter taste is not to be presented with a sensory particular: it is to taste in a suitably modified way, it is to taste bitter-ly.

There is a second important difference concerning how sensory experiences are related to the conceptual element. The difference in understanding of this relationship is crucial. On the Broad–Price view, there are two separate components that are welded in a complex act: there is the objective constituent that is sensed (of which *we are* sensorily aware), and there is a conviction or belief that there is a material object present, and there is an awareness of the objective constituent as part of the material object. On the Reid–Dretske view, by contrast, there are only two states: the having of the sensation and the perceptual thought or belief (or the acquiring of this thought) whose content is given in terms of material objects and their qualities.

For Reid (and Dretske), the perceptual experiences, as opposed to the sensations, seem to be constituted by having a certain belief or thought, whose content is expressed for example, by "there is a tree in leaf before me". This perceptual thought/belief is distinct from the sensory experience, although caused by it. For Broad, on the other hand, although there are perceptual thoughts quite distinct from the sensory experience, the perceptual experience is a complex conscious act or state, comprising both the sensory experience and perceptual thought.[12] On the Broad–Price view, a description of the sensory state can provide justification for the statement expressed in the perceptual thought, although in normal perception there isn't any inference involved. The complex perceptual experience is meant to be an integrated conscious experience.[13]

It is a core thesis of the position that I am defending that perceptual experience is an integrated state or act, and the aim of the book is to try to show how this is the case, through the theory of double awareness characteristic of representationalism. It is crucial that any adequate theory of perception should solve this integration problem. It is the prime weakness of the two-stage accounts proposed by Reid and Dretske, I shall argue, that they cannot account for the integration.

There are two other theoretical approaches to perceptual experiences, however, for which this integration problem does not arise, at least on the face of it. Both challenge the distinction between sensory experience and perceptual experience, although in radically different ways. On the first rival approach, there are perceptual experiences but there are not sensations that are distinct sensory experiences nor components of perceptual experiences. Perceptual experiences are certain acts, the acquirings of perceptual beliefs, or states that are potential beliefs or inclinations to belief, or propensities to believe. These accounts provide epistemic accounts of experience, in which the notion of belief is central. There may be sensory states that carry non-conceptual content but these states do not comprise *experience*, in the way that Dretske and Reid supposed. Defenders of this type of account include David Armstrong, George Pitcher and John Heil.

In emphasizing the role of beliefs, or potential beliefs, such accounts treat the perceptual content carried by experiences as conceptual. There is, however, another approach to perception that likewise treats the content as conceptual and rejects the Reid–Dretske separation of sensation from perceptual experiences, but takes a different view of the role of perceptual beliefs. The idea is that perceptual experiences have perceptual content in the sense that they represent things as being a certain way. Examples of thinkers in this tradition are McDowell and P. F. Strawson.

It is a key feature of this approach that perceptual experience involves the acquisition of states with conceptual content. It, too, rejects the notion of sensory experiences in the sense of the experiencing of non-conceptualized sensory states. It presents, however, a very different account of perceptual experience, from that proposed by Armstrong, Pitcher and Heil. It takes perceptual experience to be a single state in which sensory and conceptual components are inextricably entwined. Whereas Dretske takes the sensory experiences to be experiences of sensory states that carry non-conceptual(ized) content, these theorists hold that sensory (perceptual) experiences carry conceptual content. McDowell has given a very extended treatment of this position,[14] but perhaps the most memorable characterization of the view is given by P. F. Strawson. He explicitly considers, only to reject, the view that there are two distinct stages in the formation of perceptual beliefs: first, the occurrence of sensible experience, and secondly, the deployment of concepts in the formation of beliefs on the basis of this sensible experience. Instead, he holds that the concepts employed in perceptual judgement about the world and sensible experience itself interpenetrate each other more closely than this picture suggests:

> The character of our perceptual experience itself, of our sense-experience itself, is thoroughly conditioned by the judgements about the objective world which we are disposed to make when we have this experience; it is, so to speak, thoroughly permeated – saturated, one might say – with the concepts employed in such judgements.[15]

In further explication of this line of thought, P. F. Strawson writes that the candid description of experience at any moment must normally be given in terms of these concepts; and not in the restricted terms that are appropriate at moments when the subject's attention is engaged only by sensation of special interest (i.e. clinical or aesthetic) interest. McDowell, too, claims that there is only one experience, a perceptual experience, whose content is already conceptual. There is a move from perceptual experience to perceptual judgement, but it is one in which the judgement *endorses* the pre-existing conceptual content, or at least some of it.[16] One way of putting the Strawson–McDowell view is to say that sensory experiences are actually thoughts but thoughts in sensory form. That is, we can distinguish two forms in which thoughts (which are conceptual) can take place: one is a sensory form, the other non-sensory.[17]

In so far as these last two accounts stress the conceptual content of perceptual experience, the difference may be more apparent than real. It would make sense for the belief-theorists to accept that the best account of the conceptual content of perceptual experiences is in terms of representational content, rather than the more specific and implausible belief-states. Perhaps the best demonstration of this point is the very detailed account of perceptual experiences that is presented by Austen Clark in his *A Theory of Sentience*.[18] While acknowledging the importance of Pitcher's approach to perception, Clark's account is distinctive in that it proposes that sensory experiences are representational states whose content is specified in terms of "proto-referential" and "proto-predicative" components.[19] This account has the advantage in my eyes of widening the notion of "conceptual" to include what might be thought of as "proto-conceptual" components. The important difference that keeps the two accounts apart is, if I understand them correctly, that Strawson, McGinn and McDowell stress that perceptual experiences have a phenomenal character that is entwined with, but not reducible to, the intentional content of the experience.

To summarize: I have described four rival accounts of perceptual experience and have cited some illustrative examples of philosophers who have developed such accounts, or ones that closely resemble them. One account of perceptual experience is shared by a representative realist such as Broad, and by a phenomenalist such as Price. The other three accounts underpin different versions of (cognitive) direct realism:

- The first assumes a two-stage model of perceptual experience, involving a non-conceptual sensory experience and a non-sensory conceptual state. This is the theory advanced by Dretske, Evans, Reid, Sellars and others.[20]
- The second uses a one-stage model of perceptual experience: the acquiring of non-sensuous conceptual states. This has been proposed by Armstrong, Pitcher, Heil and Clark.
- The third adopts a one-stage model of perceptual experience: it involves the having of states that are conceptual and sensory. The states are sensory states "saturated" with concepts. This account is one held by McDowell, Strawson, McGinn, Searle and, before them, Kant.

One thing these accounts have in common is that they are forms of direct realism and, more accurately, direct cognitive realism, to contrast them with naive realism. They have different views about the nature of perceptual experiences, but they are all agreed that in perceptual experience we are perceptually aware of physical objects and their qualities, and not the experiences themselves, nor qualities of the experiences, nor sensory qualities that are caused by the perceived physical objects. On these theories the perceiver has the perceptual experiences or enjoys them, but is not (normally) aware of the experiences: the experiences are not "objects" for the perceiver.

The three accounts described above are, as we have seen, forms of cognitive direct realism. They are agreed that when the perceiver enjoys perceptual experiences, he or she is not normally aware of the experiences or aspects of them. This kind of account stands in contrast to the Broad–Price position described earlier. There is, however, yet another approach, a fifth account of perceptual experience, that is not only a serious contender, but, I shall argue, the right account. To be more accurate, I think that the right account of perceptual experience requires an amalgam of elements from the others.

Like McDowell and P. F. Strawson and company, I wish to reject the model that makes a sharp distinction in perception between two distinct kinds of act or experience: the first a sensation, or sensory experience, and the second a different act of perception; the first being a non-conceptual state and the second a conceptualized state – either a thought, a judgement or a belief. The model I propose, however, does not deny that there are distinct non-conceptual states and perceptual thoughts. The perceptual experience, or state of perceptual awareness, is a complex sensory and conceptual act. Understanding it requires adopting a hybrid model, as opposed to the two-stage model, according to which successful perceiving takes one from a non-conceptual state to a distinct conceptual state. On the hybrid model, successful perceiving normally involves double awareness: of physical object and sensory representation. It contains both a conceptual element, one related to physical objects, and a non-conceptual element, one with a phenomenal character. The hybrid theory presupposes not a two-stage model, but a two-aspect model.

Conclusion

There is a range of different philosophical theories about the nature of perceptual experiences. I have described the major types, drawing a contrast between the traditional account favoured by Broad and Price, and a variety of rival theories, all of which are variants of *cognitive direct realism*. These theories earn that title by virtue of the fact that they take perceptual experiences to be states with intentional content, where that content is content about physical objects and their qualities, and not sensory states or experiences. These intentional states are called by some theories "representational states" and the theory "representationalist", but these representations are not "objects" of which the perceiver is aware. On the Broad–Price theory, by contrast, the perceptual experience is a complex state having both a conceptual element and another component that has a non-intentional, non-conceptual character. The non-intentional character is something of which the perceiver is aware (or can be aware, without much difficulty).

Given this variety of positions, two major issues about the nature of perceptual experience emerge. The first concerns the question of whether it is possible to distinguish two experiences or two components of a single experience, where one experience or component is non-conceptual and the other conceptual. The second issue concerns the question of whether perceptual experiences have a phenomenal character and if so whether that is reducible to, or is distinct from, the intentional/representational content of the experience (whether that content is conceptual or non-conceptual).

Before we address these issues, however, and see how their resolution might help solve the problem of direct/indirect realism, there is a preliminary step to take. We need to clarify the distinction between direct realism and indirect realism, for here there is scope for deep misunderstanding.

Representationalism: representations as
4 # natural signs

We can, I have argued, identify primary cases of perception as ones that involve the acquiring of knowledge, both practical and theoretical. Both kinds of knowledge are what might be called "object-based knowledge" and involve knowledge by acquaintance. The practical knowledge is manifested in a variety of ways: in locating the object in space, discriminating the object from its background and in targeting one's action on the object, for example, in grasping, touching or pushing the object in question.

The description of object-based knowledge in this context suggests that the right theory of perception is some version of direct realism, and that indirect, representative theories are ruled out. This suggestion, I shall argue, ought to be resisted. It is possible, however, to formulate a representative theory of perception that will handle this kind of perceptual knowledge, a hybrid theory, to be more accurate, that contains direct and indirect components.

Direct and indirect theories of perception
One of the central questions in the philosophy of perception is whether perception is direct or indirect. This question historically has been framed within the context of the debate between direct realist theories of perception, and the representative theory of perception (representational realism), where the latter is understood as committed to indirect realism. The contrast is typically registered in the following way:

- *Indirect realism/representational realism:* The perceiver perceives physical objects and states of affairs indirectly by perceiving immediately or directly other items, standardly sensory particulars or states of affairs.
- *Direct realism:* The perceiver perceives immediately (or directly) physical objects and states of affairs without perceiving any intermediary.

It is a major contention of this book that things are more complex than this simple dichotomy suggests. And, more specifically, it is the major thesis of this book that it is possible to formulate a coherent, viable theory of perception, according to which perception of physical objects is direct (and immediate) but which nevertheless operates through awareness of intermediaries.

The way of formulating the contrast, in the first place, is very misleading. On a carefully phrased representationalist view, one does not perceive the sensory items at all. One is aware or conscious of them. One source for this misreading is that many traditional philosophers, for example, Locke, used the term "perceive" to mean (or at least to include) being aware of or being conscious of something. It is misleading, therefore, to use the mediate perception/immediate perception contrast here. Of course one can stipulate that "directly perceive" has a special sense, that is, the same as "aware of", but the problem with this, as with many stipulations, is that it is easy to forget that one has made the stipulation, and so, easy to lapse into using the term in the other sense.

The right way to present the representationalist thesis is to say that the perceiver does not perceive physical objects except by being aware of intermediaries. One does not perceive the intermediary at all. This point is not a trivial one. Perceiving a physical object is being caused by that object to have a sensory representation. Being aware of the sensory representation is not like that. Accordingly, given the way direct realism is characterized, it is possible to develop a representative theory of perception that is direct realist, in one sense, and indirect, in another.

There is a second dimension to the representative theory, as classically characterized, and this, too, needs to be challenged. The "classical" representative theory is thought of not only as an indirect theory, but as committed to a form of realism that is indirect and inferential. Inferential representational realism implies that one is aware of sensory states or sensory particulars as sensory states or particulars, and then makes an inference to the hypothetical cause of these states or particulars, some physical object. Or, if one does not actually make the inference, one could if one wished.

This way of characterizing the representative theory is widespread. An illustration of it can be found in Anthony Kenny's recent book, *Aquinas on Mind,* where he contrasts Aquinas's theory of perception with a different theory, "the representational theory of perception":

> According to some philosophers, in sense experience we do not directly observe objects or properties in the external world; the immediate objects of our experience are sense-data, private objects of which we have infallible knowledge, and from which we make more or less dubious inferences to the real nature of external objects and properties.[1]

In Aquinas's theory, on the other hand, there are no intermediaries like sense-data that come between the perceiver and perceived.

The same theme is developed by other writers, for example, Gareth Evans and Tyler Burge.[2] Burge, for example, presents his theory of perception as follows:

> our perceptual experience represents or is about objects, properties and relations that are objective . . . we have perceptual representations (or perceptual states with contents) that specify particular objective types of objects, properties or relations as such.

This view, Burge states, is a rejection of what used to be called the representational theory of perception.[3] According to that theory, he says, we primarily make reference to representations of objective entities; we make reference to objective entities only indirectly – by assuming or inferring that there are objective counterparts or causes of the representations that we make direct perceptual reference to.[4] Burge takes it that this theory is "discredited and rarely defended nowadays".[5]

Kenny and Burge, and others, are voicing the objection that the representative theory is discredited by the phenomenology of perceptual experience. This objection is a curious one. Its defects have been pointed out by a series of authors: Maund, Wright and Lowe, for example.[6] If we take the case of seeing things on television screens or on the screen at the cinema, where there is no question that what we see are images and that the images have representational content, it is certainly not the case that we make judgements about what is represented by making inferences based on judgements about states without representational content. If any of us were asked what it is we see on the television screen, we would naturally reply "a Collingwood player kicking a point", "Barry Humphries dressed up in drag", "Jennifer Capriati shaking hands" and so on. But if we were asked to "tell us what you see on the screen, tell us about the images", very few of us could say anything other than: a state (image . . .) representing a Collingwood player . . ., a state characteristic of Barry Humphries . . . and so on. The only way, in general, that we have to describe these states is by reference to football matches, chess games, lovers' quarrels and so on.

It is unquestionably true that in such situations we are aware of both, say, a cricket match in England, and states of a television screen in Australia; secondly, that it is by virtue of being aware of the latter that we are aware of the former; thirdly, that the screen states have both representational content and non-representational features; and, finally, that we cannot normally describe the screen states except in terms of what they represent. That the latter is true does not stop the television states from representing. No more should the parallel truth stop sensory states from representing.

The problem with the objection raised by Kenny and Burge is that the representative theory does not require the making of such inferences. As we saw in Chapter 1, Broad, one of the foremost modern defenders of the theory, explicitly rejects the inferential component. The answer to the objection is to say that, on the representative theory, perceiving does not involve inferences. Instead, it involves a form of double awareness: the perceiver is aware of both the sensory item and the physical object, and aware of the latter through being aware of the former.

The theory I propose to defend in this book holds that, in conscious attentive perception, one perceives physical objects and their qualities by becoming aware of sensory representations, that is, of a set of quality-instances (tropes) that are natural signs for the objects in question. The account has a number of key features. It contains the feature of double awareness that is characteristic of certain representative theories, without endorsing an inferential kind of realism. It also supports some of the intuitions of direct realism, by arguing that successful perceiving makes use of a number of beliefs that, while false, are productively false: they are beneficial illusions. Most important of all, however, is the claim that sensory representations, as natural signs, have a central role to play.

What makes the theory a representationalist one is the nature of the role that perceptual experiences play in the acquisition and exercise of this knowledge and, more specifically, the role played by sensory representations in these experiences. To understand that role we need an account of the knowledge concerned. For that I will call upon the work of Evans and McDowell. Their work is particularly useful since they reject representationalist theories of perception in favour of direct realism. What I shall argue is that not only can their account of perception be grafted onto a representationalist theory (at least the positive parts can) but the representative theory has the merit of successfully linking the practical and theoretical forms of knowledge.

Object-based perceptual knowledge and knowledge by acquaintance

In his *Varieties of Reference*, Evans develops a theory of demonstrative thought and, with it, demonstrative concepts. Central to this theory is an account of the role perception of specific objects has to play in the exercise of demonstrative concepts concerning those objects. Illustrative examples of the use of such concepts are provided by examples such as judgements such as "*that cup* is chipped" uttered while pointing at a particular cup in front of one, or "*this axe* was Grandma's favourite", in a perceptual context where I have an axe in my hands. Understanding a demonstrative concept requires having the ability to make demonstrative identification of the relevant object.

Evans examines the idea introduced by Russell, that demonstrative identification is a mode of identification quite unlike descriptive identification, one that is apt to underlie the use of a special sort of singular term, "Russellian singular terms".[7] (A Russellian singular term is one whose significance depends on its having a referent. If no such referent exists, the term lacks significance.) The general idea behind the theory of demonstrative identification that Evans develops is that "thinking about an object demonstratively is thinking about an object in a way which crucially depends upon the subject's currently *perceiving* that object".[8] Thus one simply will not have understood a normal use of the sentence "that cup is *F*" unless (a) one can perceive the cup, and (b) one thinks in a way that depends on that perception, "*that cup* is F, that is what the speaker intends saying".

It is a core idea of explaining how perceiving something makes demonstrative identification possible, that there is an information-link between subject and object "which provides the subject with (non-conceptual) information about the states and doings of that object over a period of time".[9] The existence of an information link, however, is not by itself sufficient for demonstrative identification. What else is required, at least in standard cases, is for the perceiver to have the ability to locate the object in space, upon the basis of that link. In the first instance this means locating the object in an egocentric space (a public space defined relative to the perceiver's body). Egocentric spatial terms are the terms in which the content of our spatial experiences would be formulated, and those in which our immediate behavioural plans would be expressed. As Evans goes on to say, "having spatially significant perceptual information consists at least partly in being disposed to do various things".[10]

The perceiver's ability to make demonstrative judgements is connected with his or her abilities to discriminate the object from its background, to locate the object in space, to track the object as it moves in space. These abilities are connected with the continuing information link. We must remember that here we are thinking of demonstrative identification of an object as the conscious act of a conscious perceiver. That is to say, we are thinking, in Evans's terms, of the conscious experience as input to a concept-using, reasoning and thinking organism.

Given this account, which is substantially that presented by Evans, the most plausible account of how the "conception which controls his thinking is disposed to evolve according to the changes in the information he receives from the object" is as follows. The perceiving subject has a perceptual experience in which he or she is presented with a sensory sign or representation that allows the perceiver to discriminate the object causing it from the objects in the background. Likewise, the sign changes as the perceived object's spatial relation to the object changes. It is the sensory sign that allows the subject to discriminate the object from its background, to locate it in space and to act in relation to the object, that is, to target the object in its behaviour.

This account, I suggest, is the most natural and plausible way to construe Evans's account of how there can be perceptual thoughts that have both non-conceptual and conceptual components. It enables us to see that perceptual experiences are complex activities that can be construed as embodied thoughts, where the content of these embodied thoughts contains non-conceptual components. The picture that emerges is one of a complex integrated system that unites conceptual and non-conceptual elements.

The mode of demonstrative identification described by Evans involves a form of knowledge by acquaintance, that is, perceptual acquaintance with the object perceived, say a particular cup, a particular chair, a particular fox and so on. The plausibility of the representative theory here can be reinforced by examination of McDowell's discussion of knowledge by acquaintance.[11] McDowell takes up and develops Evans's ideas, in the context of modifying Russell's account of "knowledge by acquaintance", by rejecting some of Russell's epistemological assumptions. It is intended to make the notion far more coherent, and less prey to damaging objections. For Russell, a paradigm of acquaintance was provided by perception, although for him the only objects of perceptual acquaintance were features of sense-data. McDowell proposes to extract the notion of acquaintance from Russell's epistemological framework and to "apply it to at least some perceptual relations between minds and ordinary objects".

> A typical visual experience of, say, a cat situates its object for the perceiver: in the first instance egocentrically, but granting the perceiver a general capacity to locate himself, and the objects egocentrically, in a non-egocentrically conceived world,

we can see how the placing of the cat equips the perceiver with knowledge of where in the world it is (even if the only answer he can give to the question where it is is "There").[12]

According to McDowell, it is the capacity of visual experiences to situate their objects in this way that provides the basis for a version of the notion of acquaintance, but one that abandons Russell's sense-datum epistemology. Like Evans, McDowell wishes to construct a theory that combines an insight of Russell's, that there are singular propositions that are object-dependent, with Frege's view that propositions contain senses as constituents. Russell envisaged singular propositions having as constituents besides what is predicated of their objects, simply the objects themselves. Russell held that the only possible candidates for such objects of knowledge by acquaintance were sense-data and that the only possible referring expressions were logically proper names.

His reasons for this, however, so McDowell argues, are flawed. They stem from arguing that it is necessary for the thinker to have incorrigible access to the object in question and, on the face of it, the only possible objects available are sense-data. McDowell thinks that this view goes far beyond Russell's real insight, which is that there are singular propositions that are object-dependent. Such propositions are object-dependent in the sense that the proposition would not be available to be expressed at all if the objects referred to did not exist. The insight of Russell's can be perfectly well combined with Frege's doctrine that thoughts contain senses as constituents, by claiming that there are Fregean thought-constituents (singular senses) that are object-dependent, generating an object-dependence in the thoughts in which they figure.[13]

McDowell is right in claiming that singular propositions do not require sense-data and that the objects they are dependent upon are physical objects. Accordingly, it makes sense, in giving a general account of conceptualized perception, to take perception to have propositional content where the proposition is object-dependent in this way. However, although sense-data, or something corresponding to sense-data (i.e. sensory representations) are not obligatory, they are not forbidden either. They may still play a role in allowing the perceiver to have the right kind of knowledge by acquaintance.

We need to observe that, historically, there were two major motivations for the introduction of "sense-data". One, as in the case of Russell, was epistemological. On this approach, the sense-data were connected with logically privileged epistemological access, and with providing logically indubitable foundations for knowledge-claims. There is, however, another role for sense-data, and here the motivation is metaphysical. Sense-data are postulated as having ontological existence and, while they have an epistemological role, it need not be as providing an indubitable foundation. A theorist who wishes to defend a form of indirect representationalism, and who is committed to the existence of sensory representations that are phe-nomenal items, may be thought to be committed to sense-data or something similar. If so, it is only to sense-data in the metaphysical sense that they are committed. They need no more be committed to Russell's epistemological assumptions than is McDowell or Evans.

If we understand sensory representations as having a more mod-est epistemological role, we can understand how they can play a part in the kind of object-dependent perception advanced by McDowell (and Evans). Object-dependent visual perception of, say, a fox, involves visually locating that fox in a three-dimensional space, where that space is one whose origin is located within my body. The representationalist thesis just proposed holds that what enables me to locate that fox in a public three-dimensional space is the fact that I locate a fox-representation in a subjective or phenom-enal space whose origin is placed within me, the origin.

If we go back to the quotation above, taken from McDowell's paper in which he characterizes the way in which visual experiences allow one to acquire knowledge of where in the world the perceived object is located, we can see how the modified account accommodates McDowell's description. In that passage, McDowell claims that the visual experience of a cat situates its object for the perceiver in two stages: first, egocentrically, and, secondly, in the physical world that is not centred on the "ego". Of course, we can take this "ego" to involve reference to the person's body, and no doubt this is how McDowell intends that we take it. But it is also open to us to interpret the "ego" as the personal subject of the visual experience, where the term "personal subject" does not have to be interpreted as a Cartesian ego. It can be an embodied mind of either the Aristotelian or Strawsonian kinds.

We can then modify McDowell's account in the following way. The perceiving subject locates physical objects in a space centred on his or her physical body, by means of locating phenomenal representations in a phenomenal space. The perceiving subject uses the representation to guide him or her with respect to the physical object, that is, in the behaviour that is targeted on to that physical object. The propositional content of visual experience is typically specified by a proposition or thought of the form

that dog is running away

where the term "that dog" is taken as the expression of a singular concept. What makes this particular concept a singular one is its being causally based on, or controlled by, the particular individual dog. The point here is that, by virtue of one's visual experience that is based on that particular dog, one can both act or behave with respect to that particular dog, and one is in a position to express judgements about that dog, for example, judgements that express thoughts of the form "that dog is running away". The representationalist reconstruction of the Evans–McDowell position is that the visual representation plays the intermediary role in explaining the perceiver's ability to track that individual dog, either in behaviour or in thought.

The aim of McDowell and Evans is to show how it is possible for us to have knowledge by acquaintance about physical things, for example, cups, desks, trees, apples and so on, where this knowledge does not have Russellian epistemological assumption, for example, about incorrigibility. It is easy to see how the account is meant to favour direct realism. On the face of it, the theory explains perception of X in terms of being affected by X, so as to have the ability to make demonstrative judgements about X. But this account of perception is consistent with that form of representationalism that argues that in this sense it is a physical object that is perceived, while insisting that nevertheless the way the object is perceived is through being aware of an intermediary. And this theory likewise avoids being committed to Russell's assumptions about incorrigibility.

It is important to note that my aim here is a modest one: to show how the representative theory fits easily with the Evans–McDowell accounts. There are of course objections to the notion of phenomenal fields and items, which I am appealing to, for example, most recently in Clark (2000). These objections will be examined in the remaining chapters of this book. (For a response to Clark, see Chapter 9.)

Natural signs and sensory representations

The account of perception I have presented is one in which perception, at its most basic level, is taken to be object-based and to involve the acquisition of object-based knowledge. Such knowledge involves knowledge-by-acquaintance. I also claim that such knowledge can be expressed in two forms: first, in behaviour, that is, in actions that typically are object-based (or object-directed); secondly, in thoughts that the perceiver can express with discursive concepts. This behaviour can be thought of as embodied thoughts and in so far as they require concepts, they do not require, on the part of the perceiver, discursive concepts. (The reader is referred to the earlier discussion, in Chapter 2, of embodied thoughts and practical concepts.)

It is a crucial part of the theory for how this is supposed to work that perception involves the using of sensory representations as natural signs for objects. This account presupposes a distinction between different kinds of representation, for example, between natural signs and linguistic symbols (conceptual representations). This kind of distinction is reflected in the work on signs by Charles Peirce, work that has recently been made use of by James Fetzer in his *Philosophy and Cognitive Science*.[14] There are two significant features to Peirce's account. The first is his emphasis on a sign being not just something, x, that stands for something else, y, but being a sign for S, that is, a sign for *somebody* (or possibly something). That is, signs involve at least a triangular relationship, one holding between the sign, that which is represented and that to whom it is represented, that is, the user of the sign where the user is the consumer, rather than the producer. The second crucial feature is that there are, for Peirce, three different kinds of sign: icon, index and symbol. These different kinds of representation are built on different relationships. An icon represents what it resembles, an index is a natural sign and a symbol is a conventional sign.

The distinction between natural sign, icon and symbol, is essential for a proper understanding of representative theories of perception. It is of particular importance in understanding the nature of sensory representations. Sensory representations are signs but natural signs. The three important kinds of uses for signs are to enable us to:

- communicate;
- have thoughts;
- act, that is, enable us to focus our activities, to guide our behaviour.

Standard linguistic signs, for example, sentences, of course, serve all three purposes but communication is primary. There are types of natural signs that primarily serve the third purpose. The shape and colour of clouds can be natural signs of climate changes; the states of a barometer are natural signs of atmospheric pressure; footprints in the snow are natural signs of wolves. A classical natural sign, or system of signs, is a mirror. It enables me to shave myself without making a mess of my face, to get my eye-liner on with a minimum of fuss, to get that spot on the side of my neck and so on.

The natural signs that are sensory representations are primarily action-guiding. While conventional signs do have this role, their more basic function is that of communication. To say that this is the more basic function is not necessarily to say that it is the most important one. The point is that conventional signs might not be able to serve their other important purposes except by virtue of having the capacity to serve the function of communication.

Natural signs of this kind are primarily action-guiding and not communicative. Allied to this feature is the fact that, unlike conventional signs, they do not involve rule-following. It would seem that understanding a conventional sign does require knowing how to follow an appropriate rule. This is not the case for understanding natural signs. Moreover it would seem that one could not have the appropriate knowledge involved, knowing how to follow a rule, unless one also had the capacity for understanding natural signs. This point, I would claim, is at least consistent with Wittgenstein's views as expressed in his discussion of rule-following. Indeed, it may well be implied by his views.[15] [Qualification: understanding some natural signs may require conceptual thought and rule-following. Understanding, for example, what the barometer states are natural signs of, would require such thought. However an organism might have an inner biological barometer, thermometer or clock, that is action-guiding, without requiring the possession of concepts.]

Natural signs, of the perceptual type, primarily function, I have claimed, as things that can be used to guide behaviour. As such they do not need conceptual thought, or at least discursive-conceptual thought. Nevertheless, they can also acquire conceptualized uses. A perceiver who acquires a language also acquires the ability to use natural signs in new ways, for example, as vehicles of thought. In other words, the natural signs that are sensory representations come to represent states of affairs, in that I come to recognize them as signs of cups, saucers, tables, elephants and so on. That is, I come to think of them as signs of cups. Or putting it another way, I come to use these sensory representations when I make judgements in some such form as

> I see a cup on the table.
> I see a broken saucer on the table.
> I see an elephant under that tree.

Now the sensory representations are not used simply to guide our behaviour but to make explicit judgements.

Sensory states as natural signs

In conscious attentive perception, I argue, we perceive physical objects and their qualities by becoming aware of sensory representations.[16] These sensory representations function as natural signs, performing their role through a process of double awareness. The perceiver is aware both of the sign and of what is represented, and does not have to be thought of as making inferences. Understood in this way, representationalism supports, in a back-handed way, some of the intuitions of direct realism, by arguing that successful perceiving makes use of a number of beliefs that, while false, are productively false: they are beneficial illusions.

The sensory states, as representations, share features in common with other kinds of representation. What makes them distinctively "natural signs" is that they acquire their representative role naturally and not through social and conventional means. There may be borderline cases where social factors play a role, but not an essential role. The issue is whether conventions are presupposed in the acquisition of the role of representation.

Normally, accounts of what it is for an object a to represent some object B to audience S is that a has certain features that enable in systematic manner the audience S to have thoughts about B, that is, to form mental states whose content is about B. Leaving aside how the task of representing is to be achieved, it is clear that it is essential to what it is for a to represent B that it be used, or be capable of being used, by S to enable him or her to think about B. What is easy to overlook, however, is that such conscious thoughts can include actions, that is, intentional activities. One way for a to represent B is for a to provide for the relevant person the capacity to target B in their actions: to focus their activities on B. My visual experiences, for example, can represent for me a nearby tree, in that it enables me to move within the tree's shade, to climb it, to prune it or to contemplate it. The feeling of pain in my left knee serves to guide my actions with respect to that knee, to hold it with my hand, to press it, to flex it (so as to put it back into place) as well as to have thoughts about it – to recall the time I received the injury on the rugby field.

It is a necessary condition for the a-states to serve their representative role that the audience must be capable of identifying and discriminating them. It may not be a necessary condition that a-states are causally sensitive to B-states in order to serve their representative role, but that they are causally sensitive in this way may be part of the explanation of how they acquire that role. For example, suppose that there is a causal connection between a and B (that which is represented) and states of a vary systematically with changes in states of B. This kind of causal sensitivity is not sufficient for a to represent B, but it may be an important part of the explanation of a's ability to represent. Something else is required of the audience as well. In order for a to represent B to S, a must enable S either to have thoughts about B or to guide or direct S's actions in relation to B. In the case of perceptual experiences, these two features of representation are combined. In the typical case, the perceptual experience of a nearby tree is both causally sensitive to the tree as well as functioning to enable the percipient to focus their activities on the tree.

According to the theory I am defending, a perceptual experience has sensory qualities as components that in turn are used as representations of states of affairs in the physical world. To understand, however, how they function as representations, we need to distinguish between two stages in the developmental history of any individual. A person's perceptual abilities develop through two stages before reaching the sophistication of a mature language-using perceiver. At the first stage, S uses the sign *a* as a guide for some physical object *B*: *a* serves as a sign in the sense of being used by S to guide S's behaviour, the behaviour that is sensitive to physical object *B*. At this stage the object-sensitive behaviour consists in reaching for objects, grasping objects, throwing objects at other objects, moving towards and around other objects and so on. It is at a second, later stage that S uses the sign *a* as a representation for *B*, in the sense of using *a* to have thoughts about *B* (*B*-sensitive thoughts). At this stage the perceiver has thoughts that are sensitive to *B*, without always being manifested in *B*-sensitive actions.

The sensory quality that is a component of the aspectual perceptual experience is a component that is used primarily as a guide to action, and secondarily as a means to enable one to have object-based thoughts. The sensory quality serves as a natural sign: it is a sensory representation. The sign serves this function without the perceiver being aware of it as a sensory quality, nor even aware of it as a sign or representation, in the sense of being aware of it as something distinct from that which it is used to represent. The perceiver at this stage does not distinguish between the representation and what is represented.

This feature forms a crucial part of the version of representationalism that I am defending. The normal perceiver is not held to be aware first of the sensory state *as a sensory state*, as opposed to a physical object, and then make an inference to a claim about a physical object. The perceiver is aware of the sensory sign but takes it to be the physical object. She uses the sign to grasp the object, taking the sign to be identical to that which is being grasped.

This failure to distinguish between representation and what is represented does not prevent the sign from performing its role as a sign or representation. The way to understand how this happens is to understand that the perceiver is aware of the sign under some aspect, for example, as a guide to action, and that it is possible for someone to do that while taking the sign and thing represented to be one and the same.

The human language-using perceiver, of course, is one who comes to form thoughts about what is represented. Moreover, that person in a typical perceptual situation has a complex set of thoughts about both sign and thing signified (between which the perceiver fails to distinguish). This means that one will have both true and false beliefs about the sign, and both true and false beliefs about that which is represented. The way to understand what is happening is as follows. The perceiver's thoughts about the object and sign are aspectual thoughts, that is, thoughts about the object under some description. The thoughts about the object x are true under some descriptions and false under others. For those descriptions under which they are false, they will be true of the sign (and vice versa).

Link between double awareness and causal content

On the natural-sign version of representationalism, the perceiver should be thought of as an agent-perceiver, and more accurately as an embodied agent-perceiver. The perceiver is aware of the sensory representation in that he or she uses the representation to guide his or her actions with respect to individual objects, thereby expressing his or her awareness of the representation as being caused by that object, which is at the same time awareness of the object as that which is causing the representation. In using the sensuous representation to identify and discriminate the object, he or she is ascribing the sensuous properties to that object.

The idea behind this way of thinking is similar to that developed by Moreland Perkins in his *Sensing the World*.[17] It is a central thesis of his book that we can make coherent the idea of a sensuous quality whose instantiation within consciousness depends upon consciousness of it. For my purposes, what is especially relevant is that he goes on to develop the notion of a sensuous attribution of sensuous qualities to objective states of affairs. The notion is illustrated by his example of hearing the loudness of a sound in the air. The perceiver in this case is said to be directly aware of a sensuous "loudness" internal to his or her consciousness. The sensuous quality serves as the sensuous content of our perceptual attribution of loudness to the sound before our ears, that is, to the objective state of affairs in public space.

> Being directly aware of sensuous qualities interior to consciousness is closely analogous to being directly aware of a thought that corresponds to the predicate of a non-perceptual judgement – to being aware of what one predicates in making such a judgement about some particular. But here the what that is attributed is a purely sensuous content.[18]

The idea is that in perceptual awareness there is a sensuous attribution that is comparable to the conceptual attribution typical of subject–predicate thought. In perceptual consciousness of a peach, we attribute to the cause of the sensory quality-instantiation the sensuous quality itself. An analogue case is that of a colour photograph. If I have a colour photograph of Uncle Toby showing him to be wearing a blue suit, then in depicting the suit as blue, the photo is depicting him as having the colour that is the colour of the corresponding physical part of the photograph. There are other ways we could depict the colour as blue: we could have a black and white photograph and place numerals on regions of the photograph: "1" for red, "2" for blue, "3" for green and so on. But in a normal colour photograph the picture depicts the objects as having the colours that are also colours of the photograph itself. Likewise, the pink spot on the photograph depicts Uncle Toby as having pink eyes, even though he does not in fact have them. There are other features of the photograph that we do not take to depict the objects as having: the oil mark on the blue part is not taken to represent a mark on the blue sky, the white border of the photo is not taken to depict a window frame.

The colour photograph can be used as an analogue for perceptual consciousness. In normal non-theoretical perceptual consciousness, the awareness of the sensory representation is a complex state in which the representation depicts "that which is the cause of the representation" as having certain sensuous qualities, including the sensuous qualities.

We can link this account of the content of perceptual experience with that presented by Evans and McDowell. On the account presented by Evans, perception primarily is perception of an object, whereby the perceiver receives information from the object that allows the perceiver: to locate the object in physical space, and to direct his or her actions at it; and to make demonstrative judgements, for example, that *that cup* is cracked.

It is by having visual experiences that the perceiver is so situated. The visual experience may be thought of as presenting a certain cup, *that cup*, to the perceiver as placed before him or her, and by so doing, allowing him or her to make the demonstrative judgements. The representative theory accepts this description of the perceptual situation. On the representative theory, our perceptual experiences allow us to have demonstrative thoughts about such objects as cups: what makes the thought/judgement one about a certain cup is that the experience both allows us to target the cup in our behaviour and is caused (in the right way) by that cup.

It may be thought, however, that there is a problem confronting the representative theory, which is avoided on the direct realist account favoured by Evans. The problem is that the representative theory requires a form of double awareness, of sign and object perceived, but at the level at which we make explicit, reflective perceptual judgements, there appears to be no such double awareness. Intuitively, and phenomenologically, there seems only to be one item that I am aware of.

The answer to that is that although the naive perceiver does not think explicitly of the sign as an item distinct from the object perceived, nevertheless he does (or at least can) think of the sign under one aspect and the physical object under a different aspect. The naive perceiver takes it that there is only one item there, the cup, thought of under different aspects. (Naively we are all direct realists.) The truth of the matter, however, if the representative theory is true, is that there are two items there, thought of under different aspects. The perceiver is having object-based thoughts about two items, even though he or she conflates them:

- the item that I am perceiving, that I am in causal perceptual contact with and which I can reach for;
- the item that is guiding me, and that stands out from its background.

If direct realism were true then these would comprise different aspects under which the same item is thought. On the representative theory, there are two items thought of under the different aspects, even though the perceiver conflates the two.

If the perceiver expresses the thought in the form "that cup is cracked", which is said to inform an audience, then the sentence will be understood, rightly, as expressing a thought about that very cup. This is so even if the speaker is thinking of the cup under the aspect that is not true of it, that is, is thinking of the cup as the item that is guiding him. In such cases, we may well say that the perceiver is making some sort of error in having that thought, but for practical purposes it does not matter.

There is a great danger when we think of the innocent perceiver as being in error or being confused when they conflate sign and thing signified, that we may overlook the possibility that the conflation, far from being damaging, or even harmless, is in fact beneficial. First of all, with respect to the "confusion", we should distinguish between two types: one in which you are simply muddled and little or no coherent thought is expressed; another in which you mistake one thing for another. Conflation of sign and object is of the second sort. Secondly, thinking of something as an "error" inclines us to think of it as something that should be eradicated for, after all, shouldn't all mistakes and errors be eliminated? Well, no. To think of conflations in this way, that is, as errors and mistakes ripe for eradication, is to overlook the possibility that the conflations, far from being unfortunate, are beneficial and even splendid. Far from being eradicated, they should be celebrated. The paradoxical flavour might be allayed by the following consideration. If we go to the theatre, the last thing we want from our colleague is to be told "it is only an actor on stage. It is not a Danish prince". We all know that. We all want to respond as if we believed it to be not just an actor on stage. Similarly with our experiences of colours. We experience objects in the world, I have argued, as having colours that they do not possess.[19] Our colour experiences are illusory. However, there is value in having such illusions. Even if you become convinced that objects do not have colours, there is point to acting "as if they did have the colours", at least for many purposes.

We may illustrate the point by reference to Hume's account of morality, which he compares with the philosophical opinion on colour. In both cases, we ordinarily take a feature, which was an aspect of their experience, and attribute it to the object, something that does not have the feature in question. In so doing, the person is conflating the two things and not separating them in thought. Although we are conflating two things, it would be a mistake to take it that Hume thinks that we are confused, in the sense of making an error that should be eradicated. It certainly isn't the case that Hume wanted to eradicate "the error". He thinks that the conflation serves a useful purpose.

On the view that I am defending, the perceptual process is one in which false beliefs have a role to play. These beliefs may even be thought of as productive. This idea is consonant with the idea that I have defended, in relation to colour vision; namely, that while illusions (of colour) are errors, they should not be thought of as mere errors. Illusions can be beneficial and productive. That false beliefs can play such a role seems to run counter to a view expressed by Evans. In considering contexts in which communication can or cannot take place when sentences containing singular terms that lack a referent are used, Evans writes: "if there really is something said, then it cannot possibly require a false belief for one to know what is said. Truth is seamless; there can be no truth which it requires acceptance of a falsehood to appreciate."[20]

This view may seem to contradict what I am arguing, but clear examination shows that it does not. I am happy to concede that there are no truths that, in order to be known, require acceptance of a falsehood. Nothing in my theory, however, requires such a claim. All that I have claimed is that, in certain contexts, a person will acquire a true belief in virtue of having a false belief, and that is surely non-controversial. I do not require that the perceiver could only acquire the true belief through having a false belief. I claim that a sophisticated perceiver can acquire the same knowledge that the naive perceiver acquires through his or her false belief. As far as whether the naive perceiver can be said to acquire knowledge, rather than true belief, I can defend that position by appealing to a theory of knowledge that depends on attributing to the knower the possession of a reliable mechanism for the acquisition of true beliefs. On my theory of perception, the holding of false beliefs forms part of the relevant reliable mechanism, and hence is consistent with the acquisition of knowledge on the part of the perceiver.

Conclusion

I have attempted to set out and defend, in this chapter, a hybrid view of perception, one that combines elements of the classical representative theory of perception and "direct realist" accounts of perception. According to this view, perception of physical objects is direct and immediate but nevertheless operates through awareness of intermediaries.

In conscious attentive perception, one perceives physical objects and their qualities by becoming aware of sensory representations, that is, of a set of quality-instances (tropes) that are natural signs for the objects in question. The account has a number of key features. It contains the feature of double awareness that is characteristic of certain representative theories, without endorsing an inferential kind of realism. It also supports some of the intuitions of direct realism, by arguing that successful perceiving makes use of a number of beliefs that, while false, are productively false: they are beneficial illusions. Most important of all, however, is the claim that sensory representations, as natural signs, have a central role to play.

What makes the theory a version of the representative theory is that perceptual experience contains a form of double awareness, that is, awareness of sensory item and physical states of affairs.[21] The account of double awareness, as it enfolds, displays a distinctive view of perceptual experience. A perceptual experience consists of a state of conscious awareness, one that contains both sensory and non-sensory components. The sensory component has two kinds of feature: it has a certain content, for example, it represents the world as being a certain way; and it has a certain character, by virtue of which it represents the world as being that way. Its character is best described as phenomenal: it contains those features that are intrinsic to it and by virtue of which it carries the content it does. We must distinguish, therefore, between the phenomenal features that make up the sensory character of the experiences and the features that comprise the content of the experience. For colour, for example, we can distinguish between two different but related kinds of colour: colour as a quality of physical objects; and colour as a sensory quality (an intrinsic feature of our experiences). The sensory colour quality plays a role in experiences representing physical objects as having the colours that they do.

While perception, therefore, has an indirect component, it conforms, at the same time, to the characterization above of "direct realism". The point is not a trivial one. Perception, I argue, is a process that involves causal interaction between objects and states of affairs, on the one hand, and perceivers who use sensory organs, on the other. The awareness of sensory items, characteristic of perceptual experiences, is not like that. Perception is a process that involves perception of the perceiver's environment, including one's own body – that is what perception is – but the way it works is through the use of sensory representations as natural signs. This thesis emphasizes that conscious perception typically combines direct and indirect realist components, and hence cuts across the distinction set out above between direct and indirect forms of realism. One advantage of thinking of the theory in this way, as we shall see in Chapter 5, is that it undermines the sorts of arguments in favour of that version of "natural realism" presented by Austin, and endorsed more recently by Hilary Putnam.[22]

My aim in this chapter has been to defend the hybrid theory of perception, to argue that it is a genuine competitor among the range of possible theories. It is possible, however, to construct a more positive argument in its favour. There are two parts to this argument. The first is to defend the view that, in perception, one is aware of some intermediary between the subject and the physical object perceived. This involves looking at the traditional argument from illusion. It will turn out, I shall argue, that the argument, although it has largely fallen out of favour, deserves greater credit than it is usually given. It is often dismissed without due consideration or for wrong reasons. Nevertheless, it depends on an assumption or a premise that requires further support. That support needs to come from providing an account of perceptual experience.

In Chapter 5 I shall pursue these issues. Although I shall be arguing in defence of a certain theory, outlined above, the discussion, I submit, is valuable for those who reject this position. I claim that the theory is at least as strong as the chief rivals, and that the discussion is helpful in making progress in our thinking about the issues.

Natural realism: Putnam, Austin and Heidegger

According to the indirect form of representationalism, which I have defended, when one perceives a physical object, one is immediately aware not of physical objects and their qualities, but of some items other than these physical objects. These items or intermediaries are phenomenal in character, although their metaphysical status is open to debate.[1] They may be phenomenal objects, sensory states or experiences, instances of sensory qualities, or even, I shall argue, ways of appearing (i.e. adverbially modified sensings). The thesis that one is immediately aware of such items, or is directly sensing them, is not confined to the representative theory. It is shared by prominent forms of idealism and phenomenalism. For representationalists, these items are intermediaries between the perceiving subject and the physical object or state of affairs; for idealists and phenomenalists, they are not. The idealist–phenomenalist, however, normally distinguishes between the sense of "perceive" in which one immediately perceives, or senses, the phenomenal item, and the sense of "perceive" in which one perceives the physical object. Price, for example, draws a distinction between perceiving a physical object, and sensing a sense-datum. For the subject to perceive a physical object requires two things: sensing a sensory particular and being *perceptually conscious of* a physical object, that is, taking it that there is a physical object present (to which the sensory particular is related).

The claim that the perceiver is, in the appropriate sense, "immediately aware" of some phenomenal item has been supported by a range of classical arguments in the philosophical tradition.

Unfortunately, there is a massive problem in drawing upon the classical arguments. For one thing, while the arguments are often used in support of representative realism, it is not widely appreciated that such theories can take various forms. In the second place, there are serious misconceptions about the classical arguments themselves. Misunderstandings and misconceptions are commonplace, and one of the unfortunate features of work in this field is that the mistakes tend to get handed on from one critic to another, without those critics going back to the sources, or without their dealing with the detailed responses made to the criticisms. Some of the responses are those by Mundle, Jonathan Harrison and Robinson.[2] Finally, there are fresh arguments that go beyond the classical arguments, some presented by these philosophers, and others provided by philosophers such as Lowe, Wright, Perkins and Frank Jackson.[3] Their combined sophistication exceeds anything presented in the simple expositions of the celebrated "argument from illusion" that occurs in many critical discussions. Finally, any assessment of the classical argument will need to be sensitive to the fact that a piece of reasoning may, on the surface, fit the pattern of one of the variations of the classical arguments, but may be quite different, depending on whether it is advanced by a representationalist or an idealist–phenomenalist, since their different assumptions will affect the interpretation of, and support for, the various premises.

Since there are so many variants of the argument from illusion, it is difficult to summarize it. At its heart is a claim that our veridical perceptual experiences have a certain structure and that there is a range of illusory and hallucinatory experiences that have a similar structure. The argument from illusion is best thought of, I hold, not as a straightforward argument from a stable set of premises to a conclusion, but as a piece of reasoning that tries to make best sense of the structure of veridical experiences, and of their similarity to the other types of experience. In Chapter 6 I shall attempt to set out a viable form of this reasoning. To prepare the way for this discussion, it will be important to show how misunderstandings about the traditional argument abound. Unless these misconceptions are cleared up, progress is not likely to be made.

For this purpose, I propose to take a recent discussion of perception by one of our foremost philosophers, Putnam. I propose to show how his defence of "natural realism" against indirect realism misses its mark, not least for the misunderstanding it contains not only of representative realism, but of the point of supporting arguments that it can appeal to. Putnam's discussion is especially important in view of the emphasis he places on the arguments by John Austin, arguments that have been of great influence in the philosophy of perception.

Putnam on natural realism

In his Dewey Lectures, and later in *The Threefold Cord*, Putnam argues for a thesis that I am entirely sympathetic with: that we have lost sight of the importance of perception and as a result are labouring under a range of misconceptions.[4] I agree with him on this, although we have different views of what the misconceptions are. The notable feature of the Dewey Lectures, however, is Putnam's espousal of what he calls "natural realism", a view shared by Dewey and James.

It is not exactly clear what natural realism is supposed to be. The natural realist is said to hold that "successful perception is just a seeing or hearing or feeling, etc., of things 'out there' and not a mere affection of a person's subjectivity by those things".[5] The problem with such a characterization, however, is that it is satisfied by a carefully constructed representational realism. On such a view, perception of physical objects is a seeing or hearing of things "out there" (via intermediaries) and is certainly not a *mere* affection of a person's subjectivity.

Putnam's intentions are best captured, perhaps, by the space and praise bestowed on Austin, "the philosopher whose *Sense and Sensibilia* represents the most powerful defence of what I am calling 'natural realism' in the history of philosophy".[6] This is a curious claim, not least for the fact that Austin never states in that book exactly what thesis he believes in, let alone is defending. Indeed, he says that he is not going to maintain that we ought to be "realists", to embrace, that is, the doctrine that we do perceive material things (or objects): "This doctrine would be no less scholastic and erroneous than its antithesis."[7] Nevertheless, it is this antithesis that Austin's book is directed against, or at least whose supporting arguments are dissected and rejected. This is the doctrine: "we never see or otherwise perceive or anyhow never *directly* perceive or sense, material objects (or material things), but only sense-data (or our ideas, impressions, sensa, sense-perceptions, percepts, etc.)".[8]

Accordingly, we are meant by Putnam to take it that Austin has demolished the most powerful arguments for this doctrine, which consists in the denial of natural realism. Even this formulation, however, is not clear, for what is crucial is how we understand "perceive" and "directly perceive or sense". On the face of it, the doctrine is meant to be a denial of direct realism, but in order for this to be true, we need to be clearer about what direct realism is.

As I argued in Chapter 4, the right way to present the representative thesis is to say that the perceiver does not perceive physical objects except by being aware of intermediaries. One does not perceive the intermediary at all. This point is not a trivial one. Perceiving a physical object is being caused by that object to have a sensory representation. Being aware of the sensory representation is not like that. A similar point applies to the phenomenalism defended by Price. As we saw earlier, on his account, for the perceiver to perceive a physical object requires two things: sensing a sensory particular and being perceptually conscious of a physical object, that is, taking it that there is a physical object present (to which the sensory particular is related).

Accordingly, both the representative realist and the phenomenalist can dissociate themselves from the specific doctrine attacked by Austin, for their separate positions can be formulated in such a way that only material objects are perceived, and hence only material objects are directly perceived. Given these considerations, we might reformulate the target of Austin's attack, that is, the doctrine that denies that natural realism is true, by replacing the expression "directly perceive" by "being aware of". It might be thought that such a thesis will be just as vulnerable to Austin's demolition as the earlier version. Let us see.

Austin on natural realism

Let us suppose that the doctrine Austin is attacking, the denial of "natural realism", can be formulated as:

> we never see or otherwise perceive material objects (or material things), except by being aware of, or sensing, sense-data (or our

ideas, impressions, sensa, sense perceptions, percepts, etc.), items that are not themselves material things.

We may then take it that Putnam believes that Austin has demolished the most powerful arguments for this doctrine. This belief is remarkable, however, since the overwhelming proportion of arguments Austin considers are those presented by A. J. Ayer. Ayer's argument has a different character from those of Broad and Price, for example, and in any case is directed at a special version of sense-data theories. It is true that Austin mentions Price by name but he does not discuss his arguments, apart from two references so slight as not to comprise a serious response.[9] In one of these passages, moreover, Austin seems not to be aware that, for Price, the term "sense-datum" functions very differently than for Ayer.[10] Austin does provide a devastating attack on Ayer, but the force of the devastation comes as much from the clever use of language as from the strength of argument. There is little effort given to considering what his opponent might say to respond to the devastating attack.[11]

An example of Austin's technique is his reference to the doctrine under attack as "scholastic". The major reason for this charge seems to be that there is something peculiar in attributing to ordinary language-users an abstract belief that they perceive material objects, for, Austin says, they perceive a wide range of things: dogs, tables, mountains, rainbows, flames, skies, pictures, television screens and so on. The relevance of this remark is quite unclear. The doctrine under attack from Austin can be made as precise as we wish. For example, it can take the form: when one perceives a peach then one does not directly perceive it but only a sensory counterpart; when one perceives a tomato, one does not directly perceive the tomato, but only a sensory counterpart; and likewise for dogs, apples, rainbows, flames, pictures and so on.

As Mundle has pointed out, Austin concentrates on distinctions that are used in ordinary language without attempting to explain or discuss phenomena for which such techniques are inadequate.[12] An example is Austin's discussion of double vision, something which Austin concedes is a "baffling abnormality".[13] He provides no attempt to explain this phenomenon, despite the fact that it would be the sort of experience that is likely to be of considerable importance for the argument in question, except to say that it is possible to describe the phenomenon in terms such as "I see the piece of paper double" or "I see it as two". Of course, we can use such descriptions, but what Austin overlooks is that we can examine such experiences and realize that such an experience is not exactly like seeing two pieces of paper, nor is it a case of duplicating the same experience. What we have is an experience that in some respects is like a single experience, and in some respects, like two experiences of the same object, but is not exactly like either. It is in handling the phenomenology of such experiences that the representationalist position derives much of its strength. Austin's dedication to ordinary language, while not entirely irrelevant, leaves many of the hard issues untouched.

That Austin's demolition is overrated is amply illustrated by considering those arguments from *Sense and Sensibilia* that are discussed (with approval) by Putnam.[14] The argument from illusion traditionally covers a range of arguments. One form that Austin is taken as demolishing is the following: "Perception is not infallible; therefore it cannot be direct".[15] This is certainly peculiar since it is very unclear who is supposed to have ever presented it. Even if it has some advocates, I would have thought that there were more powerful arguments. (See Broad, Price, Mundle, Harrison, Jackson, Perkins, Lowe and Robinson for some examples.[16]) The arguments that Putnam has in mind are epistemological arguments. The far stronger arguments are those that depend on phenomenology, the findings of science and a combination of these arguments and epistemological considerations.

A second argument he discusses is the argument from dreaming. This argument is taken as intended to establish that, in ordinary perceptual situations, we perceive intermediaries and not the physical object. We are asked to grant that Helen is having a very lifelike dream, which is, say, exactly like being in front of the Taj Mahal. The traditional sense-datum theorist is supposed to argue as follows:

> Helen is certainly experiencing something; what she is experiencing is certainly not the Taj Mahal . . . or indeed any physical object . . .; therefore what she is experiencing is something mental. So the immediate object of a perception is, at least some of the time, something mental.[17]

On a second, later, occasion, Helen finds herself placed in front of the Taj Mahal and now she has a perceptual experience, which from her point of view is exactly the same as the first. The traditional epistemologist is represented by Putnam as saying:

> We agreed that what Helen was immediately perceiving when she dreamt was something mental. Is it not implausible, to say the least, that things as different in nature as a physical building and a mental sense-datum could seem exactly alike? Should we not conclude that, on the second occasion, too, she was immediately perceiving sense-data exactly like the ones she was aware of on the first occasion?

Although the dreaming argument is attributed to Descartes, it is not the form of argument that he actually uses. Descartes is not trying to prove that in ordinary experience we are aware of sense-data and not physical objects. What he is trying to prove is that in ordinary experience, when we claim to perceive physical objects, for all we know, the objects may not exist and, therefore, failing certain assumptions, we do not have the knowledge we think we do.

Setting that aside, the problem with Putnam's characterization is that it leaves much out, and in any case misrepresents the argument. What is implausible is not that two things so different in nature should *seem alike*. That is not the problem and no traditional epistemologist expresses themselves in such terms. There are a number of points at issue. One is that if we have two qualitatively identical and complex experiences each caused by the brain, and if the veridical experience is caused by a complex causal process linking the physical object with the eyes and brain, then it is highly plausible that if the two experiences are such that each has its own "object", then the objects have the same nature. It is not logically required that they have the same nature, but it is difficult to understand how the process would work if they did not. The point, moreover, is not an abstract point about different natures. In principle, of course, things of different nature might share all sorts of properties in common. The problem is a special one to do with perception. It is hard to see how the brain's role could be so different in the two cases as to make one aware of a physical object in one case, and a phenomenal object in the other.

To forestall a possible objection, it is important to point out that there is nothing problematical in a defender of phenomenal objects appealing to what is known about the brain and the detailed causal links between physical objects and sensory organs. The context that Putnam describes is not one where we are trying to defeat the sceptic, nor is it one in which we are arguing against the existence of material objects in an idealistic or phenomenalistic way (although Ayer certainly was). The context is one in which it is being argued that in ordinary perception we are not directly aware of physical objects, but only of intermediaries between us and the objects. We are still aware of the objects, albeit indirectly. The theorist, accordingly, is not denying that there are physical objects and light and brains, nor that we have knowledge about them.

Putnam also points out that it is a concession to the traditional epistemologist to grant that there are non-veridical perceptual experiences that are indistinguishable from veridical experiences. Austin claims that this is a very dubious assumption:

> it is simply not true to say that seeing a bright green after-image against a white wall is exactly like seeing a bright green patch actually on the wall; or that seeing a white wall through blue spectacles is exactly like seeing a blue wall; or that seeing pink rats in D.T.'s is exactly like really seeing pink rats; . . . In all these cases we may say the same things ("It looks blue . . ." etc.) but this is no reason at all for denying the obvious fact that the "experiences" are different.[18]

We might note that the same point had been made by Price, one of the people under attack by Austin. But both Austin and Putnam have misdiagnosed the "dubious" assumption. What the traditional theorist requires is not the claim that we do actually have experiences that are qualitatively identical to veridical experiences. All that is needed is the claim that it is *possible* to have such experiences. That such experiences are actual, of course, supports the claim that they are possible, but the argument is no weaker if the premise is framed in terms of possible experiences. Even if there were no actual non-veridical experiences of the right type, we have strong reasons for thinking that they are possible. There are two major reasons. One is that we have a spectrum of experiences that are close, to greater and lesser extents, to veridical experiences. In certain respects they are very similar. There are, for example, virtual reality glasses that we can put on, which give us a wealth of experience that are very similar to actual experiences. There is the everyday example of headphones that we can put on, which give us the hallucinatory auditory experience of a chamber group in our lounge. In the second place, what we know of the brain and the eyes and of their roles in causing veridical experiences makes it highly plausible that experiences could be generated that are indistinguishable, or near enough, from veridical experiences.

My response to Austin has depended on the claim that the traditional argument from hallucination depends on the possibility of there being hallucinatory experiences qualitatively similar to veridical experiences. It will, however, be particularly important if there are some actual hallucinatory experiences of this type – for then, of course, the possibility of such experiences is clearly demonstrated. In deciding whether there are such actual experiences, we should be clear about the sense of "hallucinatory" involved. The *Oxford English Dictionary* defines "hallucination" as involving cases of "the apparent perception of an external object when no such object is present". So defined, hallucinations can be contrasted with illusions such as the bent-stick illusion and the Muller–Lyer illusion, in which there is an object, or pair of objects, that appear to have some characteristics that it does not have. Thought of in this way, rather than as experiences produced by LSD or other drugs, or by being in the DTs or through madness, hallucinatory experiences are not only common (enough) but can be reliably studied. One example is the experience of music when I put headphones (suitably connected) on. I experience a piano in the room with me, when there is none. Even if I do not have headphones on but hear through speakers on the walls, I do not experience the pianist at the place where the speakers are. There is no piano or pianist in the room. Indeed, with digitally produced recordings, there may never have existed any such pianist.

That such experiences are commonplace and quite easily understood, at least in principle, does not undercut their hallucinatory character. As far as the argument against natural realism is concerned, what is important is that the experiences are non-veridical. It seems to me undeniable that we have many such experiences that are qualitatively identical with actual veridical experiences. Additionally, knowing what we do about how, in the case of veridical perceiving, the perception depends on the causal mechanisms involved in the eye's responses to light waves, there are strong reasons for thinking that it is possible to stimulate the eyes with light waves without requiring the presence of relevant physical objects. (One does not have to depend on speculations on what might be done by stimulating directly the brain processes.) Knowing what we do, there are good reasons for thinking that it is possible to have non-veridical experiences as qualitatively similar as one likes to actual veridical experiences.

There is a further problem with Austin's discussion of hallucinatory experiences. It is true that seeing a bright green after-image against a white wall is not exactly like seeing an actual bright green patch on a white wall. However, while that experience is hallucinatory in that it has hallucinatory aspects, it is not entirely hallucinatory. In other words, the experience is a composite one, having veridical and non-veridical aspects. The bright green image is not like actual bright green patches, but it is seen against an actual wall, and it changes colour as it is seen against different walls of different colours and at different distances. Moreover, although in certain respects, for example, the colour, the after-image is not like actual coloured patches, there are other respects in which it is identical, for example, in shape and size, and being at rest. Finally, even though the bright greenness of the after-image is not like the colour of actual patches, we can say that it is more like certain patches than others. For example, it is more like a bright green circle of light than it is a green material sample. And it is more like a green material sample than a black one or a pink one.

Finally, even if Austin is right that seeing a bright green after-image against a white wall is exactly like seeing most green patches actually on the wall, it is questionable that there wouldn't be real green patches exactly like the after-image. And if there could be, the traditional epistemologist is well on his way. The route to the desired conclusion is more circuitous than was traditionally conceived, but it will get one to the end of the journey all the same.

Given that visual experiences are often not wholly hallucinatory, but rather are hybrid experiences with a mixture of veridical and non-veridical aspects, the claim of Austin that it is possible that in non-veridical experience we are aware of phenomenal objects such as sense-data, and in veridical experiences we are aware of physical objects, becomes increasingly incredible. Given what we know of the role of the brain, it seems to require a series of miracles. The point can be illustrated by the simple expedient of pressing on an eyeball, so as to produce an image of the objects in front of us. Now it would seem that we are aware of two intermediaries between us and the actual objects. It is ludicrous to say that one is the actual pen with which I am writing and the other is a phenomenal object. Just as significantly, we can say in this example that neither experience had by either eye, working by itself, is exactly the same as the experience enjoyed when using the two eyes in unison. But it would be absurd to say that we are no longer aware of two new phenomenal objects that are similar to the material objects. That, we should note, is not a logical impossibility. The point is, as Broad and Mundle have argued, it is so fantastic that the representative theory according to which one is indirectly aware of a single object, a pen, by means of being aware of two phenomenal objects, is so simple, natural and straightforward that it is the reasonable position to adopt.

Not only do Austin and Putnam misdescribe the argument they are trying to cope with, but Austin actually provides support for the opponents of "natural realism". This support comes from the point about the differences between veridical experiences and many of the actual hallucinatory experiences such as the having of after-images and so on. I think that Austin is dead right that many of these are quite unlike actual veridical experiences. But this makes things harder, not easier, for Putnam's natural realist, for now we have to admit that there are two types of experience that are different in nature. And even if phenomenal objects and sense-data only occur in non-veridical experiences, some account needs to be given of these experiences. The standard way of dealing with them is to explain the experience in terms of the acquiring of perceptual beliefs or thoughts or of sensory states with content. The argument of cognitive realists is to say that the two experiences are similar in having the same content, but if Austin is right, then that answer cannot be given, for on his account, veridical experiences and these types of non-veridical experiences are not the same.

It is considerations such as those above that enable us to see that the strongest argument for the existence of phenomenal objects is not a demonstrative argument but rather an argument that the existence of such objects helps make most sense of the perceptual facts and of certain general considerations. The reasoning has more in common with inferences to the best explanation. That this is so should cast a long shadow over the importance bestowed by Putnam on Austin. Austin is credited with destroying the argument just discussed by questioning its key assumptions. To a large extent what Austin does is show that the argument is not deductively valid. This can hardly be the great achievement that Austin gets credit for, since the invalidity was pointed out long before by Broad. He devotes a large part of *Mind and Its Place in Nature* to considering the range of alternative theories that are consistent with the premises of the argument. Broad is trying to decide which of the theories makes most sense of the range of phenomena. A more recent example is Mundle's *Perception: Facts and Theories*. We can hardly fault Austin for not knowing of Mundle's book, but he might have known of Broad's.

There is a distinctive and illuminating dialectic followed in Mundle's book. After first setting out and strengthening classical arguments against natural realism, in the second part of the book Mundle presents detailed criticism of those arguments in defence of natural realism. In the final section, he draws attention to the weaknesses of his defence, which force him reluctantly to admit the merits of a representative theory, at least with respect to vision. The reason for the reluctance rests, I would claim, on a misconception of the epistemological problems for representationalism. If my account of those problems, and how they may be resolved, is right, then Mundle's detailed analysis of natural realism and of its defects can be placed in support of a suitably constructed representationalism. Mundle's dialectic supports one of the major claims that I am making; namely, that representationalism is established by starting with something like the form of natural realism favoured by Putnam and Dewey, and modifying as much of it, and no more, as is required. What we end up with is a modified "natural" realism, one consistent with the representative theory.

Putnam does go on to discuss the type of argument that is in fact advanced by both Broad and Mundle. He considers the possibility that the opponent might retreat to saying that the appeal to intermediaries is not meant as the conclusion to a deductively secure argument, but is to be regarded as providing an explanation for a range of phenomena. Putnam's reply to this move is to say that the explanation is no genuine explanation at all. As an explanation of the fact that when she dreamed it seemed to Helen as if she were actually perceiving the Taj Mahal, the immaterialist version of the sense-datum theory is a non-starter:

> The explanation starts with a familiar fact, the fact that when I am dreaming it seems to me as if I were seeing this or that, and offers an "explanation" in terms of utterly mysterious events or processes – one that lacks all detail at just the crucial points, and possesses no testability whatsoever. Such an "explanation" would not even be regarded as intelligible in serious natural science.[19]

Putnam adds in a footnote that perhaps this is the reason that most traditional sense-datum epistemologists did not explicitly make the rejoinder that he suggests on their behalf. Well, Broad definitely does make the argument and so does Mundle. The argument, however, is far more sophisticated than Putnam gives them credit for. The explanation is not an explanation simply of facts, such as Helen's having a dream that is lifelike. The argument depends on bringing together a wide range of facts of such a nature that, given them all, the sensory particular theory makes the most sense. The important facts are not so much cases of dreaming but the wealth of perceptual experiences we enjoy. For example, there are a vast number of perceptual experiences that have both veridical and non-veridical character. For example, I experience an after-image on a wall, where the image changes colour and size, as I look at different walls. We do not have to resort to dreaming to find non-veridical experiences that are qualitatively identical, or approximately so, to veridical ones. We can press on an eyeball and produce two sets of images of objects in the world.

Finally, and most importantly, Putnam misunderstands the nature of the explanation involved. This is brought out by his saying that the explanation is not of the type that fits well into natural science. The proper rejoinder to this claim is to point out that we can have genuine explanations that are not scientific in the required sense. To show that we are not intellectual Luddites, it should be pointed out that Putnam is taking "natural science" to include procedures that conform to certain standards and requirements. It is assumed that these procedures cover explanations and descriptions of phenomena, from the third person point of view. The explanation that the traditional epistemologist is trying to provide is one that will make sense both of experience from the first person point of view, and of the scientific facts, that is, of the facts described from the third person point of view. This requires not only making sense of the first person perspective but also showing how the two perspectives fit together. If natural science, as is commonly assumed, does not bother about the first, it can hardly show how the two fit together. But that does not mean that we should not try to fit the perspectives together.

Putnam also makes one of the major mistakes made by many people who discuss variations of the classical "argument from illusion", and made especially by its critics. It is to treat the reasoning involved as captured by a simple, standard argument proceeding from acceptable premises to warranted conclusion. The reasoning, rather, is more like beginning with an assumption, moving to a conclusion and then going back to revise the initial assumption so as to make the best sense of things. Although there is some parallel between this kind of reasoning and arguments that involve inferences to the best explanation, there are important differences. I claim that this kind of reasoning is quite widespread and deserves greater recognition. It takes place in science and is common (enough) in philosophy.

On clarifying direct realism

In discussing Austin's treatment of non-veridical experiences, I argued that he unwittingly gives support to the opponents of natural realism. There is a further reason to think that Austin, despite his intentions, supports such opponents. In one passage, Austin directed his criticism against traditional epistemologists who drew radical conclusions from the observation that circular objects looked differently under a variety of circumstances. Austin asked what he took to be a damaging question: "If something is straight does it jolly well have to look straight at all times and in all circumstances? Obviously no one seriously supposes this."[20] Well, as

M. Burnyeat has pointed out, there have been many philosophers who have supposed that, and not just scholastic philosophers.[21] He argues that it is an assumption underlying an influential model of perception, one no less influential for being often a tacit model: what he calls the "window model of perception". Protagoras and Berkeley are offered as two examples of such philosophers, but Burnyeat implies that there are many more. On this model, physical objects are thought of as directly revealed by the act of perception. In perception we perceive the object simply as it is. Like opening a window and looking out, the act of perceiving reveals the thing perceived as it really is,

This view that Austin finds absurd is in fact quite widely held, and not just by philosophers. It is not uncommon for direct realists to criticize traditional epistemologists by pointing out that, contrary to what they believe, a white paper continues to look white not only in blue light, but in all kinds of different circumstances and lighting conditions. Moreover, the view attacked by Austin seems close to a view that is held by many psychologists and philosophers who discuss the perceptual constancies, for example, of size, shape and colour. The following explanations are not atypical. Nicholas Pastore writes: "The fact that the adult sees an object as having the same size, notwithstanding variation in the magnitude of the retinal image, defines the concept of size constancy."[22] In a textbook on psychology, we find John Darley and his colleagues writing: "Although sensory activity may vary enormously from moment to moment, you perceive many aspects of the world as stable and invariant."[23]

The phenomena of perceptual constancies are complex and deserve an extended discussion. Many discussions in psychology and philosophy leave as many mysteries as they aim to dissolve. For one thing, constancies are never perfect, and they vary from person to person, and if there are such variations, a problem remains for the direct realist who usually appeals to them. For my immediate purposes, however, the point about the appeals to constancy (which should be appeals to regression, if we are talking about the phenomenon studied by psychologists) is that they are appealed to normally by those defending something like Putnam's natural realism. However, if Austin is right, and I think that he is, that an object does vary in the way that it looks, in a variety of circumstances, then even if the variation is not as great as traditional epistemologists thought, and is not as simple as they thought, the issue becomes one of what we are to make of the variation in ways of looking. That is, we need to provide an account of what it is for an object to look red when it is not red, or for it to look metallic when it is plastic. The traditional epistemologist gives an answer. Perhaps it is the wrong answer, but some answer needs to be given. Austin gives none. If his is the best defence of natural realism, the opponents can rest easily at night.

Burnyeat's reference to the window model of perception helps us see that when many traditional philosophers used variations in the argument from illusion, they used that argument against a certain view of perception: "naive realism". This view is different from the cognitive form of direct realism advanced by philosophers such as Armstrong, Dretske, McDowell and others. Naive realism can be thought of as a form very close to the window model of perception. Physical objects are thought of as directly revealed by the act of perception. The objects reveal themselves when they appear as they are, and not under any forms contributed by the perceiver. It is this view predominantly that was argued against in the traditional argument from illusion.

It is easy to see how the window model might fit the view attributed with approval by Heidegger to the ancient Greeks, at least to the Greeks before Plato cast his spell.[24] Heidegger's thought is difficult and is open to different interpretations, but my understanding of his point is as follows. Heidegger holds that, prior to the influence of Plato on philosophical thought, the Greeks did not think of perception and knowledge in representational terms. Beguiled by Plato, the predominant Western philosophical tradition is supposed to suffer from having made the distinction between reality and representation, that is, making a sharp distinction between things as they are in themselves and things as they are represented as being. This pernicious error took metaphysics away from an early Greek notion that real things disclosed themselves in perception through manifesting or showing themselves, making themselves manifest, open to view, unconcealed. The original view that real things make themselves manifest gets transformed into a view that makes a distinction between reality and appearance: non-reality.

The view Heidegger attributes to the Greeks could be construed on the window model as described by Burnyeat. It is possible, however, to interpret it in a different way. We may think of Heidegger's contrast between the early Greeks and the Plato-inspired tradition as construing the two positions as employing two different notions of "appearing". Something's appearing, in the old sense, consists in something's becoming manifest, open to view, unconcealed.

The original Greek position can be thought of as a version of what I shall call "adverbialist realism". On this account, when we perceive an object, the object appears to us a certain way. There is no ontological gap between the perceived object and the way the object appears. On the adverbialist account, the object can be thought of as constituted by the range of ways it appears. The object is not thought of as independent of any of the ways in which it can appear. The perceiver contributes to the form in which the object appears. On the window model, by contrast, the object is thought of as existing independently of the perceiver (except on Berkeley's version). In perception, we perceive the object simply as it is. Like opening a window and looking out, the act of perceiving reveals the thing perceived as it really is, that is, as it exists independently of its being perceived.

Austin, Putnam and Heidegger, in their different ways, raise for us the question of what exactly direct realism amounts to. Our discussion of Austin clearly indicates that there are at least two forms. One is the transparent direct realism or the window model, described by Burnyeat. This seems to be the doctrine known as "naive realism". A different form is that of adverbial direct realism. Here the claim is that one directly perceives physical objects and their qualities, but not in the way suggested by the window model. Perceptual experience, on this account, consists in an object appearing to the perceiver a certain way – looking circular, tasting bitter, feeling rough and so on. A perceptual experience consists of being aware of, or conscious of, objects, of physical objects in the world. It is, moreover, an awareness of an object under an aspect, that is, awareness of, say, tea as bitter, or as brown or as motionless and so on. A perceptual experience on this account consists in hearing a drum as tinny, or feeling the cloth as rough, or seeing a plate as circular and so on. On the adverbialist account, it is a physical object that appears and that I see or taste or feel under an aspect.

There is no phenomenal intermediary that appears or that I see or feel or taste, under some aspect.

If, however, we are realists, we need to give some account of the metaphysical status of the appearances, or of the way things appear. It would seem that for the direct realist there are only two possibilities. One possibility is that being a table or a duck or a mountain and so on is constituted by its ways of appearing. I think that this is Heidegger's suggestion (on one interpretation of Heidegger). This provides one way of expressing the point that the distinction between something's being a real duck and appearing a duck is not a distinction between reality and non-reality. On this account, as far as real ducks, real apples and so on are concerned, ways of appearing are metaphysically basic. Being a real duck is constituted by the myriad number of ways in which it appears. The other possibility is that there is a distinction between being red, square and so on, and appearing red, square and so on, where what it is to be red, square, a duck and so on is fundamental. It is one thing to be square and quite another to appear square. There are certain conditions, standard conditions, under which things look square and are square, and other conditions under which things that look square will often not be square.

The first way of trying to capture direct realism cannot be right. At least, it cannot be right for a natural realist to accept it, a realist with respect to physical objects such as dogs, peaches, mountains. I take it that, for natural realism, there has to be a distinction between something's being F and merely appearing F. If being F is constituted by a myriad set of ways of appearing, then this distinction is lost. A theorist who takes this view cannot be a direct realist in the sense required. I do not deny that he or she is a realist of some kind. This point may be made clearer by considering the position of Berkeley. Berkeley is a realist, of some sort. He definitely believes that some things are real, for example, ideas and minds or spirits. He doesn't believe that trees and rivers and apples are real. At least, he does not believe that they exist independently of minds and ideas. Likewise with the adverbialists, who hold that so called "real qualities" are constituted by appearings; their "realism" is similar to the Berkeleian realism with respect to ordinary physical objects. The second kind of adverbialist is certainly a natural realist. For him or her, it is one thing for something to be square and another for it to appear square. And clearly there will be cases in which something is not square but only appears that way.

But now the issue becomes one of giving an account of "appears", "looks" and so on, that is adequate, that is, one that cannot be rejected on other grounds. What the adverbialist of the direct realist type requires is that for something to appear F, the perceiver comes to be in a state whose content is specified in terms of being F. What the property is that is part of the specification of the content must be characterized independently of any phenomenal properties. And it has to be specified independently of what it is for something to look a certain way, or feel a certain way and so on.

The reason for this requirement is as follows. The direct realist is attempting to give an account of what it is to see an object as being F. It won't do for him or her to explain what it is to be F in terms of its having the power to look F because, if that were so, then when the perceiver is aware of the object as F, he or she would need to be aware of the object as *looking F*. There are two problems with this. The first is that we haven't done what we were trying to do; namely, to give an account of what it is for something to look F. Secondly, to be aware of something as F would require being aware of it as looking F, and to say this is to line us up with the indirect representationalist. We need to remember here that on my version of representationalism, it is not necessary that the intermediary be a phenomenal object. It can be a way of sensing or a phenomenal state. On this account, a phenomenal state functions as a natural sign for the property in the physical world (our old friend F). Something's looking F to me can be a good candidate for such a natural sign.

Let us summarize the points of this discussion. The indirect representationalist who draws upon the traditional argument from illusion (in some variant of it) is fighting a battle on two fronts, against two opponents. One opponent embraces the window model of perception, or naive realism, a view that, for all its naivety, is hard to shake. On this view, one is presented in perceptual experience with the object itself, a particular specific chair, one the worse for wear, one with a history. Against this opponent, the argument is that by reflecting on hallucinatory and illusory experiences, one is led to think that what is presented in experience is a counterpart to the chair itself. The second opponent is the cognitive direct realist. On this account, perceptual experiences comprise our being presented with objects, in the sense that objects appear to us in certain ways. Against this opponent, the representative realist must adopt a different strategy. In this battle, the dispute is over what it is for something to *appear* in a certain way. The argument here is that when we reflect on the nature of experience, on what it is for something to appear to us, then we are led to conclude that the best theory is a representative theory. Clearly, to decide this last battle, what is crucial is what is the best account of what it is for something to appear: to look, to sound, to feel, to smell and so on.

Conclusion

In this chapter, I have examined the Putnam–Austin defence of "natural realism". I have argued that Austin provides no argument against a carefully constructed representational realism, and especially against the thesis that, in perceptual experience, one is typically aware of sensory–phenomenal intermediaries. At best, Austin provides an argument against a position that implies a certain view about sense-data, or about sense-data language. The irony is that representationalism, as defended here, that is, as a theory of natural signs, can be construed as a version of "natural realism", one satisfying all the requirements that a natural realist could reasonably and happily require.

One of the important lessons to be drawn from this discussion of Austin's treatment of natural realism and of the traditional epistemologist is this. If one is to defend natural realism, one has to give an adequate account of perception. Part of that account will be an account of the way things appear, the way things look, and taste, and feel and so on, and some effort needs to be made to give an account of these appearings. Neither Austin not Putnam make any such effort. At least cognitive realists such as Dretske and Armstrong and Heil attempt to do so. These attempts, I argue, fail.

One of the major problems with Austin's overall approach to perception is that it is founded on describing "what we would say and do say" and whether important distinctions and concepts required to describe perceptual phenomena can be captured in ordinary language. Such an approach is ideally suited to criticizing the views of A. J. Ayer, since Ayer treated sense-data language as providing an alternative language to physical object language, which was somehow meant to capture better the perceptual facts. Austin is very convincing in arguing that natural language is well suited to describe perceptual facts such as illusions, hallucinations, veridical perceivings and so on. There is little question that, for the many purposes that ordinary users of natural language have, there is no reason for them to change their language, let alone give it up.

However, Austin's approach leaves untouched that representationalist who has no wish to jettison natural language but rather wants to supplement it. This representationalist does not wish to say that we do not perceive tables, apples, rainbows, flames, skies and so on. What he or she wishes to do is revise our ways of thinking about how we do it. The aim is to develop a framework for thinking about perception – about the objects of perception, about perceptual experience and the content of experience – that will make sense of the perceptual facts, including the normalities and abnormalities of veridical and non-veridical perceivings. Crucial to such an account is developing a framework that enables us to incorporate an account of perceptual experience from the first person point of view with an account of perception from the third person point of view, where the latter comprises accounts drawn from physics, physiology, psychology and, above all, ordinary life.

Perception: the argument
6 from illusion

One of the dominant motifs concerning perception in the Western philosophical tradition is the argument from illusion, understood in a wide sense as incorporating a range of variants. The argument in its various forms is commonly taken to establish the following doctrine:

we never see or otherwise perceive or anyhow never *directly* perceive or sense, material objects (or material things), but only sense-data (or own ideas, impressions, sensa, sense-perceptions, percepts, etc.).[1]

This at least is the version that Austin attacks. Following our discussion in Chapter 5, let us suppose that the doctrine should be formulated as:

we never see or otherwise perceive material objects (or material things), except by being aware of, or sensing sense-data (or our ideas, impressions, sensa, sense-perceptions, percepts, etc.), items that are not themselves material things.

Despite its long history, however, misconceptions about the nature of the argument abound. This has been especially true in the last part of the twentieth century, when the argument tended to get short shrift. One of the major sources for this dismissal is the treatment the argument receives at the hands of Austin in his *Sense and Sensibilia*. This book lies at the heart of Putnam's defence of what he calls "natural realism" in the Dewey Lectures. (See also his *The*

Threefold Cord: Mind, Body, and the World.) The influence of this book is widespread, although it may not be that all the blame can be laid at the door of Austin.

In Chapter 5 I attempted to show how the alleged demolition by Austin is flawed. In this chapter I intend to try to be more positive: to articulate a version of the argument from illusion. In order to do that, it is essential to clarify first what the argument is intended to achieve, and what it is not.

The argument from illusion

To present a worthwhile version of the argument from illusion, it is important to explain what it is not. One sort of misunderstanding, that by Putnam and Austin, has already been discussed. There are, however, other important misunderstandings. I propose to discuss two recent examples, found in the writings of Harman and Dretske. These examples are chosen for their value in paving the way for a clearer version of the argument.

In his influential article "The Intrinsic Quality of Experience", Harman claims that the "notorious sense datum theory of perception" arises through failing to keep straight a number of "elementary points" about perceptual experience.[2] Before describing the points and diagnosing the consequent errors, Harman makes the false characterization of this "notorious and ancient sense-datum theory", as asserting that perception of external objects in the environment is always indirect and mediated by a more direct awareness of a mental sense-datum. The indirect theory, however, is only one version of the sense-datum theory. One of the most famous variants is the phenomenalistic version of Price (and Ayer). Price explicitly rejects and argues against the indirect version, by contrast to Broad. In the second place, many sense-data theorists denied that sense-data were mental. Broad and Price, for example, regarded them as neither physical nor mental.

There is, however, a more significant, although more understandable, mistake. Defenders of the sense-datum theory argue for it, Harman claims, by appealing to the so-called argument from illusion. This argument begins with the uncontroversial premise that the way things are presented in perception is not always the way they are.

Eloise sees some brown and green before her. But there is nothing brown and green before her; it is all an illusion or hallucination. From this the argument fallaciously infers that the brown and green Eloise sees is not external to her and so must be internal or mental. Since veridical, nonillusory, non-hallucinatory perception can be qualitatively indistinguishable from illusory or hallucinatory perception, the argument concludes that in all cases of perception, Eloise is directly aware of something inner and mental, and only indirectly aware of external objects like trees and leaves.[3]

Harman's diagnosis of the fallacies in this argument is instructive. An analogous argument about paintings, he points out, would start from the premise that a painting can be a painting of a unicorn even though there are no unicorns. From this it might be concluded that the painting is "in the first instance" a painting of something that is actual, for example, the painter's idea of a unicorn. To see why arguments such as these are fallacious, we only have to consider a corresponding argument:

Ponce de Leon was searching for the Fountain of Youth. But there is no such thing. So he must have been searching for something mental.

Harman is obviously correct that this last argument is fallacious. He is also correct in the claim that the argument about the painting of the unicorn is analogous and likewise fallacious. The particular argument from illusion that he has described may also be fallacious, but that argument is not the same as the traditional argument. The classical argument does not take the form:

(1) Something which is not metallic appears metallic to me,

Therefore

(2) There is something, of which I am aware, which is metallic.

Nor an argument with the premise:

(1*) It seems to me as if I am seeing something metallic.

When they describe perceptual experience, traditional theorists such as Broad and Price made a distinction between two components of experience, which we might call the "experiential component" and the "intentional component", respectively. The intentional component is the intentional content of the experience and is typically expressed in terms of the qualities of physical objects in a public space and time, for example, trees and leaves in a garden. The experiential component is non-conceptual and non-cognitive (although it is a component of a cognitive state). In keeping with this distinction, a carefully formulated argument from illusion presupposes a distinction between two forms, or concepts, of "appears", "seems", "looks" and so on. One sense is a sensible or phenomenological sense; the other is an epistemic or judgemental sense. In the words of Broad, "The plain fact is that 'looking elliptical to me' stands for a peculiar experience which, whatever the right analysis of it may be, is not just a mistaken judgement about the shape of the penny."[4]

Given that the traditional argument from illusion presupposes this distinction between two uses of "appears" and that the argument employs a special sense of "appears", the experiential or phenomenological sense, then Harman's objection to the argument is misplaced. He has constructed a straw-man argument. There is a different objection that he might have given to the argument: that the key premise that the argument takes to be non-controversial is not so benign. It might be questioned whether there is a significant legitimate sensible use of "appears", or it might be that there is a legitimate phenomenological use but one that is different from the required sense of "sensible". I think that this premise, with these uses, can be sustained, but I concede that it requires argument. Harman, however, should not dismiss the argument so cavalierly.

A more powerful critique of the argument from illusion was given by Dretske in his *Seeing and Knowing*.[5] Dretske points out that in many situations it is totally implausible to say that anything of which I am aware has those properties that some things appear to have:

> For example, something (a stone say) may look edible; does this mean that I sense something which is edible? I shall be told that "edibility" is not a visual characteristic, but I know of no non-circular way to specify what is to count as a visual characteristic.[6]

Dretske cites a range of features that are used ordinarily to describe the way things look: rough, hard, hot, far away and larger than the moon. To these we may add features such as metallic, rusty, emaciated, . . . It is not easy to see what criteria we can use to pick out the sensible qualities, in the sense required by the traditional philosophers. What Dretske is averting to here is that the argument from illusion, as it needs to be formulated, is framed in terms of sensible qualities, which, in the case of visual perception, will of course be visual characteristics. If we concentrate on the classical candidates, for example, colours such as red and shapes such as circular and square, then it is easy to think that there are no problems. But it is far from clear how we should handle such terms as "rough", "far away", "hard", "rusty" and so on. It would seem that there will be difficulties in providing a criterion to exclude these from the list of visual characteristics. Dretske has put his finger here on a key problem that will need to be resolved.

One way to resolve the problem is to distinguish between two senses of "sensible quality", even for colour terms and shape terms. That is to say, we should distinguish between physical colour and phenomenal colour, physical shape and phenomenal shape (and physical edibility and phenomenal edibility). The visual characteristics that are relevant are the phenomenal properties. (I shall return to this point later.) A more promising solution may be to simply grant that Dretske is right. There isn't a non-circular criterion to distinguish between obvious visual (phenomenal) characteristics and characteristics such as rusty, emaciated and so on. However, that might not matter very much. It may still be the case that the argument will go through, if enough properties count as visual (or, more generally, as sensible). Or at least we may be able to reconstruct a carefully formulated argument that will suffice. All this formulation of the argument requires is that there will be some sensible qualities, for which there are corresponding veridical and non-veridical situations. Providing that there are robust central cases, it will be sufficient for the weight of the argument to go through.

This point is related to another important problem for traditional theorists that Dretske draws our attention to. Dretske discusses traditional accounts of the distinction between indirect and direct versions of realism. Like many other authors, he regards the distinction as inspired by certain kinds of epistemological considerations. One is said to *directly see*, or *sense*, D only if one cannot be mistaken about D, about the fact that one is seeing (or sensing) D, or about the properties of, D. Dretske then proposes to concentrate on the proposal that S sees D directly if and only if there are some properties of D about which S cannot be mistaken.[7] He treats the argument from illusion as resting on a key premise about direct perception or direct awareness:

> S sees D directly if and only if there are some properties of D about which S cannot be mistaken.[8]

The intent, he adds, seems to be that there is a certain class of properties, visual properties, about which I cannot be mistaken. The sense in which I cannot be mistaken is that if I do believe that D has (or lacks) one of these "visual" properties, then I cannot be mistaken in my beliefs about D.

There is no doubt that the sorts of epistemological considerations referred to by Dretske have played an important role in the long history of treatments of the traditional argument from illusion. However the nature of the role needs careful consideration. First of all, there have been two motivations for the introduction of sense-data, or their recent reincarnations (phenomenal qualities, qualia-instances, . . .). One motivation is epistemological. Sense-data or sense-data statements are intended to serve as an epistemological foundation or bedrock upon which the edifice of knowledge is to be (re-)constructed. A second motivation is metaphysical: they are thought to be required in order to provide an accurate account of the phenomenology of perceptual experiences. With respect to the metaphysical motivation, it is still true that these elements have an important epistemological role, but it does not have to be one that requires infallibility or incorrigibility. In the second place, even if the sense-data are intended to play a fundamental role epistemologically, they might play such a role, even if the requirement of infallibility is relaxed. Dretske is still right, even given the metaphysical role of sense-data, that :

> S sees D directly if and only if there are some properties of D about which S cannot be mistaken.[9]

However, this claim is much more benign, given the metaphysical motivation, for it is not required that all of the properties of D be of this kind, or even that many are. The point, rather, is that it is part of knowledge by acquaintance that acquaintance requires some knowledge of D. If the subject has no knowledge of D, then he or she cannot be acquainted with D. The same principle holds about acquaintance in general. If there is nothing I know about Bill Clinton or nothing about Paris, then it is hard to see how I could be said to be acquainted with either. It is commonly thought that there is a form of beliefs that comprise *de re* beliefs: beliefs whose content is object-dependent. What I am claiming is that for someone to hold such a belief, that someone must have some knowledge about the object.

We should note that the sense of the term "sense-data" changes from the sense in which it is introduced to a later sense. The term "sense-data", as introduced, is meant to be a neutral term, neutral between different theories of perception.[10] It is meant to be non-committal about whether sense-data are mental or physical or neither, and also about what categories they fall under.[11] The point behind the use of "sensa" and "sense-datum" by Broad and Price is that sensa and sense-data are things that I sense, that is, am directly acquainted with, and it is an open question whether that which I sense (in this use) is a physical particular or a sensory–phenomenal or mental particular. Further argument is required to show that it is not physical. Broad and Price think that extra arguments can be provided. That is, they think that it can be shown that sense-data are not, in fact, material objects or parts of them. They are sensory items or phenomenal items. That is to say, it is argued that sense-data are not physical objects but rather phenomenal items. These phenomenal items that, it turns out, are sense-data, are then referred to as sense-data. This practice is quite common. In other contexts, we may refer to what a person brings on the trip as "baggage". What she brings are trunks, cases and tennis racquets. For the rest of the trip, however, they are referred to as "baggage".

We must distinguish, therefore, between "sense-data" = that which is given, and "sense-data" = sensory items. Even if to be a sense-datum in the first sense is to be something for which, for *some* of its properties, one cannot be mistaken, it does not follow that in order to be a sense-datum in the second sense it must have properties about which one cannot be mistaken.

Robinson's defence of the argument from illusion

Whatever the problems with the traditional argument from illusion, there are ways of formulating it that are much harder to defeat than is commonly supposed. One of the most sophisticated and subtle treatments, in recent times, of traditional arguments concerning the existence of sense-data is that of Robinson in a book entitled *Perception*. The focus of his book is the widely held philosophical claim that in perception one is aware of some items other than the physical object that one takes oneself to be perceiving, items that have been variously described as ideas, impressions, representations, sense-data, sensa and so on. As Robinson points out, this claim was held by most philosophers in the Western philosophical tradition, from the middle of the seventeenth century until the middle of the twentieth century.[12] Through a detailed analysis of the traditional arguments, and the various objections levelled at them, Robinson develops a sophisticated argument, designed to establish the existence of sense-data: private, non-physical items of which, in perception, one is directly aware, and that have sensible qualities and possess no intrinsic intentionality.[13]

After arguing that the traditional argument from illusion, properly formulated and understood, is far more plausible than it is currently given credit for, Robinson goes on to present his own formulation of the argument for the existence of sense-data. It is based upon a combination of elements from two traditional arguments (that are each sometimes described under the umbrella of "argument from illusion"): the traditional causal argument and the argument from hallucination. Central to the reasoning behind this argument are two claims, whose plausibility depends on findings from science:

1. It is theoretically possible that, by activating some brain process which is involved in a particular type of perception, one can cause an hallucination which exactly resembles that perception in its subjective character.

2. It is necessary to give the same account of both hallucinating and perceptual experience, when they have the same neural cause. Thus, it is not, for example, plausible to say that the hallucinatory experience involves a mental image or sense-datum, but that the perception does not, if the two have the same proximate – that is – neural cause.[14]

These two propositions, Robinson claims, are crucial in showing that perceptual processes in the brain produce some object of awareness that cannot be identified with any feature of the external world; that is, they produce a sense-datum. With respect to the first claim, it is important to point out that the possibility mentioned here is a theoretical possibility, not merely a logical possibility. What is being claimed is that there are good theoretical reasons for claiming that such a possibility exists. These theoretical reasons depend on what is known of the brain and what is known of its role in pure acquiring and exercising perceptual capacities that we possess. Thus we can see how the argument draws heavily upon the findings and theories of science.

Two important points emerge, in my view, from consideration of the role of science in this argument. First, the argument cannot simply be an argument from the first person point of view, in the way that was presented by some traditional philosophers. Secondly, the dependence on science would seem to support representational realism over the form of idealism–phenomenalism favoured by Robinson and other philosophers. This last point would no doubt be denied by Robinson and the others, who would claim that idealist–phenomenalist analyses can be provided of the objects of science. I would argue that these analyses are not successful, but there is, I believe, a more fundamental point. Even if such analyses are theoretically possible, that is not enough to sustain the idealist–phenomenalist position. That position is established, I would argue, only if it can be shown that realism, with respect to the objects of science, is unacceptable. In other words, the plausibility of idealism–phenomenalism depends on the alleged unsustainability of realism. It is the thrust of my argument to show that there is a form of realism, representative realism, that is acceptable, and for which there are no major objections. It is the aim of this book to present such an argument.

The argument Robinson defends does not, of course, establish indirect realism, but, if successful, it establishes an essential part of the theory; namely, that what the subject is directly aware of in veridical perception is something other than the perceived physical object.[15] I propose to provide a different version of the argument making modifications to his argument. In part, the new premises are easier to defend. In part, the argument is drawing upon different ways of defending key premises.

The full version of the argument from illusion, as presented by Robinson, is as follows:

(1) In some cases of perception, physical objects appear other than they actually are. That is, they appear to possess *sensible* qualities that they do not actually possess.

(2) Whenever something appears to a subject to possess a sensible quality, there is something of which the subject is aware and which does possess that quality.

Therefore:

(3) In some cases of perception, there is something of which the subject is aware, which possesses sensible qualities, which the physical object, which the subject is perceptually perceiving, does not possess.

(4) If *a* possesses a sensible quality that *b* lacks, then *a* is not identical to *b*.

Therefore:

(5) In *some cases* of perception, that of which the subject is aware, is something other than the physical object which the subject is purportedly perceiving.

(6) There is such continuity between those cases in which the objects appear other than they actually are, and the cases of veridical perception, that the same analysis of perception must apply to both.

Therefore:

(7) In *all cases* of perception, that of which the subject is aware, is something other than the physical object which the subject is purportedly perceiving.

There are two key premises to this argument, premise 2, the *Phenomenal Principle,* and premise 6, the *Continuity Principle.* Premise 2 applies to those cases in which there exists something that appears to a subject. To cover cases of hallucination as well, premise 2 can be replaced by the wider premise 2*:

(2*) If there sensibly appears to a subject to be something which possesses a particular sensible quality, then there is something of which the subject is aware, which does possess that quality.

Robinson goes on to describe this type of use, *sensibly appears*, as a phenomenological use, by contrast to what he calls a *judgemental use*, whereby for something to appear F to me is for me to judge, or be inclined to judge or to believe that something is F.[16]

We might note that, as the argument is formulated, it does not necessarily apply to all illusory and hallucinatory experiences. Premise 3 maintains that there are *some cases* of perception in which there is something of which the subject is aware, and which possesses the sensible qualities that the relevant physical object lacks. For this premise to hold, it is not necessary that premise 2 universally holds. All that is required is that it applies to enough of the perceptual situations, or better, to central cases or to enough robust cases, which will serve for the continuity considerations to carry through. This point is particularly important for the contexts in which the aim is not to provide incorrigible pieces of foundational knowledge. It is important, that is, in those contexts in which the aim is not to provide epistemological foundations but to understand how perception works, and how it is that perceptual knowledge is acquired.

We can see how Robinson's appeal to science, especially to the role of neural processes, ties in with this argument. The appeal to science is relevant to establishing premise 6, concerning the continuity between veridical and non-veridical cases. Historically, this Continuity Principle has largely been based on phenomenological considerations, that is, from reflection on what it is, from the first person point of view, to perceive and to be a subject of illusion and hallucination. The phenomenological considerations are still important, but they are reinforced by the considerations from the argument from science.

There are other points to be made about Robinson's version of the argument from illusion. The argument is formulated so as to apply to all cases of perception. However, it surely is the case that the argument only works if applied to each modality in turn, say first to seeing, and then to hearing, and then to smelling and so on. We would expect that once the argument goes through with respect to one modality, the same argument will work with the other modalities. However, once the situation is spelt out in these terms, the possibility is raised that there is some variety of perception for which the argument does not work. Two plausible possibilities are touch and kinaesthetic perception.

Kinaesthetic perception is of particular interest. Kinaesthetic perception involves knowledge about the position of our limbs and bodily parts, usually acquired through the control of those limbs and parts. While we do have kinaesthetic sensations, it is plausible that much of our kinaesthetic perception occurs without the sensations, or, if there are sensations, they play little role. As far as bodily sensations are concerned, it seems here that the perceiver exercises a body-image, that is, a sensory representation of the body, and thus, as far as these bodily sensations are involved in the perceiver's knowledge of his or her body, he or she is directly aware of a representation. However, for those instances of kinaesthetic perception without sensation, it would appear that the perceiver is directly aware of the body, and is not aware of any intermediary. Thus, the Continuity Principle (premise 6) would not apply.

As far as touch is concerned, we should perhaps distinguish between two forms of perception: touch proper, which is an active form of perception requiring the perceiver to use his or her limbs, hands, legs and so on, to find out about objects in the world, for example, through their resistance to pressure, forces and so on; and touch or feeling experienced through objects acting on the perceiver's body, for example, wind, air, weights. The complication with touch is that since it involves exercising control over one's body, it is tied up with kinaesthetic perception.

Setting aside, if we can, the kinaesthetic dimension to touch, it would seem that Robinson's argument goes through, although the illusions are perhaps less common for touch than for vision. The argument still works, I maintain, because the sense of touch involves me being aware of things exercising pressure on my body. The sense of touch requires me being aware of my body's being affected by the object concerned. Thus perception of that external object requires me being aware of an intermediary between the object and me, the perceiving subject. It is important to stress here that the argument from illusion does not have to be interpreted as denying that, in exercising the sense of touch, I am aware of external bodies.

Actually, to make this point, a modification needs to be made to the way Robinson has formulated his argument. Fortunately, not only does this modification fit my point, it makes his argument better. The main conclusion (7) is expressed as:

(7)   In *all cases* of perception, that of which the subject is aware, is something other than the physical object which the subject is purportedly perceiving.

In using the clause "that of which the subject is aware", this conclusion follows the intermediate conclusion (5). However, premise 3, which led to the latter conclusion, did not use this phrase. Instead it stated that, in some cases of perception, "there is something of which the subject is aware", which has certain qualities that the perceived object lacks. The difference is subtle but important. Phrased in the last way, the statement requires the perceiver to be aware of something other than the physical object but it does not deny that the subject is also aware of the physical object. In other words, the argument allows for double awareness. On the way that Robinson has formulated conclusions 5 and 7, however, it is easy to think that the perceiver is not aware of the physical object. What is important is that the cogency of the argument depends on interpreting the statement so as to allow for double awareness.

The assumptions of the Phenomenal Principle

The argument from illusion, as set out by Robinson, depends on a crucial premise, which he calls the "Phenomenal Principle". The application of this principle assumes that there are certain sensible properties, for example, being red, being circular, being irregular, being singular and so on, that physical objects appear to have. The Phenomenal Principle can be formulated as follows:

(PP)   Whenever something appears to a subject to possess a sensible quality, there is something of which the subject is aware and which does possess that quality.

With this principle in place, Robinson argues, a coherent argument from illusion can be mounted, one that is different from and much more powerful that the ones often attacked by hostile critics.

I am largely sympathetic to Robinson's treatment. However, I think that further work needs to be done before the Phenomenal Principle is acceptable. There are three crucial terms (concepts) that the principle employs: *sensible quality*, *aware* and *appears*. To accept the principle, we need to be clear about how these expressions are to be understood. And we must ensure that the terms are not understood in such a way as to beg the question at issue. The argument from illusion is intended, after all, to establish that there is some contradiction or at least important problems in our ordinary thinking about perception and perceptible objects. Given that the Phenomenal Principle is a central part of the argument, then that principle should be either plainly acceptable or easily established without making controversial assumptions. Likewise, its key terms, even if not already understood, should be capable of being clearly and readily explained, free from controversial philosophical assumptions. (It would be too stringent to require that the terms be free from all philosophical assumptions. It is the ones that are controversial, in this context, that we need to be careful of.) What this means is that either we use the terms "appears", "sensible quality" and "aware" in the normal way they are used, or, more realistically, in one of the ways they are used, or if we use them differently, perhaps as a modification of these senses, the use is defensible.

Take the term "sensible quality". On the face of it, sensible qualities are qualities that physical objects possess and that can be detected by perceivers' sensory systems. For vision, there are visible qualities: ones that physical objects have and that perceivers can tell, by looking, that they possess. Likewise, there are other sensible qualities that objects have that we can tell by smelling – and by tasting, and by listening for and feeling. In the case of visible qualities, they are qualities such as shape, number, contour, colour, size. Some of these sensible qualities are intrinsic qualities of physical objects, for example, shape, colour, intrinsic size; some are dispositional, for example, odours, sounds, warmth.

If we understand "sensible quality" in this way, however, then the Phenomenal Principle is in trouble. Not only is it not plausible, but it is obviously false that, whenever a physical object appears to a subject to possess a sensible quality, there is something of which the subject is aware and which does possess that quality. One way of highlighting the problem is to point out that sensible qualities, in this sense, have causal powers, or if they are dispositional properties, they are related to other properties that have causal powers. In perceptual cases, in which a physical object lacks the shape or the taste it appears to have, it is most implausible that there is anything that has that shape or taste.

The principle might be more plausible if by "sensible quality" we mean "phenomenal quality". So that in the case of shape, for example, one should distinguish between visible shape, which has causal powers, and "visual shape" which is a phenomenal quality, that is not connected with same causal powers as those connected with the physical shape. Following this line of thinking, we need to distinguish between physical shape and visual or phenomenal shape; physical size and phenomenal size, and so on.

Now there is no doubt that traditional epistemologists, such as Price, Broad and Moore, did think that there were phenomenal qualities such as these and that they were distinguishable from the kind of physical qualities contrasted above. There may be a problem with whether they are justified in thinking that way, but for the moment the important point to note is that the Phenomenal Principle is neither obviously true nor non-controversial. It requires being formulated in terms of phenomenal qualities and its acceptability will turn on at least two things: the viability of phenomenal qualities and the language for describing them; and some training or education in the art of phenomenology. Those problems may not be insuperable but it is important to acknowledge that we are no longer in the business simply of bringing out problems in the ordinary way of thinking.

Similar considerations apply to the term "appears". This term is understood in a special way, "sensibly appears", which is taken to be a *phenomenological use*, by contrast to what he calls a *judgemental use*, whereby for something to appear F to me is for me to judge, or be inclined to judge or to believe that something is F. There is a problem, however, to do with whether the phenomenological use is an ordinary everyday use, or whether it is a technical use invented by philosophers and/or psychologists. There is reason to think that it has to be a technical use. (On the ordinary use, the principle is implausible.) But if it is a technical use, then it needs to be explained, presumably by appealing to the phenomenology of perceptual experience.

Besides depending on such key terms as "sensibly appears" and "sensible quality", the Phenomenal Principle uses the notion of being *aware*. Take a case of veridical perception, one in which I see a bunch of grapes, say, before me, identifying them as grapes. In this situation it is said that I am presented in experience with something (or some things) that I am *aware of*, as standing out from background, made up of globular, blue and bluish-red objects with smooth contours. This account raises the question of how we should understand the sense in which, in this perceptual experience, I am aware of the bunch. Traditional epistemologists take it to be the same as "see". But it cannot be our ordinary sense of "see". First of all, for someone to see a bunch of grapes is for them to causally interact with the grapes so as to acquire a perceptual state that allows one to discriminate the object. The awareness is more tied in to the account of discriminating than seeing. Secondly, it cannot be this sense of "see" that is equivalent to "aware of" if we are to accommodate hallucinatory experiences. Finally, there is reason to think that we need a distinct sense of "aware" anyway. While, in seeing a bunch of grapes, I am aware of the object as being there, in front of me, I may see them being crushed and hear them pop. I am aware of the crushing just before the popping. We need to acknowledge that just as we are aware of the grape as being crushed we are aware of its being crushed before it pops. Our awareness takes in, that is, what we see and what we hear (and feel, etc.). Thus, just as with "sensibly appears" and "sensible quality", so with "aware of", the phenomenological principle needs support from phenomenological considerations. This is not to suggest that it is not forthcoming, but, as we shall see in the next chapters, there are alternative accounts offering such support.

What this discussion of Robinson's formulation of the argument from illusion brings out is that there is a plausible version of his argument but it depends on a key premise, the Phenomenal Principle, and that principle, when properly understood, stands in need of support. The kind of support, if it comes at all, will come from the phenomenology of perception. That is to say, we reflect on the situation of veridical perception and try to describe the structure of perceptual experience. We do the same with illusory and hallucinatory experiences. It is through trying to capture the extent to which these different types of experience are, or can be, subjectively identical, that the Phenomenal Principle emerges. For the first part, we argue that in normal veridical perceptual situations when, say, I see a bush before me, there exists something that I am aware of, in the sense that there is something that is presented to me, that I am perceptually acquainted with, and about which I *can* make judgements and in relation to I *can* act. The second part is to argue that in such situations of veridical perception, my judgement that the something, X, is F, for a range of suitably specified properties, is based on X's being F. With respect to both parts, we then compare the situation in veridical perception with that in hallucinatory and illusory perceptual experience. It is in virtue of this process that the Phenomenal Principle, or something like it, will emerge. One of the advantages of breaking the argument into these two parts is that it allows us to see that the principle has different parts, and hence that one part may be better supported than the other.

It is a real possibility, it seems to me, that one of the results of this process is that we shall discover tensions in our thinking about perceptual experiences, and as a consequence, we shall be led to revise our phenomenological descriptions of veridical perception. This result should not be surprising. It is a pattern of reasoning that is familiar enough in philosophy and science. We begin with certain premises, but, as a result of our reasoning, we are led to revise the initial premises and perhaps the evidence we had for them.

A problem that this defence of the Phenomenal Principle raises concerns the viability of the language for phenomenal qualities, the "phenomenal language". This language, it might be thought, runs foul of the "anti-private language argument", or some version of it. I do not think that the problems here are insuperable. One response that the traditional epistemologist might make is to ally himself or herself to that body of philosophers who have questioned Wittgenstein's argument, arguing that his argument relies on certain assumptions that can be challenged. That is one possible response, but I prefer not to rely on it.

A better defence of phenomenal qualities is to argue that the language for describing them is not necessarily private. If it is private it is so in a benign sense that does not run foul of any cogent form of the anti-private language argument. First of all, some clarification is needed. There are (or have been) two major and different motivations for introducing phenomenal qualities (or their equivalents, depending on the vocabulary). One is to introduce them with the aim of providing foundations in epistemology, where often they are introduced as items that are known as certain, infallible, incorrigible and so on. The second aim is different. It is to provide us with an account of how in fact we do acquire knowledge. Phenomenal qualities are supposed to play a role in the acquisition of knowledge, and in the justification of knowledge claims, but not necessarily as infallible and incorrigible foundations.

The important point is that if the language for phenomenal qualities is introduced as part of achieving the second aim, we do not have to think of the qualities as known with certainty and infallibility, and we do not have to think that the only kind of knowledge we can have must be justified completely in terms of descriptions of such qualities. Given the first aim, on the other hand, it is easy to see how tempting it is for the language for phenomenal qualities to be construed as necessarily private. (See Robinson (1994) and Maund (1995) for more detailed treatment of the anti-private language argument.[17])

Conclusion

I have suggested that there might be a plausible version of the argument from illusion, along the lines presented by Robinson. However, things are more complex than either Robinson or the critics of the argument think. The argument depends on a key premise, the Phenomenal Principle, and that principle, when properly understood, is controversial; at least, it stands in need of support. I have suggested that the support has to come, if at all, from reflecting on the phenomenology of perceptual experience, both veridical and non-veridical. This point is reinforced when we remind ourselves that the Phenomenal Principle presupposes the viability of a special use of "looks" and other appears-terms: the phenomenological use. That use will require defence from reflecting on the phenomenology of perceptual experience.

There is a related problem. Besides employing such key terms as "sensibly appears" and "sensible quality", the Phenomenal

Principle uses the notion of being *aware of*. Take a standard case of veridical perception, one in which, say, I see a bush before me. In this situation, there exists something that I am aware of, in the sense that there is something that is presented to me, that I am perceptually acquainted with, and about which I *can* make judgements and in relation to I *can* act. An objection that can be raised is with the notion of *presentation*. It might be argued that nothing is presented in the way required by the sense-datum theorist. There is, admittedly, a certain sense of "being presented", according to which a physical object and its physical features are presented, but what it is to be presented, in this sense, is for the object to cause in the perceiver a certain perceptual cognitive state, or an adverbially modified cognitive state, or way of sensing. For example, it may be claimed that when I have a perceptual experience I have a sensory state with non-conceptual content. I am not, however, aware of the intrinsic qualities of the sensory state. Rather by being in the state with its non-conceptual content, I am thereby aware of the physical object in question.

To conclude, to succeed the argument from illusion depends on a defence of the Phenomenal Principle, and the defence of that principle will require a defence, and proper analysis, of the phenomenal use of "appears", and a defence of a certain view about the structure of perceptual experience, and defence against rival accounts. In the remaining chapters of this book I shall try to address these issues. Given my earlier defence of indirect representationalism, this position is one that I wish to resist. I shall take up the challenge in Chapters 8 and 9.

The aim in this chapter, I should add, has been to examine the argument from illusion and to show that it has far greater strengths than it is commonly given credit for. I have also tried to show how it needs to be supported and to indicate the direction from where that support should come. In so far as the version of representational realism that I am defending depends on the argument from illusion, it seems to me that enough has been done to establish a modest thesis: that it is a viable competitor in the contest, at least on equal terms with the major players.

The phenomenal and phenomenological senses of "looks"

There is a common thread to the Austin–Putnam discussion of natural realism, and the more general discussion of the argument from illusion: that understanding what it is for something to *appear* to perceivers, of what it is to taste, feel, look, sound, smell and so on, a certain way, is of vital importance. Not only is such an account important in understanding the epistemological role of perception, but it is crucial for the assessment of the forms of realism – direct, indirect and natural – and especially of adverbialist theories of realism. Indeed, it is crucial to providing a satisfying philosophical account of perception.

In discussions of perception it is common to find a distinction drawn between the phenomenal (phenomenological) sense of "looks" (and of tastes, etc.) and other senses, for example, an epistemic (or doxastic) sense and a comparative sense. It is the phenomenal sense that is crucial in the setting out and defence of most theories of perception. Not only is this sense relied upon in the argument from illusion, but it has a central role to play for those who reject the argument from illusion, for example, Dretske and Tye.

In this chapter I shall attempt to set out a framework for thinking about the different uses of "looks". Within that framework, I shall attempt to provide an account of the phenomenological sense of "looks". In concentrating on "looks", I shall take it as a model for other "appears" terms: sounds, feels, tastes, smells and so on.

Although my central concern is with philosophical approaches to perception, it is reassuring to find the psychologist Irvin Rock, in his book *Perception*, saying that the goal of the science of perception is to understand the act of perception itself, and to discover how and why things appear as they do.[1] His assessment of the major theoretical approaches to visual perception is based on how well they may be taken to answer Kurt Koffka's famous query "Why do things look as they do?"[2] Philosophers and psychologists have, in my view, broadly speaking, different aims in studying perception, but there is considerable overlap on issues of interest. Both should benefit from getting clearer about the range of the way things appear, and of the significance of these ways.

Ambiguities with "appears" and "phenomenal"

It is common to find, in the philosophical literature on perception, reference to three different uses of "looks" (or "seems" or "appears" used in visual contexts): epistemic, comparative and phenomenal (or phenomenological). Unfortunately, not all writers mean the same by these terms and, in any case, there is a need for greater complexity in the understanding of these uses than most allow. Two of the best characterizations of the threefold distinction are those given by Chisholm and Jackson, but even their accounts require substantial amendment.[3] There is a need to recognize more than the three uses identified by them, and there is, I shall argue, a better way to characterize the various uses.

One important ambiguity concerns the question of whether the phenomenological (phenomenal) sense of "looks" discussed, and heavily relied upon, in philosophical contexts is a technical use or is an ordinary, uncomplicated use found in everyday, humdrum contexts, as Dennett suggests. It sometimes appears that for traditional philosophers such as Broad and Price, the term is used in a technical sense, but we need to be careful. It may be that what looks to be a technical use in the hands of a philosopher is simply a device for clarifying an ordinary use, and that the philosopher is making explicit something that is implicitly recognized by ordinary competent language users, and would be readily accepted by them, once it is pointed out. Some philosophers, however, do regard the phenomenological use as a technical one. Anthony Quinton, for example, no friend of sense-data, seems to think it is. He writes of the phenomenological use of "appears" as involving a description of one's experiences, but as one that is a sophisticated procedure, seldom called for: "It is an essential accomplishment for painters, broadcast engineers, doctors of the eye and ear, cooks and experimental psychologists. But unless we fall into their hands, there is little need for us to become proficient in it."[4]

To describe one's experiences, Quinton says, would require a radical change of attitude. "I am not in a position to describe my experiences unless I am in the appropriate, sophisticated, phenomenological frame of mind."[5] Quinton's claim stands in sharp contrast to that expressed by Evans. For Evans, to describe our visual experiences is to look at the world and describe what we see. All one has to do is add the operator "it seems to me that . . ." to say "I am seeing a black horse" or "there is a black horse in front of me facing away".[6]

I propose to argue that there is both a technical use, and an ordinary use, for "looks" (and other appears terms) in the phenomenological sense. However, the technical use reflects the fact that there is a phenomenal sense in which things look, whose existence is presupposed by the ordinary use and is implicitly recognized by ordinary perceivers. The technical use comes into play, so to speak, when philosophers, psychologists, doctors and so on try to make explicit what is implicit. Contrary to Quinton, then, I propose to argue that there is an ordinary, phenomenological sense of "looks", which is reflected in ordinary practice. It is as the result of analysis of that use that we are led to acknowledge the other sense in which there is a phenomenal way that things look.

There is a further ambiguity arising with terms such as "phenomenal" and "phenomenological", especially with respect to uses of "looks", "tastes", "feels", "sounds" and so on. First, the terms in most philosophical contexts are used interchangeably. Secondly, and more importantly, there is a difference between a neutral sense and a strong, robust sense. In the latter sense, to speak of phenomenal states or aspects of experience, I take it, is another way of speaking of qualitative, intrinsic states or aspects of experience ("qualia"). These aspects are ontologically subjective (to use Searle's phrase). They are intrinsic properties of experiences or sensory objects; they are not epistemic properties or representational properties.

There is strong opposition to this position. There is a group of philosophers who, while denying that there are phenomenal states in the strong sense, do admit that there are phenomenal states in a weaker sense. It is in this vein that Tye, for example, argues that perceptual experiences have phenomenal character, but do not have intrinsic phenomenal qualities of which the perceiving subject can become aware. Among these philosophers, it is common to hold that there is a proper "phenomenal" or "phenomenological" use of "looks", which can be contrasted with an epistemic use but, they claim, this use can be explained away satisfactorily.[7] This sense of "phenomenal" is a neutral sense, which makes no commitment to phenomenal states in the full-bodied, strong sense.

To overcome the problems with the ambiguity concerning "phenomenal" and particularly with the phenomenal uses of "appears", I propose to adopt a certain strategy. I shall use the term "phenomenological" to cover phenomenal states in the weak, neutral sense, keeping the term "phenomenal", unless otherwise stated, for the strong sense. I shall argue that while there is a neutral phenomenological use of "looks", which is distinct from the phenomenal use, nevertheless, the phenomenological use presupposes a phenomenal sense of "looks", in the stronger sense.

In this chapter, I shall examine the attempts to dispense with the phenomenal sense of "looks", arguing that they are unsuccessful. There is a sense of "phenomenological" that is neutral in that it makes no explicit commitment to states which are phenomenal, in the strong sense. There is, however, an implicit commitment.

The three uses of "looks"

It is clear that there is a wide variety of ways in which the perceptual expressions "looks", "tastes", "feels", "sounds" and so on function. The expression ". . . looks . . .", for example, is used in different contexts: "looks F", "looks as if it is F", "looks like an F", "looks just like an F", "looks the way things which are F look" and so on. We can list the variety of ways by the following illustrative examples:

1. Harry looks distinguished (pale, hostile, tall, lean, healthy, . . .)
2. Harry looks the way triumphant people characteristically look.
3. Harry looks like an English bulldog.
4. Harry looks as if he has lost the contract.

5. It looks as if Harry has lost his bet.
6. It looks (i.e. seems) as if Harry won't be joining us.

Statements 1 to 6 are objective in that they are open to argument from other people, in straightforward ways, but they presuppose that there are perceptual experiences that are reported through the sentences, which add the qualifier "to me" or "to Alice" to each of the sentences above.

In trying to provide a systematic account of these uses, one important distinction to make is between the epistemic, or judgemental, use of "looks", and the phenomenological use. One of the earliest philosophical contexts in which this distinction is important is in those debates in which the ancient sceptics engaged. Julia Annas and Jonathan Barnes provide a detailed discussion of the distinction in their *The Modes of Scepticism*.[8] Annas and Barnes write that the sense in which the sceptics say how things appear is "to say how they impress us or how they strike us", and they (Annas and Barnes) contrast this use with the epistemic use of "appears":

> In English we sometimes use the phrase "That appears so and so" to indicate a guarded belief: I may say "The claret appears corked" or "The defendant appears guilty" in order to evince a belief, tentative or guarded, that the claret is corked or the defendant guilty. The Greek verb *phainesthai* is also used in the same way to express tentative belief. But that use of "appear" and of *phainesthai* must be sharply distinguished from the use we have previously described. The Pyrrhonist, when he talks about appearances, is saying nothing at all about his beliefs, tentative of form: he intends to register how things strike him, not how much confidence he is putting in the way they strike him.[9]

As they go on to say, "in the phenomenological sense, the verb expresses the way things impress us, while in the judgemental sense, it expresses our beliefs". Actually, things are more complicated than this would suggest. We need to distinguish between "pure" epistemic uses, where "looks" functions as a synonym for "seems", and has nothing special to do with perception, and other epistemic uses that are linked with perception. I shall, however, postpone discussion of this complication to the next section.

Besides the phenomenological and the epistemic (pure and perceptual) uses of "looks", there is a clear need to specify a comparative sense. There is clearly all the world of difference between "Tom looks (to Susan) like a poodle" and "Tom looks (to Susan) as if he is a poodle". In one statement we are making a comparison between two ways in which something looks, and in the other we are either citing a reason for a belief, or are expressing a belief in a guarded way. I might very well accept "Andy Warhol's mother looks to me like Andy Warhol in drag", but deny "Andy Warhol's mother looks to me as if she is Andy Warhol in drag".

The epistemic sense is to be understood as having a propositional content, for example, that something is *F*, and it is usually understood in terms of the perceiver's expressing a belief, or an inclination to belief, or alternatively as expressing a belief in a guarded way, allowing oneself a hedge or a way out. A crucial difference between the epistemic sense and the comparative sense is that, for the epistemic sense to apply, the perceiver must possess the concept of being *F*, whereas for the comparative sense he or she does not. It could well be, for example, that things that share a certain molecular structure should look the same distinctive way to someone, without that person having the concept of a molecule, let alone the concept of that molecular structure. Although, as we shall see, there are different kinds of epistemic senses, there is little doubt that all epistemic senses are different in this way from the comparative sense.

Things are more complicated than is suggested by the neat distinction Annas and Barnes draw between the epistemic and phenomenological senses of "looks". Depending on the context, the judgements "the claret looks corked" and "the defendant looks guilty" can function quite differently, even if each is used to express a tentative or guarded belief. In one context, the expression functions as a synonym for the more general, purely epistemic expression "seems", and has nothing special to do with perceptual contexts at all. There are other contexts in which "the defendant looks guilty" is used not just to express guardedly a belief, but to indicate that one has perceptual reasons, of a certain sort: that the reasons relate to the way the defendant is looking. That is to say, there are two kinds of epistemic sense: a pure sense and a special perceptual-epistemic sense.

Jackson has characterized an epistemic interpretation for "looks" that is fitted for perceptual contexts. This epistemic use is propositional in that statements containing this use of "looks" can be naturally cast into the form "it looks as if p", where p is a sentence expressing a proposition, for example, "it looks as if the sun is sinking into the sea", "it looks as if it is about to rain" and so on.[10] To use "looks" in this way, says Jackson, is to express the fact that "a certain body of visually acquired evidence . . . supports the proposition". Jackson contrasts this use with the kind of epistemic use that is put in terms of tentative, guarded assent.[11] To say that the people in the house I am visiting appear to be away is to assert "in a guarded, tentative, qualified way that they are away".[12] We might mark the two senses as:

(1a) it seems$_e$ to me as if p (e.g. X is triangular);
(1b) it looks$_{p\text{-}e}$ to me as if X is triangular.

There is a further complication. Jackson presents the perceptual-epistemic sense in this form:

(1b) it looks$_{p\text{-}e}$ to me as if X is triangular.

There is, however, another important "looks" construction, for which there is an epistemic construction. Take sentences of the form:

(2) X looks to me as if it is triangular.

There is a significant difference between saying "X looks as if it is rubbery (red, square . . .) to me" and "it looks to me as if X is rubbery (red, square . . .)". The first says something about the way X looks, about its appearance. The second is compatible with my not seeing X at all: it looks to me as if rain is coming. Sentences of the same form as (2) imply that there is a certain distinctive way that X looks, such that it provides a reason for a certain belief. We have two distinct, although related, things: the way of looking and the belief that that way of looking supports.

Summarizing, the difference can be registered by the sentences:

(2) X looks to me as if it is triangular, and
(1b) it looks to me as if X is triangular.

For each of these there is a propositional content. The important feature about (2) however, is not only that X is part of the propositional content but also that X plays a causal role, not only in the person's having a state with that propositional content, but in him or her having the relevant visual evidence as well. On the other hand, "it looks to me as if Bill Clinton is guilty" might be true if the visual evidence is provided by my looking at a witness's face, and not at Bill Clinton.

Taking the epistemic (perceptual) sense in these two ways, it would seem that the proper analyses of these two uses is as follows:

Epistemic (perceptual)
  1. It looks$_{p\text{-}e}$ to Alice as if X is rusty:
      1a.   From the way something looks$_d$, it seems$_e$ to Alice as if X is rusty.
  2. X looks to Alice as if it is rusty:
      2a.   From the way X looks$_d$, it seems$_e$ to Alice as if X is rusty.

Once we spell out the analyses in this way, we can see that the per-ceptual-epistemic senses presuppose a more basic sense of "looks"; let us call it a "non-epistemic descriptive sense".

The intentional phenomenological sense

I have just argued, with respect to the comparative use of "looks", that not only can we identify a phenomenological use for looks, looks$_{pg}$, which is distinct from the comparative use, but also that the comparative use presupposes a non-comparative, descriptive use. (We should resist the temptation to identify this automatically with the phenomenological sense.) In the same way, we can appeal to two analogous arguments to establish, with respect to the epistemic (perceptual) use, that there is a distinct phenomenological use, and a non-epistemic, descriptive use. There is an important difference, for example, between

(1) this wine looks yellow to me
(2) this wine looks to me as if it won't be drunk

and between the corresponding objective judgements. The difference rests on the fact that (2) has a certain propositional content.
Statement (2) takes the form "the wine looks to me as if *p*". It might
be thought that (1) is a special case of (2). That is, it might be
thought that (1) could be expressed as

(1*) the wine looks to me as if it is yellow.

This suggestion, however, cannot work. There can be a situation in
which it is true that it looks as if the wine is yellow, but false that it
looks yellow to me. Suppose I am looking at bottles of wine in the
near dark, in which I cannot tell the colour of wines, or cannot tell
the colour properly. Knowing that there are only red wines and
yellow wines in the room, I may say of a certain wine that it looks to
me as if it is yellow because it looks lighter in colour than the others,
but not because it looks yellow (because it does not). Or it may be
that the wines are all in dark bottles, the yellow wines with labels,
the red ones without. Viewing the label, I say that the wine in the
bottle looks to me as if it is yellow, but I could not truthfully say that
it looks yellow to me.

In the case of expressions of the form "*X* looks *F* to me", unlike
those of the form "*X* looks to me as if it is *F*", there is an implication
that there is a characteristic and distinctive appearance that
F-things have; there is a distinctive way that things that are *F* look.
The point about such expressions as "looks red", "looks metallic",
"looks rusty", "looks angry", "looks sharp" and so on is that they
are used to form sets of conceptually related pairs: looks red/is red,
looks metallic/is metallic, looks rusty/is rusty and so on. To look
yellow, rusty, emaciated, hostile and so on is, in each case, a sign of
something's being yellow, rusty, emaciated, hostile and so on. It is
not, of course, an infallible sign, but it is a sign nevertheless. In such
cases there is a characteristic way that things that are yellow or rusty
or emaciated and so on have of appearing. On the other hand,
when one says that the wine looks as if *p*, what is normally meant is
that there is a way that the wine looks that, given special knowledge, supports the claim that *p*. For example, I say that the wine

looks as if it won't be drunk, because I know that it has been standing unopened on the table. The point of making this remark is to
say that I have certain visual evidence concerning the wine such
that, given what I know, it supports the judgement that *p*.

To take another example: the difference between "the briefcase
looks weather-beaten" and "the briefcase looks as if it is weather-
beaten" is that the former implies that there is a certain way of
looking, one that can be characterized as a "weather-beaten" way: it
is a distinctive way of appearing. There is no such implication in the
statement that it looks as if it is weather-beaten. To assert the latter
is to say something about the kind of evidence we have but it leaves
it quite open what that evidence is. What we can say of the perceptual-epistemic case is that it implies that there is a certain way that
the briefcase looks, and judging by the way it looks there is reason
to believe that it is weather-beaten.

The examples of the conceptual phenomenological sense that I
have given are of predicates, for example, as in "looks yellow",
"looks square", "looks rusty", "looks hostile" and so on. There is
another kind of example, for example, that "that building looks like
a church to Susan", "that dog looks like a bulldog to Helen" and so
on. Those are uses that require the perceiver to possess the concepts
bulldog, *church* and so on. (There are other uses of "looks like" that
are comparative, and that can be applied to someone without that
person needing the concepts.) The difference between these types
of cases reflects the fact that one type refers to properties such as
being blue, oblong, emaciated, tall and so on, and the other refers
to objects, for example, a church, a bulldog, a horse, an apple and
so on. It would seem that, with respect to the latter, there is a gestalt
character to the way something looks that is peculiar to the type of
object in question. This gestalt is connected not to a single property
but to an arrangement of features.

It seems clear that we can identify an independent, phenomenological use of "looks", quite separate from the comparative and
epistemic uses (perceptual and pure). This phenomenological sense
is intentional and conceptual. That is to say, for something to look
rusty to Alice, or look red to her, or metallic, it is necessary for Alice
to possess the relevant concept, that is, of something's being rusty,
or red, or metallic, as the case may be. This use of "looks" is the one
we commonly use when we say of someone, Harry say, that he

looks distinguished, or looks pale, or looks hearty and so on. The point about such expressions as "looks red", "looks metallic", "looks rusty", "looks angry", "looks sharp" and so on is that they are used to form sets of conceptually related pairs: looks red/is red, looks metallic/is metallic, looks rusty/is rusty and so on. The normal perceiver who is competent with looks red, looks metallic and so on is someone who operates with the conceptually related pairs: looks red/is red, looks metallic/is metallic and so on.

Although the phenomenological sense is conceptual, it is possible that its use presupposes a descriptive, non-conceptual way of looking, for, as we saw earlier, just as the comparative sense of "looks" presupposes some non-comparative, descriptive way of looking, so the perceptual-epistemic sense presupposes some non-epistemic, descriptive way of looking. In the next section, I shall explore that possibility.

Two phenomenological senses: intentional and non-conceptual

The discussion in the previous section brought out two important things. First, there is a perfectly ordinary phenomenological sense of "looks", one that is independent of the various epistemic uses and the comparative sense, and, secondly, there is a descriptive sense of "looks" that is presupposed by the perceptual-epistemic use and the comparative use. While the phenomenological and descriptive senses might be the same, they haven't been shown to be the same, and we should not assume that they are so. One possibility is that the phenomenological sense, like the other two, also presupposes a descriptive sense. It might be that the phenomenological use is intentional, reflecting the conceptual content of one's experiences, whereas the descriptive use applies to the non-conceptual content.

There are several reasons for taking this possibility seriously. The first concerns features that are built into the conceptual practices in which "looks like" and "appears" expressions function. As I pointed out previously, in contrasting the use in which "X looks rusty (metallic, square, red, . . .) to me" with the case in which "X looks to me as if it is rusty (metallic, . . . etc.)", there is, in the former case, an implication that there is a characteristic and distinctive appearance for things that are rusty (metallic, . . . etc.), a characteristic way that these things look. In the second place, some-one who operates with the conceptual pairs – looks rusty/is rusty, looks metallic/is metallic, looks square/is square – recognizes that the fact that something looks rusty is a reason for thinking that it is rusty, that something looks square is a reason for thinking that it is square and so on. But in combination with this knowledge, the person is aware that there are circumstances in which something that is not rusty may look rusty, that something that is not square may look square and so on.

There is an additional reason. Take the earlier example where it is supposed that I am looking at bottles of wine in the near dark, in which I cannot tell the colour of wines, or cannot tell the colour properly. Knowing that there are only red wines and yellow wines in the room, I may say of a certain wine that it looks to me as if it is yellow, but not because it looks yellow (because it does not). There is an important aspect to this example. The wine certainly does not look yellow to me. What way does it look? It may well be that I cannot describe the way it looks. This is not because this way is essentially ineffable. It is just that I do not have the concept. I might get trained to describe it. I certainly know that the wine does not look yellow, or red, or blue. This example supports the claim that the intentional conceptual phenomenological sense of "looks" presupposes a descriptive sense of "looks". In this respect, the phenomenological sense is similar to the comparative and percep-tual-epistemic senses. In this descriptive sense something may look F to subject Sally without Sally's possessing the concept of being F.

To explore more fully the possibility that the phenomenological conceptual sense of "looks" is consistent with the presence of a non-conceptual descriptive way in which things look, let us reconsider the way the phenomenological use of "looks" is introduced by Annas and Barnes. They explain the phenomenological use of "looks" in terms of one's being *struck in a certain way*. The point of this formulation is to contrast the case in which I have a (guarded) belief about what I am seeing with the case in which I want to abstract from what I know or believe about the things I am seeing, and report simply on how "it is with me". There is, however, a complication with how we should understand "strikes" in this context.

When we report on how things look to us, in the sense of report-ing "how things strike me", we are describing our perceptual experiences. There are two quite different things we might be aiming to do. One is to express the *content* of that experience: "there is before me a red lantern"; "there is a fox turning towards me" and so on. Another is to describe the intrinsic non-representational qualities of that experience itself. Annas and Barnes write that the sense in which the sceptics say how things appear is "to say how they *impress* us or how they *strike* us", but that is compatible with our describing either the content of our experience (how things are represented as being) or how we are affected. To describe the latter is to describe the grounds there are for accepting the propositional content (of the experience). Traditionally it has been claimed that to describe these grounds is to apply a phenomenal sense, one that is non-conceptual. These grounds are non-representational, intrinsic qualities of the experience, or are intrinsic quality-instances (tropes) that are qualities of either physical objects, or phenomenal items.

An important issue is whether it is possible to report on the intrinsic qualities of our perceptual experiences. There are many philosophers, for example, Harman, Tye, Evans, Dretske and Armstrong, who argue that it is not. In his "The Intrinsic Quality of Experience", for example, Harman takes the view that, in reporting our visual experience, all that we can report on is the content of the experience, that is, the intentional content, not the intrinsic character of the experience itself.[13] If he is right, all that anyone can report on, in saying how things strike them, perceptually, is the content of the experience, that is, that there is a green and brown tree before me.

Quinton, on the other hand, says of the statement "it looks to me (here, now) elliptical" that we say of a plate we know to be tilted and round: "This statement answers the question 'how does it strike you, look to you, what exactly do you see?' It is replaceable by 'there is an elliptical patch in the centre of my visual field'."[14] He goes on to say that, in this case, the description of what appears is a description of one's experience. It is clear that Quinton's description of the phenomenological use is similar to the sensible use described by Broad:

> When I judge that a penny looks elliptical I am not mistakenly ascribing elliptical shape to what is in fact round . . .

The plain fact is that "looking elliptical to me" stands for a peculiar experience which, whatever the right analysis of it may be, is not just a mistaken judgement about the shape of the penny.[15]

It has become something of a commonplace for philosophers to criticize Broad on the grounds that a penny does look elliptical when viewed obliquely. The penny continues to look circular as you turn it in your hand. In Broad's defence, however, we can say something like the following: it is perfectly true that as we turn the penny over it continues to look, from the various positions, as a circular body does from those positions, but, nevertheless, it is also true that as the viewing angle changes, the penny does look different, and it is by reference to the elliptical shape that we try to capture the difference. In Broad's defence, we might say that as the penny changes, my inclination to believe that the penny is circular is unchanged, and that in the perceptual-epistemic sense, the penny continues to look the same, but still there is a sense in which it looks different, and that is the "sensible" use of looks, that is, the phenomenological sense. Perhaps things are more complex than Broad and Quinton take them to be. However, the point that they are making cannot be dismissed as cavalierly as it commonly is.

The two ways of interpreting what it is for something to strike one reflect two different phenomenological uses of "looks". If our perceptual states (experiences) are thought of as vehicles that carry intentional content, then we would expect that both uses are legitimate. The difference between the two uses is that one is intentional and the other not. Each of them can be contrasted with the epistemic and perceptual-epistemic uses, where these uses involve beliefs (judgements), either guarded or fuller. (The claim that this is not the right way to think of experiences is examined in Chapter 8.)

When we use "looks" in the phenomenological sense, we are doing two things: reporting on the content of the experience; and referring to the way we are affected. In the normal course of events, in so far as we are referring to the intrinsic qualities, we are doing so by relation to their content and not describing them. Traditional philosophers who employed the phenomenological use of "looks", in the technical sense, were attempting to describe those qualities. According to the argument that I develop, the description of those qualities is parasitic on our being accomplished in the use of "looks" in the intentional, phenomenological sense.

If I am right that there is a phenomenological sense of "looks" that is intentional and conceptual, but it presupposes a descriptive sense of looks, as is the case for the comparative and perceptual-epistemic senses of looks, then it follows that this descriptive use can become a second kind of phenomenological sense. The point is that if the function of the standard phenomenological sense is to describe our experiences (how they "strike us" perceptually) then there are different aspects of the experiences that we might want to describe. In the normal course of events, what perceivers are interested in describing is the conceptual content of their experiences. However, if there is another aspect to the experience, say a non-conceptual aspect, then in some circumstances, there may be a point in describing them.

Summary

There is a framework within which we describe the variety of ways in which perceptual terms such as "looks" and, more generally, "seems" operate. Within that framework, there is a place for phenomenal uses of "looks", ones that express phenomenal, sensuous, qualitative aspects to perceptual experience. Also contained within that framework is a range of other uses for "looks", including ones that presuppose or refer to these sensuous, qualitative aspects.

The variety of uses of "looks" is as follows:

A. *Epistemic (pure = non-perceptual):*
(1) Epistemic (pure):
    1. it looks to Alice as if p (e.g. X is rusty)
        = it seems$_e$ to Alice as if X is rusty.
    [The phrase "it seems" indicates guarded belief.]

B. *Perceptual:*
(1) Epistemic (perceptual):
    1. X looks to Alice as if it is rusty:
        1a. From the way X looks$_d$, it seems$_e$ to Alice as if X is rusty.
    2. It looks$_{p\text{-}e}$ to Alice as if X is rusty:

> 2a. From the way something looks$_d$, it seems$_e$ to Alice as if X is rusty.

(2) Comparative:
1. X looks to Alice the way rusty things look:
   1a. X looks$_d$ to Alice the way things which are rusty typically look$_d$, in standard conditions (where "standard" is contextually defined).

(3) Phenomenological:
1. X looks$_{pg}$ rusty to Alice:
   1a. X looks$_d$ to Alice the way that signifies to Alice that there is something rusty before her.

It seems to me that "looks$_d$" refers to a phenomenal way of looking, one that is non-conceptual.

Conclusion

In this chapter I have set out a framework to cover the variety of ways in which perceptual terms such as "looks" and, more generally, "seems" operate. I argued that there is an ordinary, phenomenological sense of "looks" (and other "appears" terms) that stands in contrast to comparative and perceptual-epistemic senses. I further argued that this phenomenological sense presupposes a descriptive, phenomenal sense of looks: "looks$_d$". This descriptive sense is a non-conceptual, phenomenal sense: for something to look F to Alice does not require that Alice possess the concept of F.

One of reasons for pursuing this account is to help with assessing the argument from illusion. The argument, in one of its strongest formulations, that is, as presented by Howard Robinson, depends on a key premise, the Phenomenal Principle:

(PP) Whenever something appears to a subject to possess a sensible quality, there is something of which the subject is aware and which does possess that quality.

This argument presupposes that we interpret "appears" in a special sense, the phenomenological sense. If we interpret the Phenomenal Principle as referring to the first, ordinary phenomenological sense, then the principle is clearly false. But if we take it to be adopting the descriptive sense, then it is more plausible. That is to say, it is plausible that to say that something looks$_d$ in a certain way is to report on the intrinsic phenomenal qualities of our experience that the something causes. However, before we can draw that conclusion, more work still needs to be done.

The descriptive sense of "looks" is a non-conceptual, phenomenal sense. Even if this sense is legitimate, however, it is a further step to go on to claim that, given this descriptive sense, if something looks$_d$ F to a perceiver then the perceiver is presented with something that is F. Whatever plausibility it has will be derived from an appeal to the phenomenology of perceptual experience. However there are a number of theories of perceptual experience that challenge the plausibility of the claim. There are, for one thing, other ways to try to account for the non-conceptual phenomenal character of perceptual experiences. In the chapters to follow, I take up that challenge.

8 Types of perceptual content

When we perceive a physical object we have a perceptual experience caused by that object. It is common to hold that such experiences have two aspects: a sensuous, sensory aspect and an intentional aspect. The experience is intentional in the sense that it carries intentional content: it represents (things in the world) as being a certain way. A perceptual experience is typically an experience that represents a cup before me, a tree through the window, a police siren heard in the distance, the burning toast in the kitchen and so on. It is commonly held that besides having intentional content, the perceptual experiences have a sensuous, sensory aspect: there is something to the taste of a Shiraz wine, the smell of burning onions, the look of a Perth blue sky, that is not captured in the intentional content.

The difference between the intentional and sensory aspects of perceptual experience is reflected in the different senses of "looks", "tastes" and so on. As I argued in Chapter 7, there is a perfectly ordinary phenomenological use of "looks", one that is intentional and conceptual. There is, however, a more technical, phenomenal sense of "looks". This use depends on the fact that the ordinary phenomenological use depends on there being a descriptive, non-conceptual way in which things look.

When, therefore, we report on how things look to us, in the sense of reporting "how things strike me", we are describing our perceptual experiences. There are two quite different things we might be aiming to do. One is to express the *content* of that experience: "there is before me a red lantern", "there is a fox turning towards me" and so on. Another is to describe the intrinsic non-representational qualities of that experience itself. Annas and Barnes write that the sense in which the sceptics say how things appear is "to say how they *impress* us or how they *strike* us", but that is compatible with our describing either the content of our experience (how things are represented as being) or how we are affected. These two ways of reporting on our experiences reflect the ordinary phenomenological sense and the more technical phenomenal sense. Or so I argue.

There is, however, a group of philosophers who reject the claim that the two aspects of experience, the sensory and the intentional, answer the description that I have given. They deny that there are two uses of "looks" that function in the way I have claimed. It is argued by Dretske, Tye and others that there are sensory, phenomenal states, ones that are non-conceptual, but they are states whose intrinsic qualities the perceiver is not aware of. These states are thought to have phenomenal character only in the sense that they carry non-conceptual content. The issue between us, it seems to me, rests on the question of whether, in perceptual contexts, there are two senses of "non-conceptual content".

In this chapter I wish to examine the ways in which experiences might be thought to have a non-conceptual character. This issue is important not only in its relation to the account of the way things appear, but also in the related topic, of whether perceptual experience has an indirect component in the way that I have suggested, that is, of whether some version of indirect realism can be supported over direct realism.

Two types of perceptual content

One common view of how the two aspects, the sensory and intentional, are connected is that position defended by Lowe.[1] He writes that a perceptual experience must always have an intentional object, that it is an experience as of perceiving something. However, while perceptual experiences are intentional states of mind, it is important to recognize that they also involve a sensational or sensuous element. These two aspects, Lowe holds, make different contributions to the perceptual experience. For Lowe, the intentional content is conceptual but the perceptual sensation constitutes "a wholly non-conceptual component of perceptual experience". The intentional content is not intrinsic to it, in the sense that its possession of just that content is a non-contingent feature of the experience.

There is an alternative view of perceptual experience that is also common, for example, as presented by McGinn.[2] McGinn also writes that perceptual experiences have different aspects, a subjective aspect and a world-directed aspect – they present the world as being a certain way – but he holds that these aspects are linked: "Perceptual experiences are Janus-faced: they point outward to the external world but they also present a subjective form to the subject . . . they are *of something* other than the subject, and they are *like something* for the subject".[3] But these two faces, he holds, are linked together: these two faces do not wear different expressions for what the experience is like is a function of what it is of, and what it is of is a function of what it is like. In linking these two aspects in this way, McGinn offers us a very different position from that of Lowe.

A possible resolution of this difference between Lowe and McGinn might run as follows. The passage that I have quoted from McGinn does not spell out the nature of the intentional (representational) content of the perceptual experiences. There are two ways of thinking about this content. One is to think of it as conceptual in nature; the other is to think of the content as non-conceptual. We might treat Lowe's account as drawing attention to two aspects of perceptual experiences that are connected with two kinds of content: conceptual and non-conceptual. The non-conceptual content is linked with the sensuous, sensational element of perceptual experiences, and the conceptual content is linked with something else, for example, the judgements and beliefs that the perceiver acquires, or would be likely to acquire. The position now would be that there first occur sensory experiences with rich non-conceptual content. There then occurs a transition to being in a state with conceptual content. What has happened is that some of the rich non-conceptual content has been selected and expressed in the conceptual content of the conceptual state.

That this suggestion would keep faith with the spirit of Lowe's account is confirmed by his characterization of the (kind of) intentional content that is separated from the sensory/sensuous element.

This intentional content is conceptual since, as he writes, with respect to the visual experience of seeing a snake: "to say that the experience has this intentional content is to say that it is an experience of the sort one typically enjoys when, because of the experiential state one is in, one is inclined to believe that one is seeing a snake".[4]

This proposal to link the sensory/sensuous aspect of perceptual experience to non-conceptual content is in fact presented and defended by a range of theorists, for example, Martin Davies, Tye, Dretske and Harman. Davies, in his account of perceptual experience, first considers the possibility of construing the representational content of visual experience, the way it presents the world as being, in terms of "the content of the judgment that the subject would make if he or she were to take the experience at face value".[5] He rejects this proposal, however, in favour of taking the content in a different way:

> On the view that I am adopting, the perceptual content of an experience is a kind of *nonconceptual content*. What this means is that a subject can have an experience with a certain perceptual content without possessing the concepts that would be used in specifying the content of that experience.[6]

Enjoying experiences with perceptual content, he writes, does not require the possession of concepts, nor the employment of such concepts that may be possessed. This content, Davies goes on to add, might very well be linked with the conceptual content (of the sort characterized by Lowe).

Davies explains the notion of non-conceptual content that he has in mind by allying it with Peacocke's notion of *scenario content*:

> One basic form of representational content should be individuated by specifying which ways of filling out the space around the perceiver are consistent with the representational content being correct. The idea is that the content involves a spatial type, the type being that under which falls precisely those ways of filling the space around the subject that are consistent with the correctness of the content.[7]

As Davies points out, it is not necessary that the concepts we use in specifying this kind of content need be concepts possessed by the subject himself. Accordingly, if we exploit this notion of non-conceptual content, we could link the phenomenal character of perceptual experience with its perceptual (non-conceptual) content, thus reconciling the views of McGinn and Lowe.

There is a serious problem, however, with this attempted resolution of the dispute. Neither McGinn nor Lowe would be happy with it. Lowe would reject the claim that there is nothing more to the phenomenal character of sensory experience than its non-conceptual content (as just defined) and McGinn, while holding that content and phenomenal character are intertwined, would be unhappy with the suggestion that the content is non-conceptual.

What we have, in fact, is a three-cornered contest between three different ways of construing the phenomenal and intentional aspects to experience. On two points of the triangle are the positions defended by Lowe and Davies. Both accept that, within standard perceptual situations, we can distinguish between two acts or states: a non-conceptual sensory state or sensation and a conceptual state with conceptual content. Where they differ is how they construe the phenomenal character. Davies and Dretske and Tye and others hold that the phenomenal character can be identified with the representational non-conceptual content that the sensory states (sensations) carry. This is denied in the other position.

The position I attributed to McGinn, which is also defended by McDowell and P. F. Strawson, is different from both of the other positions. To be clear how different it is from the other positions, it is useful to refer to the more explicit characterization given by Strawson:

> The character of our perceptual experience itself, of our sense-experience itself, is thoroughly conditioned by the judgements about the objective world which we are disposed to make when we have this experience; it is, so to speak, thoroughly permeated – saturated, one might say – with the concepts employed in such judgements.[8]

In order to be in a position to settle this dispute we need, at the very least, to do two things: settle the issue about the way non-conceptual content is to be characterized; appreciate that the term "perceptual experience" can be understood in both a wide sense and a narrow one.

With respect to the first task, let us note that there is a problem with Davies's presentation of non-conceptual content. What his account tells us is how we may specify the representational content of a perceptual experience. It does not tell us what it is for a state to have that content in the first place. This distinction is one that McGinn stresses in his article. To acknowledge this distinction does not mean that we think that it is not important to be able to individuate the content. Important as it is, it does not tell us what it is for a state to have non-conceptual content.

We need, therefore, some account of what it is for a state to have non-conceptual content. This is an issue that has been addressed, and in some depth, by Dretske. In the next section, I shall examine his account, arguing that in addition to the two types of non-conceptual content identified by him, there is another kind that is important, especially in perceptual contexts.

Dretske: experiences and representational content

In *Naturalizing the Mind*, Dretske presents a theory of experiences, and of how they have representational content, that is, how it is that they represent things in the world as being a certain way.[9] He distinguishes between perceptual experiences of k (as f) and perceptual thoughts about k (that it is f) – between sensory and conceptual representations of k as f. "One can experience blue (the shirt's colour) – and in this sense, be aware of blue – without being conceptually aware that anything is (or looks) blue."[10] Dretske describes these two forms of awareness as sensory awareness and conceptual awareness, respectively. Each form of awareness involves representations and the content of each type of representation is specified, in part, by the same property, for example, that of being blue.

The representational content carried by sensory experiences is non-conceptual. Dretske has provided a detailed account of this kind of non-conceptual content. It is a type of informational content, but Dretske is at pains to point out that representational content is not mere informational content. Dretske's account of representational content thus presupposes an account of informational content, although it requires more.

Informational content can be carried by a variety of states of organisms, mechanisms and natural objects, none of which need possess the concepts required to specify the content: rings on trees, footprints in the snow, sensory systems in perceivers. What makes it true that these states carry informational content about P (i.e. that object X is in state F) is that the states stand in an objective relation to P (usually a certain type of causal relation). The way states carry informational content is that the states form part of a system of states that standardly stand in certain causal relations with certain independent physical states. For example, the optic array striking a perceiver's eyes carries information about objects in the distance in that the optic array has a configuration that is of a type that is generally related causally to the type of objects in the distance, and, in this instance, is carried by the instances of those objects. To carry information about a that it is F, it is not essential that the feature F itself cause the corresponding state in the optic array. It could be that F is related to some other property that is causally responsible.

None of this informational content, by itself, is yet representational content. Dretske has a theory about what makes relevant pieces of the informational content representational content. There is a problem, however, not so much with the theory itself, but with the way it is formulated. Dretske overlooks something that is implicit in the account; namely, that representational content is, in an important sense, user-relative. In so doing he draws entirely the wrong conclusion.

On Dretske's account, what it is to be a representation is to be a state, within a system, with a certain function: an indicator function. A state represents a property F in so far as it has the function of indicating or providing information about that property, with respect to a certain domain of objects. Such functions can be assigned or fixed either naturally or conventionally, for example, in natural language. Of the natural functions, some are acquired and some are systemic, where the latter are functions that, for biological systems, are fixed by the evolutionary history of the organism type. (Some acquired functions are learned.)

Experiences, it is claimed, have their representational content fixed by the biological functions of the sensory systems of which they are states. The reasoning adopted by Dretske is as follows. The experiences or sensory states carry all sorts of informational content, not all of which is representational content. What turns informational content into representational content is the fact that the function of the experience or sensory state is to provide the information in question. What determines the function is the evolutionary history of the organism type. The function is determined by what the organism was designed or "designed" to do. On this account, a sensory state will have acquired non-conceptual representational content, in that the sensory states of the organism have acquired, through the organism's evolutionary history, the function of providing certain non-conceptualized information about a certain range of objects. The crux of Dretske's position is that experiences are those natural representations that service the construction of acquired (conceptual) representations. They are the states whose functions it is to supply information to a cognitive system for calibration and use in the control and regulation of behaviour. Thought of in this way, a sensory state becomes a natural representation that represents something as blue in that it supplies information, about something's having the property blue, to that part of the organism that regulates the organism's behaviour. In particular, it provides information that can be exploited by the organism in blue-related behaviour.

Clearly, not all the informational content carried by a set of states can be exploited by the organism whose states they are. In some cases the information is of a type that a person with sufficient knowledge of the right kind, for example, of the causal relationships involved, could exploit the information, but not the organism itself. There are two ways in which the information that is carried by a sensory state, for example, that a is F, can be exploited by the organism. One is that it can be used by the organism in behaviour that is centred on that object, a. Information that a peach is of a ripe colour can be exploited by the organism's reaching for, or eating, the peach. This behaviour need not involve conceptualization, at least not in a linguistic way. (There may be practical concepts involved.) A second way in which the information can be exploited is that the sensory state plays a causal role in leading to the organism's acquiring a conceptual state, for example, a thought that embodies the information in conceptual form. What gives that conceptual state its conceptual content, presumably, is that it is a state that plays a certain role, including the fact that it provides the basis for the disposition to behave in a range of appropriate ways.

What emerges from this account, although Dretske does not notice it, is the important point that however the relevant informational content of a sensory state is exploited, what makes the content *representational content* is that the information is, or can be, exploited by the organism.[11] A representation of x is a representation of x for someone or something. (That is to say, representational content is user-relative.) It is only in this way that information can bestow an evolutionary advantage and this allows us to identify that role as the function of the state. This point is reinforced by reflection on how the biologist is in any position to identify the evolutionary function of any feature of an organism. Usually the biologist has to construct a likely story on the basis of examining how a current instance of the organism in question operates in its environment. In other words, the biologist can only calculate what is the function of one of an organism's characteristics, from an evolutionary point of view, by calculating what is the functional role of characteristics in a typical individual organism.[12]

For Dretske, what turns informational content into representational content is the fact that the informational content has been selected. However, in order for the content about a certain property, say colour, to be selected, the organism has, in some way, to exploit the fact that an object has the property of colour. That is, supposing that the sensory state has a certain character by virtue of which it carries content that something is F. Then in order for the information to be selected, it must make a difference to the organism that there is present some object that is F. The organism must behave in an F-sensitive manner. In the case of colour, that is in a colour-sensitive manner. It is clear that an organism that can discriminate colours will be in a position to take advantage of the colour of certain bodies. That its sensory states carry information about colour will obviously be of evolutionary importance. However, in order to be of such importance, the organism has to be able to discriminate between the different colours, that is, to be sensitive to the colours. To say all of this is another way of saying that in order for the colour information to be selected, it has to be the case that for a typical organism its sensory states represent colours, that is, the sensory state carries content about colours that the organism can exploit.

Hence, contrary to Dretske's wider analysis, according to which the content only becomes representational content through its evolutionary history, the content only becomes selected if first of all it is representational content for individual organisms. The upshot of this discussion is that we can only identify the representational content in terms of the appropriate evolutionary history of the organism type if we can identify the representational content in terms of the behaviour of the organism-token. And we can do the latter in terms of the kind of information that the organism can exploit. Despite this limitation, we can agree with Dretske that there are two types of non-conceptual content, and that representational non-conceptual content is more than just informational content.

Two types of non-conceptual representational content

Representational content, I have argued, is user-relative. A state can only have representational content for someone (or something). A map of New York carries information about that city. It represents New York only to someone capable of reading the map. A book carries information about, say, the telephone numbers of residents of Sydney, but it represents those numbers only to those who can interpret the book. A painting or a picture can represent Napoleon on his horse, or the Grand Canyon at dawn, but only to those with the right kind of visual system. My visual experience carries all kinds of information, not only information about physical objects that are present, but information about my retinal states, my neural states and so on. However, much of this information does not matter to me. The information that is relevant is the information that I use (or am capable of using).

There are different ways, however, in which there can be representational content that is non-conceptual. One is the sense described by Dretske: the experience carries non-conceptual content which is informational content that does not require the exercise of, and possibly not the possession of, concepts. The informational content is of a kind that the perceiver is capable of extracting and exploiting, or is suitably related to information that can be extracted. The second sense is that according to which the *representing* is non-conceptual. That is to say, the state represents in a non-conceptual way. In both cases the experience carries representational content only in the sense that the perceiver is in a position to utilize that content.

In this second sense, "non-conceptual content" is short for "non-conceptual component or ingredient of content". Lowe suggests something along these lines when he says that he takes perceptual sensations to "constitute a wholly non-conceptual component of perceptual experience".[13] It is this sense that is crucial in understanding how representational content for perceptual experiences is non-conceptual. To explain why, we need to be clear about the difference between the two senses of "non-conceptual content".

To illustrate the difference between these senses of non-conceptual content, consider the case of a vinyl record, one that is a recording, say, of the London Philharmonic Orchestra playing a Mozart symphony (or, if you prefer, Elvis at Memphis). The record has a series of grooves, which carry information about the original playing of that symphony. It carries that information by virtue of the fact that the marks on the grooves are causally related, in the right kind of way, with the sounds made on the original occasion. That information can be conveyed into other media: the markings on a digital tape, those on a compact disc and so on.

The markings on the vinyl-record grooves carry information not only about the events in the Royal Festival Hall, but about the markings that would be produced on each of the different media. They also carry information about certain dispositional properties that the event at the Royal Festival Hall possesses: the power to produce markings of the distinctive kind on each of the recording media. None of these kinds of informational content yet amounts to representational content. However, take the vinyl record and place it on a turntable – and set the needle in place. Now the record represents to the hearer a certain event: the playing of the Mozart symphony. Clearly, in this situation, the record does have representational content. What kind? It has non-conceptual content. It represents the room in which it is being played as containing the playing of the Mozart symphony. It represents a certain event as being a certain way: it represents the original playing as if it were happening now, as it was played in a certain way, as on the original occasion (or something like it).

This kind of representational content is non-conceptual. The record represents something as being a certain way, as sounding a certain way. Perhaps the record has the representational content it does only if the hearer possesses some concepts – the hearer is aware of the music as occurring now, as carrying from a certain direction – but to a large extent, the content is non-conceptual. The way the record represents is as follows: it announces (in effect) "This is the way the Mozart symphony was played in 1969. Listen!"

Given the second kind of non-conceptual content, the representation can be used as the basis of demonstrative concepts in a way consistent with the accounts of demonstrative concepts set out by Evans and McDowell. That is to say, the sensory representation is used in locating the object in space and in tracking the object as it or the perceiver moves through space. The idea here is that the representation is used as a guide, that is, as a tool by the perceiver.

On Dretske's account of representational content, it would seem that the way the non-conceptual content is used is through the perceiver extracting the content and putting it in conceptual form, for example, in a belief or thought. There is no doubt that such a process can take place in perceptual contexts. Dretske implies, however, that this is the only type of perceptual non-conceptual content. I submit that there is a different type of non-conceptual (representational) content as well, and, moreover, that this type is much more plausible as providing a more accurate phenomenological description of what the situation is in normal conscious perceptual experience.

The non-conceptual components of content

The claim that I am making is that we have, or can have, certain kinds of thoughts, for example, perceptual thoughts, that have non-conceptual components. We can, that is to say, distinguish between two senses of "non-conceptual content" and "non-conceptual representation". To understand this claim properly, and what it entails, however, we need to be clear about how terms such as "content" and "non-conceptual content" have different senses and, in consequence, how this makes a difference to how we should understand "non-conceptual representation".

When we think about how thoughts (and mental states in general) can have content, there are two different things we can have in mind. One way of understanding what the content of a thought is can be expressed in terms of the satisfaction conditions. Beliefs, for example, will have truth-conditions: these are states of affairs that will make the beliefs true. Not only beliefs but other mental states, for example, desires, hopes, wishes, commands, intentions, requests and so on, will have satisfaction conditions. Given that content is understood in this way, then representational states can carry non-conceptual content in the sense that they carry content but not in conceptualized form. The representation has a certain character that is causally related to some objective state of affairs, for example, that x is F. Someone who knows the type of relationship involved will be able to draw the inference that x is F. The system that has the representational state does not need to possess either the concept that individuates x, or the concept *being F*.

There is a second way of understanding how a thought can have content. A given thought has content in the sense that it involves the exercise of concepts. Typically, a thought involves the exercise of at least two concepts. The thought "Clinton was a lucky President" involves the exercise of a concept that individuates Clinton, and the exercise of a general concept of *being a lucky President*. Some of these concepts, it is plausible to hold, are object-dependent. The exercise (and possession) of the concept that individuates Clinton requires, it is plausible to hold, that the thinker is in a special relation to a certain person, that is, Clinton. That relation is a causal one, even if it is not wholly causal (i.e. there are descriptive components to it.)

There are, therefore, two ways of understanding what the content of a thought is and, hence, two types of content. No doubt these two ways are related, but it is still important to distinguish between them. In the second sense of *content*, the content of a thought involves the exercise of concepts. Some of these concepts, and the exercise of the concepts, are object-dependent. What makes a certain act an exercise of a given concept requires the agent to be related in a suitable way to that object. Once we think of content in this second way, an important possibility opens up. It is possible to think that there are some thoughts such that, while they do involve the exercise of concepts, they involve something else:

the use of objects, or events. The thought is made up of a joint activity with two constituents: the exercise of concepts and the use of an object or event. Some theorists, for example, Bertrand Russell, wanted to go further, and say that for some thoughts all of their constituents were objects. This last suggestion seems to me to be wildly wrong. It doesn't make much sense. The first suggestion, on the other hand, makes more sense. It seems highly plausible that in some thoughts, for example, one's identification of an object, is an act or activity that involves the object itself. The thought is made up of a joint activity with two constituents: the exercise of concepts and the use of an object or event,

It seems to me that there are many examples in which a person expresses a thought where it is coherent to hold that an ingredient of the thought, of both the vehicle and the content, is an actual object or event, or a quality-instance, an instance say of red or of looking amused. The object or quality-instance is both displayed or shown, and attributed to another object. If I point to a hat on the table saying "that — [pointing] belonged to Lloyd George" then the particular hat is the object of thought and is part of the content. It is, as well, the vehicle, or part of the vehicle, by which that content is expressed. It is the act of pointing to that specific hat that carries the content, not just the utterance of the sentence. Likewise I might say to you, say, "After Gloria left, Robin whistled this tune —", where the blank is filled by my whistling the very tune. Now, there are cases in which I could name it, but there are other cases in which I could not, for example, I do not know the tune, or the tune does not have a name. The point is that I can talk about certain objects or events not by using a name or description but by displaying the object in question.[14]

It is helpful in this context to refer to Nelson Goodman's example of representation by exemplification.[15] A painter may represent the red colour of a brick house, and the yellow colour of the road, by exemplifying the red and the yellow, respectively, in the picture he is painting. Likewise two actors may represent two characters in a play as kissing by actually kissing each other. They could, of course, simulate the kiss, but actors usually don't. The characters are represented as kissing by exemplification. Likewise a film could portray John Malkovich looking surprised by John Malkovich's looking surprised.

Let us now turn to perceptual experiences and perceptual judge-ments, based (in some sense) on experiences. Given our under-standing of how there can be thoughts whose content contains non-conceptual and conceptual components, we can apply this understanding to the special case of perceptual experiences. It is possible to think of experiences in the following way. They contain sensory representations, sensory items, that are naturally connected to our behavioural dispositions. As far as perceptual judgements based on experiences are concerned, the perceptual judgement can be thought of as a complex thought that contains the sensory repre-sentation as a component. It is a non-conceptual component in the sense that its occurrence does not involve the exercise of concepts.

A typical perceptual thought, that is to say, is a complex inte-grated act that contains various components, at least one of which is the exercise of a concept (or concepts) and another which is not. I am aware of sensory representations as signs for physical objects, and I am aware of those objects in a number of ways: as being there before me, as being within reach, as being graspable and so on. In saying that I am aware of sensory representation as a sign, what I mean is that I am aware of the representation as present before me and treat it as a sign of the object. The sense in which I treat it as a sign is that I use it, to guide me in my actions. I do not, normally, intellectualize it as "a sign". I do not, normally, distinguish it from the object, that is, the thing that I reach for, the thing that I grasp.

Conclusion

I have argued that perceptual experiences do have a type of repre-sentational content that is non-conceptual, but there are two senses in which the representation might be non-conceptual. One is the sense described by Dretske: the experience carries non-conceptual content that is informational content that does not require the exercise of, and possibly not the possession of, concepts. The informational content is of a kind that the perceiver is capable of extracting and exploiting, or is suitably related to that information that can be extracted. The second sense is that according to which the representing itself is non-conceptual, that is to say, the state represents in a non-conceptual way. The representation can be said to have a non-conceptual ingredient. (In both cases the experience carries representational content only in the sense that the perceiver is in a position to utilize that content.)

The difference between these types of non-conceptual content is important in getting clear about the nature of perceptual experience. It is particularly important when we consider those accounts that identify the phenomenal character of perceptual experience with the non-conceptual content. On one account, the phenomenal character will be analysed in terms of the informational content carried by the experience. Admittedly, it will be a special kind of informational content that constitutes the representational content, but it will be informational content nonetheless. On the account that I am proposing, the phenomenal character cannot be analysed in that way. On this account, to acknowledge the phenomenal character of our experiences is to acknowledge the existence of intrinsic qualities of the experiences, qualities that are accessible to introspection and to phenomenological descriptions. I shall pursue these issues in Chapter 9.

9 The representationalist–intentionalist thesis

On the face of it, we can distinguish between the phenomenal character of perceptual experiences, and their intentional (representational) content. There are, as we have seen, however, two very different ways we might construe the phenomenal character. On one theory, to acknowledge the phenomenal character of our experiences is to acknowledge the existence of intrinsic qualities of the experiences (or of phenomenal items contained in the experiences), qualities that are accessible to introspection, and to phenomenological descriptions. The phenomenal character, on this account, consists of intrinsic qualities of subjective experiences, that is, of what are sometimes called "qualia". Or so it seems. There is, however, an alternative way of construing the phenomenal character of experiences that does not admit the existence of qualia, or such intrinsic phenomenal qualities. On this account, the phenomenal character is analysed in terms of the representational character, that is, the representational content, of the experiences. Almost everyone accepts that, in some sense, perceptual experiences have representational (intentional) content, but what is at issue is whether there is, in addition, phenomenal character to the experiences.

The representationalist thesis, or the *intentionalist thesis*, as it is sometimes called, is that we are, in normal perception, not aware of the intrinsic qualities of experiences; we are instead aware of those objects and their qualities that are specified in the content of our experiences. One major proponent of the representational theory of phenomenal character is Dretske, whose views we looked at briefly in Chapter 8. Other advocates are Tye, Evans, Millikan,

Harman and Clark. In this chapter, I shall examine this thesis, examining the kinds of reasons that these various authors have given in its favour.

One of the major problems with the way this thesis is explained and defended, I shall argue, is that advocates of the thesis do not recognize the possibility of there being two kinds of representational, non-conceptual content as described in Chapter 8. Accordingly, they do not appreciate how there can be a type of representational content that is consistent with the perceiver being aware both of the intrinsic qualities of the experiences and of its representational content.

Millikan: on conflating content with vehicle

The defender of the representationalist thesis must explain why the rival theory has seemed so plausible, that is, why it has seemed that there is a phenomenal character to experience besides the representational character. One explanation, which Evans and Millikan have provided, is that those who think this way are victims of a beguiling fallacy, "the sense-datum fallacy". This fallacy consists in conflating the content of the experience, or properties expressed in the content, with intrinsic qualities of the experience itself.

This fallacy, Millikan writes, is just a special case of a type of confusion that is widespread and dangerous, particularly in philosophical theorizing: that of mingling the intentional contents of a representation with attributes of the vehicle of representations, that is, of attributing to the vehicle of representation qualities that are qualities of the object represented.[1] It is the error, for example, that Kant accuses Hume of committing: of conflating successions of representations with the representation of succession. It is just this type of conflation that is said to lie behind the sense-datum fallacy.

This fallacy, Millikan points out, was diagnosed earlier by Evans, who refers to it sometimes as the "homunculus fallacy":

> when one attempts to explain what is involved in a subject's being related to objects in the external world by appealing to the existence of an inner situation which recapitulates the essential features of the original situation to be explained . . .

by introducing a relation between the subject and inner objects of essentially the same kind as the relation between the subject and outer objects.[2]

Before proceeding, it is important to note that the sense-datum fallacy is not thought to be confined to those who believe in sense-data. The position that is opposed by Evans and Millikan is the view that in perceptual experience we are presented with certain quality-instances (e.g. instances of redness, circularity, hard-edgedness, etc.) that, on some accounts, represent physical objects or, on others, are taken to be constituents of physical objects. One form such theories take is that of sense-datum theories. The sense-datum fallacy that such theories are alleged to commit is that they conflate the content of experience (or properties expressed in the content) with intrinsic qualities of the experience itself. Not all defenders of such theories see themselves as defending sense-data. We might note that the term "sense-data" was used in a variety of senses originally, and while the term has been avoided like the plague by modern philosophers, it could plausibly be argued that the more modern terms, for example "qualia" or phenomenal qualities, are equivalent to the qualities of sense-data.[3] However, we need not chart these troubled waters. It is sufficient to interpret Evans as holding that the theories he is against commit the same kind of fallacy as that characteristically committed by advocates of sense-datum theories. This is certainly the view of Millikan, who argues that a range of theories commit the sense-datum fallacy in attributing properties that are in fact properties that our experiences represent physical objects as having to internal objects: "sense data, or percepts, or phenomenal properties, or visual fields, etc.".

Millikan's discussion of the sense-datum fallacy is of special interest for the way she extends and modifies the characterization provided by Evans. I shall argue that Millikan's account of the sense-datum fallacy is flawed: that she herself commits a fallacy, what might be called the "fallacy fallacy". This is the fallacy of thinking that because someone might commit a fallacy, that they thereby have committed the fallacy. I shall try to explain and defend these dark thoughts.

In theorizing about perception, Millikan writes, there is an impulse to take acts of perceiving objects ("visaging a scene or object") to have corresponding to them something that exemplifies the properties that the world would have to have, for the visaging to be veridical. This is the first part of the process. The second part is to take visaging as like having pictures in the mind and, simultaneously, to take pictures to be literally like what they picture. From these ingredients out falls the irresistible theory:

> that visagings involve items appearing before the mind that have the properties they represent. The properties claimed by visagings to characterize the world exist as "objective reality" (Descartes), or they, or doubles of them, are true of sense data, or percepts, or phenomenal properties, or visual fields, etc. When and only when the world resembles the inner picture, then the visaging is veridical, showing how things really are.[4]

Millikan's discussion is particularly interesting to the extent that she goes beyond Evans but before examining that, we should note that her account is questionable as a description of traditional theories. Broad and Price, to take two famous sense-data theorists, far from saying that sense-data (sensa) have the properties of physical objects, assert the very opposite. They begin by defining "sense-datum" or "sensa" in neutral terms, leaving it open whether they are physical or non-physical, for example, phenomenal. They then argue that, because the sense-data have certain properties that physical objects do not have (and vice versa), they cannot be physical objects. It would seem, therefore, that whatever they may be committing, it is certainly not the "sense-datum fallacy". And Descartes seems entirely the wrong target.

It may be, of course, that Millikan has identified a genuine and worrying fallacy even if it is not the one committed by the theorists above. There are, however, serious problems with her characterization of the fallacy. First of all, there is an important possibility that Millikan overlooks. In describing the fallacy as one of conflating vehicle and content, she overlooks the possibility that the fallacy is one built into the perceptual process. She is, of course, critical of philosophers who construct a theory of perception in which they conflate vehicle and content. But for all that she has shown, it may well be that it is a naive perceiver who commits the fallacy in conflating idea with object. This is what Hume claimed, and it is the theory that I am defending. The point of the fallacy is that it is beneficial: it helps the perceiver achieve many of the perceiver's purposes. In other words, the fallacy serves an important function. Accordingly, if the theorist of perception is providing an account of naive perception or natural perception, that is, of how perceivers actually perceive, it may be that the account should describe the fallacy. Presumably it is open to the theorist to combine the naive or natural account with a more sophisticated account.

It is in connection with the more sophisticated account that the more important difficulty arises with the account provided by Millikan and by Evans. The more important point is this: of course, in a case where there is a vehicle that represents objects, we must be careful to distinguish between the properties of the vehicle and those of the objects represented (as specified in the content), and not to conflate them. However, this distinction is a conceptual one. It does not mean that the vehicle and object cannot have the same properties. Nor does it rule out that the possibility that it is by virtue of the vehicle having certain properties that the state has the specific content that it does, that is, that the content (what is represented) can be specified in terms of those properties. (This is compatible of course with there being other factors that also contribute to the content.) Consider some examples.

A. *Pictures of red-coated man on a white horse*. Things being what they are, it is a red patch on the picture that is used to represent the man's coat as red; and the fact that the man-part of the picture is above the horse-part represents the man being above the horse.

B. *Map of the London underground*. Things being what they are, and maps being what they are, that the Tottenham Court Road spot is between the Oxford Circus and Holborn spots represents Tottenham Court Road station being between the Oxford Circus and Holborn stations. (Other features, for example, colour and size of the spots do not represent in this way, nor does the distance between the spots.)

C. *Actors*. Actors on the stage represent characters as doing many things, as having arguments, as fighting, as killing people. Often the actors are pretending or at least simulating. They can represent a killing without actually killing anyone.

Nevertheless, there are many occasions where what they represent is done by actually exemplifying what is portrayed. Actors
may simulate a kiss, but I have it on good authority that they
actually kiss, at least often enough. Likewise someone may
portray John Malkovich in a movie by being John Malkovich,
or the Clintons by being the Clintons.

Millikan may respond to this argument by saying that these
examples, the map and the pictures, only represent what they do
because there are people who have conceptual abilities, who interpret the maps and pictures. The sense-datum theorist, it would be
alleged, claims that being aware of the sense-data is in itself
sufficient for it to represent the object. But this is simply wrong.
Price and Broad, for example, insist on perceptual experience
containing both an objective constituent that is sensed, and an act of
perceptual consciousness of a physical object. Moreover, as I have
argued, there is no reason why a representationalist cannot argue
that the sense-datum requires conceptual abilities for representation to go through.

Finally, it is important to acknowledge the way in which
Millikan's analysis differs from Evans's. As she points out, Evans
says that the main error with the sense-datum fallacy (homunculus
fallacy) is the invoking of an infinite regress: "how will the inner
eye then perceive the inner picture? In the same way that the outer
eye does?".[5] It is particularly interesting that Millikan herself does
not rely on this infinite regress problem that Evans's questions
suggest (in the same way that Dennett has proposed). The more
important problem with the theory, she suggests, is that it provides
a "passive picture theory" of inner representation, which makes it
difficult to understand how it can explain how the pictures can
move the mind so as to constitute a grasp of them as what is
represented. "Having projected the visaged properties to the inside
of the mind, the assumption is that there can be no problem about
how they manage to move the mind so as to constitute a grasp of
them as what is represented."[6] It seems now that the real source of
the error is not that the theorist has conflated vehicle with object
represented, but rather with the way the "inner object" is conceived. Millikan assumes, similarly to Dennett, that someone who
uses the picture metaphor is committed to thinking of the pictures

as passive. She fails to consider the possibility that the metaphor might involve the perceiver being active in his or her awareness of the picture, for example, being active in using the representation to guide the action or thought.

If we refer to the discussion in Chapter 8, where I distinguished a sense of representational content, a non-conceptual ingredient sense, as opposed to the informational content sense, then we can see how Millikan fails to appreciate the possibility of the first sense. If experiences carry content in this sense (as well as the other) then those who are charged with committing the "sense-datum fallacy" are committing no fallacy at all. On this alternative approach, there is an element in the experience itself that plays a part in the representing. Part of the vehicle of representation contributes to the content. Of course, it may be that Millikan can appeal to arguments that show that her theory of representational content (understood as ruling out the alternative) should be favoured over the alternative. There are other arguments but, as we shall see, they are less than persuasive.

The transparency of experience

Some of the strongest arguments in favour of the intentionalist thesis are those provided by Tye and Harman. These arguments involve appeals to the phenomenology of perceptual experience, principally to the well-known "transparency" or the "diaphanous nature" of perceptual experience. Tye sets out his argument, most recently, in his book, *Consciousness, Color and Content*.[7] (I shall concentrate on this book, although I shall also briefly discuss Harman's arguments.[8])

Tye's principal aim in this book is to defend what he calls "strong representationalism", a view that aims to tell us precisely what the phenomenal character of our perceptual experiences is: it is the same as (a certain kind of) representational content. More precisely, phenomenal character is one and the same as poised, abstract, non-conceptual, intentional content (a theory that runs by the title PANIC). It is non-conceptual in the sense that the subject need not possess any of the concepts that we, as theorists, exercise when we state the correctness conditions for that content. It is abstract in that it is content into which no particular concrete object or surface enters. It is in defence of this thesis that Tye makes vital use of the transparency phenomenon. The argument is that our perceptual experiences do have phenomenal character: there is "something it is like" to have these experiences. The phenomenal character is revealed when we introspect our experiences. But, so the argument runs, when we reflect on what such introspection reveals, and discover the transparency of perceptual experience, the only viable explanation is that it is the *content* of the experiences that is revealed.

The transparency of perceptual experiences is explained by Tye as follows: "Focus your attention on the scene before your eyes and on how things look to you. You see various objects by seeing their facing surfaces."[9] In seeing these surfaces, he holds, you are immediately and directly aware of a whole host of qualities. You experience these qualities as qualities of the surfaces. You do not experience any of these qualities as qualities of your experience. There are no qualities of the experience that you are aware of; you are simply aware of the qualities of the objects seen. The experience of seeing is transparent.

Since you are not directly aware of any qualities of your inner experiences, your experience is transparent to you. But when you introspect, Tye argues, you are certainly aware of the phenomenal character of your visual experience. "Via introspection you are directly aware of a range of qualities that you experience as being qualities of surfaces at varying distances away and orientations; and thereby you are said to be aware of the phenomenal character of the experience."[10] By being aware of the external qualities, you are aware of what it is like for you.

What, then, is the visual phenomenal character? One possible hypothesis, Tye remarks, is that it is a quality of the surface experienced. But that hypothesis is intelligible, he adds, only if it is assumed that the surface is an immaterial one of the sort the sense-datum theorists posited. This hypothesis, he thinks, can be quickly dismissed: the theory is "unacceptable, however, for a whole host of familiar reasons". The best (and only remaining) hypothesis, he suggests, is that visual phenomenal character is representational content of a certain sort: content into which certain external qualities enter. The theory is that when we introspect our perceptual experiences, that is, when we reflectively attend to them while having them, we do not become aware of the intrinsic qualities either of these experiences, nor of phenomenal items that are components of the experiences. Rather we become aware of the representational content of the experience: we become aware of the way objects are represented as being.

Tye does not claim that transparency requires the intentionalist theory: it is the best explanatory hypothesis. What can be immediately ruled out is the possibility that the qualities that we do have direct access to are qualities of experiences, and not the hypothesis that the qualities are qualities of phenomenal items (the sense-datum hypothesis.). Separate reasons, it is held, can be brought into play to rule out the sense-datum hypothesis. It is not so clear, however, that the sense-datum hypothesis can be so quickly dismissed. Most of the "familiar reasons" usually given are either bad ones or not relevant to the most carefully formulated versions. An example is the reasons given by Austin in *Sense and Sensibilia* ("the best arguments against sense-datum theories", according to Putnam), where he almost exclusively concentrates on Ayer's version and then often not fairly. In any case, most critical arguments against sense-datum theories are not arguments that sense-data do not exist. They are arguments against arguments for their existence. This means that we should be careful before dismissing sense-datum theories if they can provide an alternative account of the transparency of experience. The objections are, moreover, often framed in terms of showing that arguments for sense-data are not demonstrative arguments. They seldom consider the possibility that the sense-datum hypothesis is best construed as providing the best explanation for the phenomena.

The sense-datum hypothesis, or a hypothesis framed in terms of a phenomenal field, deserves greater consideration. Take, for example, the suggestion that Tye puts before rejecting it; namely, that the phenomenal character of the experience is a quality of the surface experienced. That hypothesis is intelligible, Tye writes, "only if it is assumed that the surface is an immaterial one of the sort the sense-datum theorists posited".[11] But why shouldn't the quality be a quality of the material surface itself? Clearly, Tye takes that to be "unintelligible", but why exactly is it so? Traditional sense-datum theorists took it to be intelligible but false. Indeed, they took it to be the view of "naive realism", a view that is so intuitively attractive that it needs arguing against. On this kind of view, there is an experience of "seeing a cat", and it has phenomenal character. What "it is like" to have such an experience is to be confronted visually with a cat – and this experience really is transparent: one is aware of the cat itself, and not of any feature of the experience. The transparency of the situation is brought out neatly by Burnyeat's label, the "window model of perception". On this view, perceiving a cat is placing one immediately in contact with the cat, like opening a window on the world. This view, we all think, is false, no doubt. But why exactly do we think it false? And even if it is false, it is surely not unintelligible, as Tye suggests. Take, for example, his own description of the transparency of perceptual experience when, as he says, we see various objects by seeing their facing surfaces:

> Intuitively, the surfaces you see directly are publicly observable physical surfaces. In seeing these surfaces, you are immediately and directly aware of a whole host of qualities. You may not be able to name or describe these qualities but they look to you to qualify the surfaces; you experience them as being qualities of the surfaces.[12]

In his own terms, this is the intuitive view. Why is it wrong to think that these qualities are actually qualities of the surfaces? It seems to me that the sense-datum theorist was trying to capture the intuition that they are publicly observable qualities, while at the same time, reinterpreting that intuition.

The significance of this point is magnified if it turns out that the intentionalist thesis does not give a very good explanation of transparency at all. Indeed, I shall argue, it does not. Part of the reason why is that Tye has misdescribed the phenomenon of transparency. Another part is that there are difficulties with his account of what "introspective awareness" and "awareness of qualities of external objects" consist in.

In developing his theory of what phenomenal character is, Tye relies upon an account of *introspective awareness*. Introspection of phenomenal character is said to be a reliable automatic process that takes us from being in one state to being in another, from having an experience to being in a conceptual state. It is a process that takes, as input, *awareness of* external qualities, and yields, as output, *awareness that* a state is present with a certain phenomenal character. There are thus two kinds of awareness involved, comprising two distinct states: an experience or a feeling or a pain, which is an *awareness of* some objective quality, either a property of an external object or a disturbance in one's body; and a conceptual state – a state of *awareness-that*. The first state is a non-conceptual state, one that is apt to give rise to the conceptual state. If we introspect our experiences or feelings, we come to form a conceptual state: a state of awareness that an experience with a certain character is present.

There are several problems. The first has to do with the claim that introspection is a reliable process that takes as input *awareness of* external qualities, and yields as output *awareness that* a state is present with a certain phenomenal character. This is puzzling, since Tye also says that what it is to be aware of the phenomenal character is to be aware of the external qualities: "by being aware of the external qualities that you experience, you are aware of what it is like for you".[13] It would seem that "awareness of the external qualities" is both input and output. This may be a slip of the pen. Perhaps the output is best expressed as a state in which we are aware that a state is present with a phenomenal character. But this misdescribes the process that shows that the experience is transparent. If I am asked to reflect on my experiences of seeing a tiger and report on the experience, then it is simply not true that in general I become aware that a state is present that has a certain phenomenal character, nor that I am aware of being in a state that represents things as being in a certain way. Unless I have read some fairly sophisticated philosophy books, I am aware of no such thing. I am aware that there is a tiger, a large, tawny cat before me, or that I am seeing such a cat.

It may be true that I have such a state, and one with such a phenomenal character and, moreover, it may be true, as Tye suggests, that it is because I have such a state that I report what I do, but it is simply not true that I am aware that I have such a state. The phenomenon of transparency is best explained, much as Moore originally explained it, in the following way:

> We say to the perceiving subject: "Look, I want you to describe two things in turn. First, I want you to look over there, in that direction, and tell me what it is that you see." After the subject does that, we then ask now for the second task: "Now look

again and tell me not what you see, that is, tell me not about the object seen and its qualities, but about the experience of seeing itself. Tell me about the characteristics of this experience."

In such a situation, there seems nothing to report other than what I have already done. The experience has no other qualities that I am aware of. The subject does not become aware that I have an experience with a certain content. I reiterate that I am aware of a tiger. Accordingly, Tye's account of introspective awareness does not match the phenomenology of the situation.

There is a second difficulty. The output of the introspection is said to be a state of awareness-that, a state that is conceptual. But what exactly is the content of the state? Do I become aware that I am having an experience with a certain non-conceptual content? That seems bizarre. More plausibly, what I become aware of is the (non-conceptual) content although perhaps I am not aware of it as content. But how exactly is "awareness of a certain non-conceptual content" related to the state of awareness-that? Plausibly, I am aware that there is a tiger before me, which has more features than I can describe – but now it is unclear how this state of awareness-that is different from the state when I do not introspect, but simply see and report what I see.

There is, it seems to me, an alternative that fits better the phenomenology of experience, that is, that fits what happens when we introspect. When we introspect our visual experiences, we are aware of an instance of a quality. It is this quality-instance that the naive realist takes to be an instance of a quality-type possessed by physical objects, and instantiated in the very object being perceived. Likewise, for the phenomenalist, it is this quality-instance that is instantiated in a phenomenal object presented to the subject in experience. Similarly, the indirect representational realist construes the quality-instance as something that represents the presence of another quality-instance, an instance of a quality possessed by the physical object. Each account can handle the transparency of perceptual experience. Other reasons are called for to decide between them. Moreover, on these theories when we formulate the cognitive states with conceptual content, then we express content that is (in part) abstract. We takes these quality-instances to be instances of property-types.

The intentionalist/representationalist makes a sharp distinction between two sense of "awareness": one non-conceptual and one conceptual (one involving thing-awareness, the other fact-awareness). I suggest that there is a third sense of "awareness of", one that combines elements of the other two, that is, of the non-conceptual and conceptual senses. Intuitively, I am presented with an instance of a quality (or complex of qualities: redness, round-ness, hard-edgedness, . . .) and I am aware of it as, say, being present and before me, and perhaps as an instance of red. In accepting the phenomenon of transparency, I suggest, we are adopting some such sense. This account, I submit, makes better sense of the phenom-enology of perception, even as Tye himself describes it, when he points out that we are immediately and directly aware of a whole host of qualities, even though we "may not be able to name or describe" these qualities, ones that look to us to qualify the surfaces.

Not only does the intentionalist thesis not give the best account of the transparency of perceptual experiences but, as I shall argue in the next section, it has other problems. Before examining them, we should note that Harman's discussion of the "diaphanous nature" of perceptual experience is subject to the same criticisms that apply to Tye's arguments.[14] Like Tye, Harman argues that attempts to describe the intrinsic phenomenal features of perceptual experi-ences get the phenomenology of experience all wrong. Typically, when someone, Eloise say, sees a tree before her, the colours she experiences are all experienced as features of the tree and its sur-roundings. "None of these are experienced as intrinsic features of her experience. Nor does she experience any features of anything as intrinsic features of her experience." To confirm this, Harman asks us to perform a simple thought-experiment:

> Look at a tree and try to turn your attention to intrinsic features of your visual experience. I predict you will find that the only features there to turn your attention to will be features of the presented tree, including relational features of the tree "from here".[15]

The alternative view, that what we are aware of are intrinsic features of our experience, is not the result of phenomenological study, Harman claims, but rather is the conclusion of an argument, for example, the argument from illusion. But this argument, it is claimed, is either invalid or question-begging.

Now, Harman may well be right that this argument is invalid, which will come as no surprise to those who do not present it as a logically compelling argument, but as one that makes best sense of the phenomenology of the situation. But there is a more important point. Harman's intentionalist theory does not fit his description of the phenomenology. What he says we will find when we engage in the phenomenological exercise is that you will be aware of the *features of the tree itself*. I agree. It seems to us that it is the tree itself. But this is not what the intentionalist theory says. What it says is that when I see the tree, I have an experience that has content, and what I am aware of is the content of the experience. In particular, if the experience is illusory and I experience the tree as blue when it is green, then I am not aware of any feature of the tree.

We should note that, as the sense-datum theorist is at pains to stress, it seems, from the point of view of the perceiver, that one is presented with the very features of the tree itself. This is one step in the argument that leads us eventually to the conclusion (admittedly not a logically compelling one) that what one is directly aware of is not in fact a physical object. The sense-datum theory is well suited to handling the phenomenology of the situation. Indeed, that is one of the prime motivations for the theory. It is important also to remember that most criticisms of the theory are objections to the arguments for the sense-datum hypothesis, and are usually objections to the effect that the arguments are not logically compelling. They seldom address arguments that are intended to make most sense of the phenomenology of the situation. Given the range of difficulties the intentionalist account has, it would appear that Harman and Tye have much more to do to show that this account provides the best explanation for the transparency/diaphanous nature of perceptual experience.

Reasons against the intentionalist thesis

There is an important issue that the accounts by Tye and Harman glide over. In trying to get clear about the nature and role of perceptual experiences, one technique is to apply introspection. That is, you deliberately attend to how things look to you on a given occasion, attempting to discern the relevant features of the perceptual experience. Tye and Harman place great emphasis on this procedure, arguing that the theory that best respects the phenomenology, that is, the fact of the transparency of perceptual experience, is that one is aware of the content of the experience, that is, the way things are represented.

Phenomenology, however hard it may be to delineate precisely, is wider than introspection. One can also reflect on the role perceptual experiences play when one is not introspecting. There are many situations, for example, in which veridical perception (or perception that one assumes is veridical) plays an important role. If I am looking through the window, thinking about whether the trees need pruning and the grass needs cutting, and whether I could do enough of the pruning before someone comes who knows what they are doing, then my perception of the trees and grass plays a role. And they play a role, it is important to stress, at the conceptual level. I am trying to decide whether those branches that are before me are too long for me to manage and so on. I am not introspecting. I am having perceptual experiences and, on the basis of them, trying to make a decision (sort of).

In such a situation, I am not introspecting my experiences and I need not be aware that I am having experiences (in the sense that I am not thinking about my experiences, I am thinking about trees and grass). But, presumably, on the intentionalist thesis, in these cases I must be aware of the content of my experiences, that is, the way the trees and grass are represented, in the same way that I am aware of the content of my experiences when I introspect. This point is important to avoid the possibility that the intentional theorist maintains that I am only aware of the content when I introspect, and that when I perceive without introspection, I am aware of objects, not the content of experiences.

The important point is that when one has perceptual experiences, one is aware of the content, of the way things are represented in experience, whether we are introspecting or not, providing we are perceptually engaged in the world, that is, acting on the basis of our perception, or thinking about the objects seen, or being thrilled about what we are seeing and enjoying or fearing what is seen. Tye and I are agreed on this point. It is brought out in an example that he has given:

Standing on the beach in Santa Barbara a couple of summers ago on a bright sunny day, I found myself transfixed by the intense blue of the Pacific Ocean. Was I not here delighting in the phenomenal aspects of my visual experience? And if I was, doesn't this show that there are visual qualia?[16]

He is not convinced. It seems to him:

that what I found so pleasing in the above instance, what I was focussing on as it were, were a certain shade and intensity of the color blue. I experienced blue as a property of the ocean not as a property of my experience. My experience itself certainly wasn't blue. Rather it was an experience that represented the ocean as blue. What I was really delighting in then were specific aspects of the content of my experience. It was the content, not anything else, that was immediately accessible to my consciousness and that has aspects I found so pleasing.[17]

We may agree with Tye that when we are thrilled with a glorious sunset or the magical, intense blue of the Pacific Ocean, then the perceiver is aware of the content of the experience, and being thrilled at that. The issue is how that content, that is, how that representing, is to be characterized.

What is crucial, however, is the form this representing takes. We should note that the indirect realist can agree with (and indeed insist upon) the claim that what the observer delights in is the way the sun's setting is represented: for the observer, this way of representing consists in the sun's setting causing a representation and that is highly enjoyable. More importantly for our immediate purposes, however, is that the intentionalist must tell us whether the way the sun's setting is represented is either a non-conceptual or a conceptual representing. It is hard to see how he or she could have in mind a conceptual representation. It is hard to see how we could be so delighted in that. (I may have some quiver of delight if my brother tells me on the phone that there is in Sydney a wonderful sunset, while in Perth the sun is beating down, but that does not compare with my delight three hours later when I go down to Cottesloe Beach.)

It would seem that the delight would have to be at the non-conceptual representing of the sun's setting. This seems right, but now we have to clarify the sense in which there can be a non-conceptual representing. I described one such sense that an indirect representationalist can appeal to: there is in experience a representation that shows what things are like. This type of non-conceptual representing easily makes intelligible the delight that we experience at the sunset. Clearly, however, this is not the sense of non-conceptual representing that the intentionalist relies upon. But his or her sense of *non-conceptual* makes a mystery of the delight.

The naive realist and the phenomenalist and the indirect representational realist all agree on one thing: that there is an actual quality instantiated and that is being enjoyed, whether it is a quality of a physical object, an experience or a phenomenal sensed item. When I delight in the sunset and its colour, I am delighting in that instantiation of a quality.

On the content theory, on the other hand, it is not a quality-instance that I am enjoying. I am thrilled at the way the sunset is represented, its being represented as a certain type of quality. Now that type of quality need not be instantiated at all on the theory. Why not? Well, first of all, if we accept the teleosemantic theory of content, the property is the property that the state was selected for indicating, and that feature of the environment need no longer be around. At the very least it need not be present in the current environment.

Even if we reject the teleosemantic theory, and assume that the function of a representational state can be specified in other terms, for example, in terms of current dispositions, it can still be the case that the property in question is not actually instantiated in the environment. Let us say that the colour of my bunch of grapes in the light I am viewing it is illusory. Then it may be that this colour is wonderful. Here I am thrilled to have the illusion. But I am not enjoying an instantiation of any quality. I am enjoying, on the theory, the way the bunch of grapes is being represented, that is, as having a property it does not have. The property in question is one that can be specified in counterfactual terms; it is the property that would, under certain conditions, cause the state in question.

Tye, Harman and others insist that I am not aware of the intrinsic qualities of this state. Instead I am aware of the content. What this means is that I am aware of a certain property of a certain type: the type that under conditions would cause the state in question. This strikes me as grossly implausible. There is a better explanation readily available. Given that the representationalist theorists have not given good reasons for rejecting that explanation, and given that the positive reasons for the representationalist thesis are so weak, there seems to me to little doubt which theory we should adopt. I say the positive arguments for the representationalist thesis are weak, because either they have little support, or else they depend on the rivals having already been ruled out on other grounds. Most of the positive reasons for the representationalist thesis are consistent with major rivals.

Pain and the projection theory

Whatever plausibility the intentionalist theory has concerning the transparency of, say, visual experience, it is hard to see how it can have any plausibility when applied to the experience of pain, which, Tye and Harman both claim, is transparent. I acknowledge that our experiences of pain have representational content and that they represent a bodily region, say a leg or head or tooth, as being a certain way, and that they *can* be used to represent a bodily disturbance, but how could it be thought that the experience is itself transparent? The experience of pain has content all right: it represents the intrinsic quality as going on in the body. The ache is experienced in the head, behind the eye, say. Of course, we do not believe that the feeling is there, but the phenomenology of pain is that we experience the pain *as if it were there*. I feel the pain in the foot just as I feel movement and pressure in the foot. Indeed, the feeling of pressure in the foot can quickly become a feeling of pressure and pain in the same region in the foot. The natural account of pain is surely that we are aware of the bodily disturbance through being aware of the intrinsic quality of the pain.

It may well be that the account of pain given by both Harman and Tye is intended not as a description of the intentional content of pain experiences but as a proposal that this reflects the proper way to think about pain. Possibly the ordinary intentional content of pain experience should be treated as confused. That, however, is not the way Harman describes what he is doing, nor Tye, and it would be irrelevant to their project, which is to appeal to the phenomenology of experience.

Once again, an alternative explanation of the content of pain experience is available. In arguing that the phenomenal character of an experience is given by the content of the experience, Tye and Harman do not consider that the perceiver might be aware both of intrinsic qualities and content. It may be that the intrinsic qualities contribute to the content. It could be, for example, as Hume and others have suggested, that we project (or "project") some of the intrinsic qualities on to the object. Tye does say that projectivism, upon reflection, seems incomprehensible.[18] He claims that he does not understand how subjective qualities can be projected, and especially on to physical objects. The answer to this is that the projection is not literal, but metaphorical: it is a case of "projection". One example is that a picture of a man in a red coat can be such that the red in the picture is used to represent the red of the man's coat. That is to say, the red in the picture exemplifies the red of the coat represented. Likewise, two actors kissing on stage can exemplify two characters kissing. In the case of pain, the pain one feels in one's leg is a subjective feeling that one "projects" on to the leg. It is not a real projection. One has a body image that represents the body. The pain is projected on to, is located on, that part of the body image that represents the leg. Likewise with colours. There is a subjective quality that we "project" on to an external object, the moon, say, to represent it as yellow. We do not actually project the quality on to the physical moon: we project it on to that part of our subjective visual field that represents the moon. The basis of the metaphor is that the perceiver automatically and naturally takes the representation of the leg to be identical to "that which I reach for when trying to ease the pain", that is, the part of the leg that is the source of the pain. Likewise, he or she takes the moon-representation to be identical to "that which I point at when indicating the moon".

Indeed, the notion of *projection* seems perfectly fitted to Tye's representationalism, or to a suitably modified version of it. The intrinsic quality of the subjective experience need not be thought of as projected on to a physical object, or on to the subject's leg: it is "projected" on to the representational content of the experience. That is to say, it contributes to, or is a part of, the content, in the way that a property of a photograph *may* contribute to the content of the photograph.

Austen Clark's theory of sensory experience

Clark has produced an important piece of work that, on the face of it, may be thought to decide the dispute between the compet-ing theories of phenomenal character that I have just described.[19] Clark's work is very important since it provides a detailed analysis of sensory experience and its representational nature. He defends an account of sensory experience, sensory representation and phenomenal charac-ter that, on the face of it, supports the intentionalist theory, and he explicitly rejects and argues against the position that I am defending. However, I shall argue, much of his argument can actually be turned in support of the theory that I am advocating, and his explicit argu-ment against this position is not cogent (although the details are too great to include fully here).

Clark begins by distinguishing between two senses in which we can talk about the "qualities of [sensory] experiences". This distinc-tion reflects the difference between ascribing a property to some-thing experienced, and ascribing a property to the *experiencing* of it. This distinction, he writes, can be found in different terms, in the works of Reid, Sellars and, more recently, G. Strawson.[20] Following G. Strawson, Clark distinguishes between "phenomenal proper-ties" and "qualitative properties". Phenomenal properties are all those that characterize how things *appear*, and qualitative proper-ties are properties of those internal states "in virtue of which things out there, dangling in front of one's grasping fingers, appear as they do".[21] The phenomenal properties are those specified in the way things *look*, *sound*, *feel* and so on. If an apple looks red, feels cold and tastes sweet, then the terms *red*, *cold* and *sweet* express phe-nomenal properties. Clark is using "appears" here in the non-con-ceptual sense. Understood in this way, Clark's use of "phenomenal" fits Tye's interpretation of "phenomenal character" as non-concep-tual, representational content. (As Clark also points out, there is a danger of confusion since some people often use the terms "qualita-tive" and "phenomenal" in different senses, and there is one tradi-tion that treats them as equivalent. His usage is different from my usage that applies to phenomenal items, for example, phenomenal fields or sense-data, as discussed in theories of phenomenalism, and sense-datum theories.)

Having made the distinction between phenomenal and qualita-tive properties, Clark goes on to distinguish between two senses of "quality space": one in which relative similarities and differences between phenomenal properties (qualities) are presented, and one in which similarities and differences between qualitative properties (qualities) are presented. Qualitative properties are not properties of the things seen, heard, felt and so on, nor are they properties that characterize how those things appear. They are properties of states of mind that help to explain why things appear as they do. We do not know these properties through "knowledge by acquaintance". We come to know what they are, if we do at all, through inference. Clark connects this knowledge with Dretske's account of the knowledge of qualitative character as "displaced perception".[22]

> By attending carefully to the variations in shades among inked patches of paper in front of one's eyes, one can come to apprehend something about the variations in qualitative character among visual states that we find somewhere behind those eyes.[23]

The qualitative properties among which these variations hold, so Clark claims, are complex neural properties: "we must find a neurophysiological interpretation for the dimensions of variations in qualitative properties".[24] This claim marks a crucial step in Clark's account since it means that, by making it, he has automatically ruled out those accounts of qualitative character that are given in terms of "phenomenal fields" or "phenomenal" properties, as in phenomenalism and traditional sense-datum theories. The "projection" theory that I have just sketched (and for which the supporting grounds have been laid in previous chapters) is one such theory. That such theories are automatically ruled out is illustrated by what he says when he writes of seeking a psycho-physical interpretation for our quality space. In so doing, we seek to know how those dimensions of variations in quality space are actually registered by the nervous system.

> In a sense it is only after this is done that qualitative properties have been identified. Until then, we know at best that there are some k distinct dimensions of variation in the qualitative character of states in the given modality, but we do not know what those dimensions are.[25]

Clark's assumption is legitimate if these theories can be ruled out on independent grounds, but Clark's theory cannot be used to rule them out, for it presupposes that they are wrong. These other independent grounds, as I and others, for example, Robinson, have argued, have not been forthcoming. Those rival theories, let it be said, do not deny the importance of uncovering and describing the underlying neural mechanisms. They differ in how we should interpret the "qualitative character" of sensory experiences.

Clark explains his account in terms of colour vision. Although, as he points out, the identification of the relevant neural processes is sketchy, there has been considerable progress in the task. Clark points out, as have C. L. Hardin and Thompson, that what has become known as the "opponent process" theory has become something of the "standard model" in colour vision science (although the situation is not entirely clear-cut).[26] Clark argues that the emerging model is one that should elicit quiet surprise when we discover which dimensions of variation in phenomenal appearances are actually registered by the nervous system:

> Colours of a given brightness are not registered by separate coordinates of hue and saturation; the latter are not the differentiative properties on which chromatic discriminations actually proceed. Indeed the gamut is described by two "opponent" axes. One axis registers where the colour is in a series from yellow through grey to blue, and the other where it is in a series from red through grey to green. Both opponent axes carry information about both hue and saturation, but mathematically the result is the same: they describe a plane. The pair of coordinates yield a unique position in the 2-dimensional order of hues and saturations of a given brightness.[27]

Clark asks the question of how it is possible "to be surprised by such facts as the way in practice the dimensions of variation in phenomenal appearance are actually registered by the nervous system". This, to my mind, is a crucial question. Unfortunately, it seems to me, it is a question Clark does not answer. However, he does give an important analysis of facts about colour vision. It is important, he writes, to admit the existence of "qualitative structure". For example, the fact that orange is between red and yellow is not a straightforward physical fact, but a fact of "qualitative structure". A sensory system can register similarities between instances of orange and of red, but the qualities themselves are not objects of discrimination. Clark goes on to point out that there are good reasons to think that all the facts that could be mentioned in defining a particular qualitative term are found among such facts of qualitative structure.

Given this claim, it becomes highly significant that, as Clark argues, the structural properties (relations of similarities and differences) that hold in the phenomenal and qualitative colour spaces are not matched in any quality space concerning actual properties of the "stimulus class", that is, the objects that are perceived, normally, as having colours. (This point is one that a number of authors have regarded as highly significant, for example, Hardin, Thompson, and Maund.[28]) Since, as he argues, colours are defined in terms of their structural relations, it follows that physical objects do not have colours. Clark goes on to argue that the qualitative properties are relational ones. Given this claim, and the claim that there are no actual, intrinsic (non-relational) colours possessed by physical objects, and the further phenomenal fact that colours appear to be intrinsic properties, two conclusions would seem to follow: experiences of colour are illusory; and to explain how this is so, we need a theory that employs sense-data, or phenomenal fields, much as required in the "projection" theory.

Clark explicitly rejects this conclusion, but it is hard to see how he can. Take, for example, his discussion of the consequence of his account that qualitative character is a relational affair. He admits that this is counterintuitive, since qualitative properties seem to be intrinsic properties but they are not: "When one sees a patch of orange, the experience seems to involve an intrinsic monadic quale: the quale orange. But this experience is an illusion."[29] But this passage conflicts with his own distinction between phenomenal and qualitative properties. It is the phenomenal properties, the way things *appear*, that seem to involve the quale. Therefore, the qualitative properties are not part of those properties that the objects seem to have. It may be thought that because, on Clark's theory, if the qualitative properties are relational then so are the phenomenal properties, but rather than draw that conclusion, the appropriate conclusion to draw, surely, is that the theory is wrong. But in any case, if the theorist ends up saying that "the experience of orange is illusory since it seems to involve an intrinsic monadic quale", then we had better have a theory of how the illusion comes about and of what it consists. On the face of it, that there is such an illusory experience with this character supports what the sense-datum and phenomenal-field theorists are saying about perceptual experience. Clark would seem to have conceded set and match to the opponent.

Clark does consider a similar criticism raised by David Chalmers: "this method does not explain the intrinsic nature of a colour experience".[30] Clark's response is, "Guilty as charged, Your Honour. There is no such nature to be explained." He goes on to say: "Not only is there no intrinsic nature to colour experience, but given what we know about vertebrate sensory physiology, it is difficult to see how intrinsic properties could account for the qualitative character of any sensory experience."[31] But, once again, Clark is appealing to the wrong aspect of experience. If what we are trying to do is to give an account of the phenomenology of experience, then it won't do to say that experience does not have intrinsic properties, if that is the way things appear. If experience does not have the intrinsic nature, then one will need a theory to explain why they appear to have one. It is the same mistake as the one he makes when he says "the appearance of black is a relational affair, even though it appears to be intrinsic".[32]

These issues surface again when Clark presents, and defends against rivals, his positive theory of sensory experience, and of its representational character. The idea here is that sensory experience has a representational character for which there are underlying mechanisms. Clark provides a theory of what those mechanisms are. In this vein, he develops what he calls the "Feature-Placing hypothesis", according to which, sensory representation, when successful, proceeds by picking out place-times and characterizing qualities that appear at those place-times.[33] We have here a "primitive variety of mental representation".

The argument is complex but, for our purposes, the crucial part of it concerns his discussion of different concepts of *visual field*. Clark, first of all, identifies for a given perceiver, a *field of view* at time *t*, that is, at the time at which the perceiver is having the experience. This field of view is constituted by the scattered totality of physical phenomena seen at time *t*. Some of these events or objects ante-date the time of experience. For example, the star I am seeing now may be a star as it existed 4.2 years ago. This field of view is a physical phenomenon that exists independently of the perceiver's experience and representation of it. This is the first sense of visual field that Clark discusses. On the necessity of the visual field in this sense, it should be noted, most theorists are agreed, including defenders of the classical representative theory. There are, however, two other senses of "visual field": one is the sum of *visual sense-impressions* and the other the sum of *intentional objects*. Putting the three senses together we have:

- visual field₁: the sum of physical phenomena seen at time *t*, that is, the objects visually impinging on the perceiver;
- visual field₂: the sum of visual representings, that is, of visual impressions;
- visual field₃: the sum of intentional objects.

Clark goes on to argue that the first kind of visual field is essential, but that there is no reason to admit the second type. He admits that there is a need for the concept of *visual field*, in the third sense, but that this sense does not require us to quantify over the "intentional objects", and that the facts about intentional objects can be handled on the feature-placing hypothesis, for which the first kind of visual field is central. The problem with his argument, it seems to me, is that first he interprets the second sense of field of view as requiring that the field of sense-impressions is two-dimensional. This is decidedly not the sort of field that I have in mind, nor is it what Price and Broad had in mind. Clark admits that his argument could be defeated by adding a third dimension to the field of impressions. If we do that, he says, "it loses much of its allure. One might reasonably wonder why the 3-dimensional structure of space outside the head has to be represented by constructing an isomorphic model of it inside the head".[34] But I fail to see the problem. Surely the point of the inner map is that it is not an isomorphic map. It maps only some of the features of the world. First of all, it presents a selection of objects and qualities in that world, and secondly, it presents the world as seen from a specific point of view. If, as Clark admits, some of the objects seen, for example, distant stars, no longer exist or, if they do, they are not in the part of the sky where they appear, then we had better have a map "inside the head" that represents them.

There is a further problem with Clark's treatment of visual fields: he does not give an adequate account of the field of intentional objects. What is required for a proper account, I argue, is that we take into account the second type of visual field, that is, the phenomenal field, as on the "projection" theory. This is to reiterate the point made earlier, that Clark admits that the experience of orange is an illusory experience of an intrinsic monadic quale: the quale orange. The same point holds for all the experiences of colour. That is why the intentional-object field needs to be combined with the phenomenal-field, for example, in the way advanced by the "projection" theory.

To summarize, Clark distinguishes between phenomenal properties, the properties objects appear to have, the qualitative properties, the properties of internal states in virtue of which the experiences represent objects as having the phenomenal qualities, and the properties of the objects that make up the "stimuli class" for the experiences, that is, the objects that cause the experiences, and which the experiences represent as having the properties in question. Since Clark admits that the properties, which objects appear to have, have a character that is not captured in the properties of the neural processes, and are not contained by the objects perceived, it seems to me that he has admitted that perceptual experiences have an illusory character built into them. Given this illusory character, there are grounds for admitting the power of a phenomenal field theory or sense-datum theory, such as presented in the "projection" theory described earlier in this chapter, and foreshadowed in Chapter 4.[35]

Conclusion

The intentionalist/representationalist thesis is the thesis that when we introspect our perceptual experiences, that is, when we reflectively attend to them while having them, we do not become aware of the intrinsic qualities, either of these experiences or of phenomenal items that are components of the experiences. Rather, we become aware of the representational content of the experience: we become aware of the way objects are represented as being. I have argued that these theorists are adopting here a false dichotomy. They have not taken proper account of an alternative form of non-conceptual representative content. There is, I have argued, a sense of non-conceptual content that should be explained in terms of a non-conceptual representing. Given this sense, it is far more plausible that when we introspect our perceptual experiences, we are aware of the intrinsic qualities of the perceptual experiences, or of phenomenal items presented to us in that experience. Indeed, this account makes more intelligible the transparency of perceptual experience than does the intentionalist/representationalist thesis.

Adverbialist accounts of
10 perceptual experience

Perceptual experiences, we have agreed, have both phenomenal (sensuous) character and intentional content. In Chapter 9 I examined the theory that attempts to explain phenomenal character in terms of the intentional content or, more accurately, the non-conceptual, representational content of the experience. I argued that it was not successful. In particular it suffered in comparison with those theories that accounted for phenomenal character in terms of intrinsic phenomenal qualities of phenomenal items. Examples of such theories are the traditional sense-datum theories but another important example is the natural-sign theory that I have championed. On this theory, the naive perceiver takes the signs as signs of physical objects and their qualities, but does not conceptualize them as signs.

According to this last group of theories, perceptual experience has a certain structure: it consists in the awareness of phenomenal items, or of quality-instances. As was discussed in Chapter 3, this structure fits an *act–object structure*. The fact that these theories imply that perceptual experiences have an act–object structure is of great importance, for there is a significant body of philosophers, both traditional and contemporary, who reject this analysis, including Reid, Ducasse, Chisholm, B. Aune and, more recently, Dretske and Tye. What they offer in its place is an adverbialist account of perceptual experience.

One of the earliest and most explicit of critics of the act–object analysis was Reid.[1] He argued that it was crucial in accounts of perception to distinguish perception from sensation. Each of these acts (activities) has an object, but an "object" in very different senses of the term:

perception: its object is distinct from the act;
sensation: its object was not something distinct from it; it could only exist while being sensed.

These sensations are sensory *experiences*, that is, states of awareness or consciousness. These states, while conscious, are ones that we need not be aware *that* we are having, while we are having them. Their "objects" only exist while being sensed; they are not distinct from the corresponding act. Pains, itches and feelings seem good examples. Pains seem incapable of being divorced from the feeling of pain. This point entails the rejection of the act–object analysis for sensations. The sensation is best thought of in adverbial terms: the so-called "object" of the act of sensation simply modifies the activity of sensing. My tasting a bitter taste has a grammatical object, a bitter taste, but that "object" is not something that can exist independently of the tasting: it is a modification of the tasting.

There are, however, two ways of interpreting the adverbialist position that ought not be confused. On each of the alternatives, the "bitter taste" component of tasting a bitter taste is construed as a modification of the tasting, but they construe the tasting and the type of modification involved differently. According to one position, the tasting is a non-conceptualized sensory state and the bitter taste is a modification of the tasting. The sensory state can occur without the perceiver exercising or even possessing the concept of *bitter*.

According to the second alternative, the tasting is a form of conceptualized awareness, and hence requires the exercise of the relevant concepts. On this account, to taste a bitter taste involves being aware of something as bitter. The account is adverbial in the sense that one does not taste, in this sense, without tasting something as F, that is, as bitter, sweet, spicy and so on. The terms "bitter", "sweet", "spicy" and so on are not used to pick out some sensory quality that we are aware of. Rather they express concepts that we are exercising in tasting. Objects such as wines and foods are bitter, sweet, spicy and so on. In tasting the wine as bitter, we are aware of the wine's bitterness; we are not aware of a sensory quality.

The conceptual version of the adverbialist account is an important account of perceptual experience in its own right. What is distinctive about it is its view that the phenomenal character and conceptual content are intertwined. It is possible to capture this account in McGinn's description of perceptual experiences as Janus-faced: "they point outward to the external world but they also present a subjective form to the subject . . . they are *of something* other than the subject, and they are *like something* for the subject."[2] A more explicit description of the account, however, was provided by P. F. Strawson. He considers, only to reject, the view that there are two distinct stages in the formation of perceptual beliefs: first, the occurrence of sensible experience; and, secondly, the deployment of concepts in the formation of beliefs on the basis of this sensible experience. Instead he holds that the concepts employed in perceptual judgement about the world and sensible experience itself interpenetrate each other more closely than this picture suggests:

> The character of our perceptual experience itself, of our sense-experience itself, is thoroughly conditioned by the judgements about the objective world which we are disposed to make when we have this experience; it is, so to speak, thoroughly permeated – saturated, one might say – with the concepts employed in such judgements.[3]

In further explication of this line of thought, P. F. Strawson writes that the candid description of experience at any moment must normally be given in terms of these concepts; and not in the restricted terms that are appropriate at moments when the subject's attention is engaged only by sensation of special interest (i.e. clinical or aesthetic) interest. It is useful to borrow Strawson's description and label the account the "concept-saturated account".

In this chapter, I propose to give brief discussions of the two versions of adverbialist direct realism: the non-conceptual and the conceptual versions.

The adverbial account of sensory experience

The non-conceptual adverbialist account is set up in opposition to those who offer a particular-analysis of sensory experience: those like

Moore, Price and (for Reid) Locke and Berkeley, who construe sensory experience in terms of the perceiver's being aware of, or "perceiving" a sensory particular.[4] Typically, we are thought to sense something yellow and circular, where "sensing" consists of being aware of the yellow, circular something, albeit in a special form of awareness: sensory awareness (knowledge by acquaintance).

The act–object analysis is held by the adverbialists to be fatally flawed since, so it is claimed, there are, in perceptual experience, no instances of sensory qualities to serve as the "object" of awareness. What there are, instead, are ways of experiencing, for example, a way of tasting, looking, feeling and so on. To think that there are sensory objects represents a failure to look beyond the grammatical similarities between "Peter tasted the tea" and "Peter tasted a bitter taste". The bitter taste is not an object that is experienced – it is a way of tasting.

The report of an experience, "I sensed something yellow and circular", is said to have a deceptive surface structure. The yellow circular "something" is said to have no more existence independently of the activity of sensing than a dance, say, has from an activity of dancing. Just as "Morris danced a merry dance" should be construed as "Morris danced merrily", so "I sensed something yellow and circular" should be construed as "I sensed yellowly, circularly and singularly".

One charge that some adverbialists level at the act–object analysis is that they are confused. They treat grammatically similar sentences as if they were logically the same (when they are not). The charge of confusion suggests that the theorists are not simply wrong, but that they go wrong because of their failure to be alert to a grammatical point. It is hard to see, however, that this charge can stand up. The possibility that people might be grammatically confused is in itself no reason to think that they actually make that confusion. Ducasse and others who emphasize the grammatical point give no evidence for the confusion.[5] The confusion is offered only as a possible explanation for why the act–object analysis makes the mistake. But this argument presupposes that the analysis is mistaken, and that needs to be shown.

It may have been the case that some act–object theorists were confused in this way. Many, however, were not, but even if they were, they do not have to be, for there are understandable reasons, even if they are not compelling ones, to support the act–object analysis. To demonstrate that this is so, we can appeal to the transparency of experience that Tye and Harman emphasize against sense-data theorists. One can cite these hostile witnesses in support of the claim that, from a phenomenological point of view, when one reflects on one's perceptual experiences, it is surely obvious that what one is presented with in experience is a specific object. This supports an act–object analysis. It is a subsequent argument about the nature of the object that, for such philosophers as Moore, Broad and Price, is supposed to lead to the conclusion that the objects are phenomenal items.

There is a more substantive criticism of the act–object analysis; namely, that the theory is simply wrong, and the adverbialist account is to be preferred as providing the best account of perceptual experience. But once again we can appeal to the phenomenon of the transparency of experience, this time to show that the adverbialist theory is wrong. It is important to remember here that the adverbialist account implies that ordinarily, when we perceive an object, we enjoy a perceptual experience, but no experience or part of it becomes an "object" for us. The only object is the external object (or part of the perceiver's body). However, the experience can become an "object" when one introspects. But surely the adverbialist account of the experience does not capture the phenomenology of this situation. When I introspect my visual experiences what is revealed is not my "sensing adverbially modified". Surely Tye and Harman are right: what seems to be revealed is "the tree itself", "a particular ocean", "a particular chair". What the sense-data theorist is arguing about is the nature of the object. What Tye and Harman agree is that it is an object that is revealed in experience: the experience is diaphanous.

It would seem that the adverbialist is faced with a dilemma: when I introspect my experiences then what I become aware of is either the content of the experience, the way an object is represented as being, or it is a collection of sense-data. He or she obviously cannot take the second option. If he or she takes the first option then either the content is thought of as non-conceptual in the way that Dretske and Tye suppose, and was rejected above, or it is conceptual as McGinn and Strawson and McDowell suppose. Either way he or she has abandoned his or her position.

There is an alternative that the adverbialist might fall back on. The thesis might be that although perceptual experiences appear to have an act–object structure, they are really adverbial modifications of a sensory experience. One is experiencing redly, circularly, at-an-angle-ly and so on, but the sensory experience takes the form of individuals spread out in space. Thus construed, the adverbialist thesis is a metaphysical thesis. But this move is surely of no help. If we are to be critical of the act–object analysis of perceptual experience, we need to be clear about the sense of "object" that is involved.

There are at least two kinds of "object" that may be in question. One model for what the object is, is that the particular is a substance, at least in the minimal sense in which pens, leaves, apples, horses, leopards, tables and trees may be said to be substances: the bearers of properties that may or may not change over time. If one construes sensory particulars (sensa, sensibilia, . . .) on this model, then it is easy to see how certain philosophical problems will arise that might be hard to resolve; for example, whether the sensa have insides and backsides, which are unexperienced, and whether they continue to exist when unsensed and so on.[6]

There is, however, a second way of construing "object". The object might be something that can serve as an object of thought and reflection, and for this it might be sufficient that it is "thing-like". It is thing-like in that we can ascribe to it certain properties: a shape, a location in space, movement through space, certain causal properties and so on. It can be the object of thought, that is, something we have thoughts about. "Thing-like" examples are mountains, waves and shadows. Metaphysically, mountains are adverbial modifications of the earth's belt. They have no existence independent of being part of the earth. Yet for all that, they have some rather strong "object"-characteristics: they are located in space, are tall, have a height, and a point, give a whack if you fly a plane into them and so on.[7]

If by "object" we mean an independently existing substance, that is, something whose essential nature is separate from the act of sensing, then the metaphysical thesis, if true, would rule out an act–object analysis of perceptual experience. But surely there is no serious theory that would be committed to this view. The view that the "objects" of our experiences are sensory particulars or sense-data is surely compatible with them being metaphysical aspects of our sensing. This situation is surely no different from that of mountains.

It is surely possible to construe the sensory particulars as thing-like, and in that sense ontological, without their being substances. According to this suggestion, sensing a sensory particular is construed as a process in which the sensory particular is a component of the process. It is a particular sustained by the activity of sensing, in much the same way as a shadow is cast by a man, a wave is sustained in a rope, a spot of illumination is produced by a torch. For sensory particulars, the model for thinking of them as "objects" is that provided by shadows, spots of light, rainbows, images, utterances, waves in the water and so on. In these cases we have activities where we can pick out an "object" of the activity and describe its features, literally, without holding that the object can exist independently of the activity. In such cases the object X is an object sustained or caused by something. The activity or process is one that involves the sustaining or holding together or producing some condition. We can, if we like, call the item "thing-like" rather than an object. It is thing-like in that we can ascribe to it certain properties: a shape, a location in space, movement through space, certain causal properties and so on. It can be the object of thought, that is, something we have thoughts about.[8]

Accordingly, if sensory particulars are adverbial modifications of sensing in the way that mountains are adverbial modifications of the earth's belt, then it leaves untouched those theories of perceptual experience that are committed to an "act–object analysis". Certainly, as far as the dispute between representational realists and direct realists is concerned, all that is required is that the sensory items are thing-like. They do not have to be objects, in the sense of independent substances.

Finally, we should note that there are two prime motivations for the adverbialist analysis. One is that it avoids commitment to sensory particulars, such as sense-data (sensa, sensibilia, etc.) and thus avoids having to solve difficult philosophical problems. Such problems however, only arise if we take the "objects" to be substances, and there is no reason to do that. The second motivation for the adverbialist analysis is that it allows us to hold on to a version of direct realism, thus avoiding the epistemological problems that are alleged to confront representational theories of perception, particularly of the indirect variety. This motivation is likewise unfounded. First of all, the version of representative realism that I have been advancing is a version of natural realism. The sensory representations are natural signs of physical objects and their qualities. Accordingly, there are no greater epistemological problems for this theory than there are for any form of direct realism. In the second place, even as far as the classical theory is concerned, it is the case that, as a number of authors (Mackie, Jackson, Maund, Lowe and Broad) have argued, these epistemological worries are unfounded.[9]

Concept-saturated perception

The conceptual version of adverbialism is the theory I have labelled, picking up P. F. Strawson's characterization, the "concept-saturated account" of perceptual experience. While Strawson and McGinn, with his description of experience as Janus-faced, give us memorable images for thinking of the theory, the strongest defence of the position has been provided by McDowell.

The concept-saturated account of perceptual experience can be explained in contrast to the two-stage version of cognitive direct realism defended by Reid and Dretske. The contrast is clearly brought out by McDowell in his book *Mind and World*, where he contrasts his account with the two-stage model of Evans. In a similar vein to Dretske and Reid, Evans had described the perceptual process of making perceptual judgements based on perceptual experiences as one in which a process of conceptualization or judgement takes the perceiving subject from being in one kind of informational state, a state with non-conceptual content, to being in another kind of state, one with content of a different kind, namely conceptual content.[10] This two-stage account naturally invites two immediate questions: what exactly is a perceptual experience; and what is the nature of the transition from one state to the other? Evans's answer to the first is that perceptual experiences are the informational states that carry non-conceptual content, but they are not *ipso facto* states of a conscious subject. Something more is needed. Such a state counts as an experience only if the non-conceptual content is "available as input to a thinking, concept-applying and reasoning system".

However, it needs to be spelled out what it is for a state to be "available as input" to the thinking, reasoning system. Two models suggest themselves. On the first, the transition between states is a causal one. The informational state serves as input by causing the conceptual state to occur. On the second, the non-conceptual state is "available to input" in the sense that it is available for inferences to be made. McDowell's criticism of Evans's theory targets the second way, arguing that for a state to serve as input to a rational inference, it has to be a premise for a conclusion, and that requires it to already have conceptual content, contrary to what Evans has supposed. Evans's account thus leads to self-contradiction. McDowell rejects the other purely causal interpretation of what it is to be "available as input", on the grounds that it is explicitly ruled out by Evans. In any case, this interpretation provides no motivation for identifying the non-conceptual state as "an experience". Why should being the last state in a chain of causal links constitute an experience?

McDowell's account of perceptual experience and his criticism of Evans proceeds in terms of a discussion of the traditional account of the mind's functions of sensibility and understanding. As he points out, the standard view of these functions is that sensibility is passive and non-conceptual, while the understanding is the faculty of spontaneity, involving "thinking, concept-applying and reasoning". McDowell argues that the traditional view is misconceived, in holding that the sensibility's function is to deliver "non-conceptualized inputs" to the understanding, which employs concepts in making judgements. This view is an endorsement of the "myth of the given": the view that states that conceptual content can be rationally supported by experiences construed as states with non-conceptual content.

In opposition to Evans's account of perceptual experience, McDowell defends a position in which the perceiver's conceptual capacities are operative in sensibility as well as in reasoning. On McDowell's account, one's perceptual experiences are essentially states that carry conceptual content, and are states distinguishable from perceptual judgements, which consist of assent to, or dissent from (or the withholding of assent from), the content of those experiences. According to McDowell's account:

> the content of a perceptual experience is already conceptual. A judgement of experience does not introduce a new kind of

content, but simply endorses the conceptual content, or some
of it, that is already possessed by the experience on which it is
grounded.[11]

McDowell insists here that the grounding of perceptual judgements
by perceptual experience does not depend on an inferential step
from one content to another: "a typical judgement of experience
selects from the content of the experience on which it is based".

McDowell shares with Donald Davidson the assumption that
the premises for rational inferences must be states already imbued
with conceptual content. This assumption has been challenged
by Millar, who has argued for an account of perceptual experiences where the process between experience and conceptual state
can be interpreted as a "quasi-inference".[12] I want to pursue,
however, another line. It seems to me that there is another possibility that McDowell has not considered. Perceptual experience is
a complex, *sui generis*, act of conscious awareness. We are
presented with non-conceptual elements which we are aware of as
being a certain way. We are aware of them as signs, in the sense
that we are aware of them as tools, which we can use. We use the
signs in locating objects in space before us, as objects we can reach
for and grasp or throw things at. The situation is not one in which
we are first in a non-conceptual state and then move into an
entirely different state, for example, by a rational inference. The
perceptual experience is a complex, integrated act with different
components: we are aware of a particular and are aware of it as
something that can be used. There is the following link between
our judgements about particular objects, that cup, that tree, the
moon and so on. Our sensory representations, the non-conceptual
items of our perceptual experience, play a crucial role in our
identifying a cup as *that cup* (which is not to say that it plays this
role all by itself).

Sensuous content: its richness and fine-grained detail

The model for perceptual experience advanced by Evans (and
Dretske) seems problematical. Does the model favoured by
McDowell fare any better? The point of his proposal is to reject
both the view of perceptual experience as a non-conceptual state

and the view of perceptual experience as the mere acquisition of belief. Instead the experience is a state with content, where the content is conceptual. The content of such experiences is that things are thus and so, for example, that there is a yellow hoop before me. The perceiver who has the experience is someone who can then either endorse or reject the content. The parallel, on McDowell's account, to the Evans–Dretske causal–rational transition from non-conceptual state to conceptual state, is a transition from a state with conceptual content to an act of assenting, dissenting or withholding assent.

A vital element in McDowell's account is that the grounding of perceptual judgements by perceptual experience does not depend on an inferential step from one content to another: "A typical judgement of experience *selects* from the content of the experience on which it is based."[13] In conceding that the judgement typically does not exhaust the richness of the conceptual content of the experience, McDowell is trying to defuse the claim stressed by advocates of non-conceptual content (Peacocke, Dretske, Evans) that our perceptual experiences, especially our visual experiences, typically have a richness and profusion of detail that far outruns our abilities to formulate judgements. McDowell argues that although it is true that the richness of detail cannot be captured in the judgements, this does not show, as the non-conceptualists claim, that the context is non-conceptual, for, he argues, it does not show that we do not have the appropriate concepts.

I would have thought that this point made by the non-conceptualists is not that we do not have the requisite concepts, but that the content, on a particular occasion, has not been conceptualized. However, the lesson the richness of visual experience teaches is this. Let us suppose, as McDowell concedes, that I select from the conceptual content of my experience to make a judgement, for example:

there is a yellow hoop before me

rather than any of the following:

there is a wooden hoop before me;
there is an upright hoop before me;

there is an upright hoop before me, facing away at an angle of 45°;

there is a slightly orangish, yellow hoop before me.

Presumably I must be aware of the experience, that is, aware of the rich full content, before I select, and McDowell's account does not have place for this awareness. Another way of putting this point is as follows. McDowell agrees that there is a strong sense in which our visual experience has a richness that is not captured in the actual perceptual judgements we make. Where he disagrees with Dretske and Evans is that he rejects their suggestion that the rich content of visual experience is non-conceptual. The richness of the experience does not outrun the potential of our conceptual resources: it outruns the actual judgements that we do make. Let us grant McDowell this. There still remains the question as to why it is that we think that the experience is so rich in this way, that is, why it has the rich content. It seems to me that our reasons are phenomenological. We know from our own visual experiences what they are like. We know that there is this superfluity of richness. We are aware of the richness of the experience.

A further point concerns the role of assent and dissent in McDowell's scheme. It is held that the perceiver has an experience with rich conceptual content, to which he or she can either assent or dissent. McDowell wants to distinguish the act of assenting from the making of an explicit judgement, for example, that "there is a yellow hoop, slightly tilted facing towards me". We obviously do not explicitly make all the judgements that we could individually make. That is, there may be one hundred judgements, any one of which we could make if we chose, but we cannot make all of them. But then it does not seem any more possible to assent to all of these propositions that are contained in the experience.

In conscious perception, I am not just aware that there is, say, a yellow hoop before me, standing out against a background. I am aware of a scene or vista, and am aware of it: as before me; or as rich, or alternatively as impoverished, as occasionally it is. Within this scene, I may be aware that there is a yellow, slightly tilted hoop. One of the things I am aware of, when I engage in conscious seeing, is that there is a scene before me, profuse in detail, among which detail I can focus on some aspect. Giving a satisfactory account of what exactly this conscious awareness consists of is not easy to do. Indeed, I think that it is one of the hardest jobs imaginable. It would be crazy though to deny that there is this conscious awareness, or ignore it, or be satisfied with an account of it that is obviously wrong. I do not pretend to be able to give a full account, but what I claim is that the best answer we have is one in which the state of conscious awareness is one that has a non-conceptual component: a rich non-conceptual state or component that we are aware of under an aspect. To say this is not to give a full answer, but it is to give part of the answer.

There is an argument for the necessity of admitting non-conceptual content that Evans places great weight on. It depends on the claim that experiences have a determinacy of detail that our conceptual abilities do not capture. It is an argument that McDowell discusses at some length, only to reject. "Do we really understand", Evans rhetorically asks, "the proposal that we have as many colour concepts as there are shades of colour that we can sensibly discriminate?" The suggestion made by Evans is that "our repertoire of colour concepts is coarser in grain than our abilities to discriminate shades, and therefore unable to capture the fine detail of colour experience".[14]

The way of thinking that informs this suggestion, McDowell holds, can be resisted, for it makes the illicit assumption that our ability to embrace colour, for example, within our conceptual thinking is restricted to concepts expressed by general words such as "red", "green" or "burnt sienna". McDowell's claim is that we are equipped to include shades of colour within our conceptual thinking with the same determinacy with which they are presented in one's visual experiences, so that our concepts can capture colours no less sharply than our experiences present them.

The conceptual capacities in question are recognitional capacities, ones that can be made explicit with the help of a sample, "something that is guaranteed to be available at the time of the experience with which the capacity sets in".[15] What reason could there be, McDowell asks, for refusing to accept that such recognitional capacities are conceptual? Evans is depending on the phenomenological point that the world as experience takes hold of it is more finely grained than we could register by appealing only to conceptual capacities express-ible by general colour words and phrases.[16]

McDowell's point seems to be that, however detailed the fine grain of the subject's perceptual experiences are, they can be expressed by a perceptual judgement and illustrated by, for example, pointing to a sample: "*that shade* of red". Likewise, if I have an experience of an elliptical counter (not a round coin viewed from an angle, but a genuine ellipse) then even if I lack the general concept "*eccentricity* 0.8", I can allow that my experience has this conceptual content since I have the capacity to express that concept by reference to a sample of ellipses. But surely McDowell's reply misses the point. It may well be true that if I lack the capacity to express the concept "*eccentricity* 0.8" in words but can point to examples of instances of this concept, then by the act of pointing I am demonstrating my possessing, temporarily, the concept. However, the crucial question is whether in having the experience itself I thereby exercise the concept. This issue is quite separate from that of whether I could, on a specific occasion, exercise the concept by exploiting a nearby sample. The point about our perceptual experiences having rich sensuous content of fine-grained detail is that we can reflect on the experience and acknowledge that there is a wide spread of qualities that we could pick out. In acknowledging this, we have not yet picked out these qualities. Accordingly, McDowell has not shown what he claims to have done: that the sensory experience itself involves the application of the relevant concept.

However, even if sensory experiences could be thought of as involving the applications of concepts, we would still need to distinguish between two different applications of concepts, sensory–sensuous applications and non-sensuous ones. And there is no reason why the indirect representational theory could not be accommodated to this situation. On that theory, the conscious, non-sensuous application of, say, the concept of ellipse is mediated by the sensory component, which itself is the non-conscious sensuous application of the concept. As a consequence, we can say the same thing about the conceptual version of the adverbialist thesis as we found we could say about the non-conceptual adverbialist thesis, interpreted as a metaphysical thesis: that it leaves untouched those theories of perceptual experience that are committed to an "act–object analysis".

(A final point: McDowell's ideas raise many complex issues that it is hard to do justice to. There is much more that I would like to do. In a fuller discussion I would hope to make greater use of the work of Evan Fales in his *A Defence of the Given*, particularly in Chapter 4, "The Conceptual Content of the Given".[17] I make reference to that book here, so that the interested reader may pursue these issues at greater depth.)

Conclusion

In this chapter I have examined the two major versions of the adverbialist thesis, arguing that those versions do not give us reason to reject those theories of perceptual experience that are committed to an act–object analysis of perceptual experience. The thesis can either be interpreted in such a weak sense as to be compatible with those theories or, alternatively, it is ungrounded.

Conclusion

There are two major interrelated problems in the philosophy of perception: whether perception is direct or indirect; and what is the best account that we can give of perceptual experiences. I have aimed in this book to provide a framework, a "natural realist" view of perception, that would provide the means for making progress towards solving these problems, and for examining the major theories that have been provided. My aim has principally been to set out these issues, although I have not disguised the fact that I think that there are solid grounds that point the way to a particular resolution of the problems.

I argued initially that the debate between direct and indirect realism should be moved from a debate about perception to one about perceptual experience. I provided and defended a theory that is a form of indirect representationalism, a "hybrid theory", which had indirect and direct components. Perceptual experiences, on this account, are complex thoughts that have non-conceptual, sensuous components and other components that are conceptual and non-sensuous. A conscious perceptual experience is an intentional activity. It is an act of (double) awareness, an activity, that consists of the perceiver taking the sensuous component to be a sign of the presence of something of a certain kind, for example, that there is a certain kind of physical object before him or her.

One path to handling the problem of direct–indirect perceptual experience is through the argument from illusion. I argued that this argument is better than it is usually given credit for, but it still stands in need of support for one of its key premises. In particular, it needs an account of what it is for something to look a certain way (i.e. to appear) and, especially, of a phenomenal use of "looks". Another path to handling the problem is trying to provide an account of perceptual experience that will handle the problem of the dual aspect of perceptual experiences: that they have both sensuous, phenomenal character and intentional content. These two paths converge. When we chart the variety of ways in which things look we find that there is a central role for a phenomenological sense of "looks", which has two aspects, a conceptual intentional aspect and a non-conceptual, phenomenal aspect.

At this stage, the major issue to emerge concerns how we should characterize the phenomenal character and intentional content, and how they are related. One important question is whether the phenomenal character can be identified as a non-conceptual aspect to our experiences, separate from the conceptual aspect and, secondly, if it can, whether it is to be characterized in terms of non-conceptual content (a type of informational content) or as a way of representing. And if it is a way of representing, should the phenomenal character of an experience be characterized in terms of the subject's being presented with a sensory–phenomenal item with phenomenal characteristics, or should it be thought of in an adverbial way, as a way in which the subject's sensing (his or her sensory experiences) is modified?

It seemed to me that there are clear answers to these questions that supported a certain view of the structure of perceptual experience, which, at the very least, is consistent with the indirect, natural-sign version of representational realism, which I had earlier presented.

Notes

Chapter 1: The philosophy of perception

1. Plato had a higher conception of knowledge, which concerned the Eternal forms. Still, he recognized the role of sense perception in telling us about the world of flux, the world of phenomena.
2. The views of the Stoics and Aristotle are discussed respectively in the articles by Frede and Block, cited in the next note. Aristotle's views can be found in "De Anima", Book II, in J. Barnes (ed.), *The Complete Works of Aristotle*, (Princeton, NJ: Princeton University Press, 1984), pp. 656–75.
3. See M. Frede, "Stoics and Skeptics on Clear and Distinct Impressions", in M. Burnyeat (ed.), *The Skeptical Tradition* (Berkeley, CA: University of California Press, 1983), pp. 65–94; and I. Block, "Truth and Error in Aristotle's Theory of Perception", *Philosophical Quarterly* 11 (1961), pp. 1–9.
4. Indeed, it seems to me that evolutionary epistemology as pursued by philosophers of science such as Popper, Lakatos and others, falls within this field.
5. Introduction in H. Kornblith (ed.), *Naturalizing Epistemology* (Cambridge, MA: MIT Press, 1985), pp. 3–13.
6. C. D. Broad, *Scientific Thought* (London: Kegan Paul, 1923), p. 268.
7. E. J. Lowe, *Locke on Human Understanding* (London: Routledge, 1995), p. 62.
8. C. McGinn, *The Subjective View* (Oxford: Oxford University Press, 1983), p. 129.
9. See, for example, J. Yolton, *Perceptual Acquaintance from Descartes to Reid*, (Minneapolis, MN: University of Minnesota Press, 1984), and Lowe, *Locke on Human Understanding*, pp. 42–7, 59.
10. M. Burnyeat, "Conflicting Appearances", *Proceedings of the British Academy*, 65 (1979), pp. 69–111.
11. J. J. Gibson, *The Ecological Approach to Visual Perception* (Boston: Houghton Mifflin, 1979).
12. H. H. Price, *Perception* (London: Methuen, 1932); H. Robinson, *Perception* (London: Routledge, 1994).
13. J. Dancy, *Introduction to Contemporary Epistemology* (Oxford: Blackwell, 1985), pp. 156–63.
14. T. Crane, *Elements of Mind* (Oxford: Oxford University Press, 2001).
15. Crane, *Elements of Mind*, p. 137.

16. I. Gordon, *Theories of Visual Perception* (New York: Wiley, 1997), p. 1.
17. I. Rock, "The Concept of Indirect Perception", in *Indirect Perception*, I. Rock (ed.), (Cambridge, MA: MIT Press, 1997).
18. Rock, *Perception* (New York: Scientific American Books, 1995).
19. *Ibid.*, p. 3.
20. *Ibid.*, p. 4.
21. J. Haugeland, *Having Thought* (Cambridge, MA: Harvard University Press, 1998), p. 221.
22. *Ibid.*, pp. 221–2.
23. E. Thompson, *Colour Vision* (London: Routledge, 1995).
24. Indeed I would like to defend a fourth type of theory, one that contains representations but ones that are action-centred.
25. D. Marr, *Vision* (New York: Freeman & Co., 1982).
26. *Ibid.*, p. 4. Austin reference is to J. Austin, *Sense and Sensibilia*, reconstructed by G. J. Warnock (Oxford: Oxford University Press, 1962).
27. I. Hacking, *Representing and Intervening* (Cambridge: Cambridge University Press, 1983).

Chapter 2: A theory of natural realism

1. J. Campbell, *Past, Space and Self* (Cambridge, MA: MIT Press, 1994).
2. *Ibid.*, p. 41.
3. *Ibid.*, p. 47.
4. *Ibid.*, p. 45.
5. *Ibid.*, p. 45.
6. G. Warnock, "Seeing", in *Perceiving, Sensing and Knowing*, R. Swartz (ed.), pp. 49–67 (Berkeley, CA: University of California Press, 1965); F. Dretske, *Seeing and Knowing* (London: Routledge, 1969); K. Mulligan, "Perception", in *The Cambridge Companion to Husserl*, B. Smith & D. Woodruffe-Smith (eds), pp. 168–238 (Cambridge: Cambridge University Press, 1995), esp. pp. 170–74; C. Landesman, *The Eye and Mind* (Dordrecht: Kluwer, 1993).
7. Dretske, *Seeing and Knowing*, p. 29.
8. *Ibid.*, pp. 6–9.
9. Landesman, *The Eye and Mind*.
10. *Ibid.*, p. 3.
11. See also C. W. K. Mundle, *Perception: Facts and Theories* (Oxford: Oxford University Press, 1971).
12. Landesman, *The Eye and Mind*, p. 3.

Chapter 3: Theories of perceptual experiences

1. For further support, see S. Zeki & A. Bartels, "Towards a Theory of Visual Consciousness", *Consciousness and Cognition* 8 (1999): pp. 225–59.
2. G. Ryle, "Sensation", in Swartz, *Perception, Seeing and Knowing*, pp. 187–203. The quote is from p. 202.
3. P. M. S. Hacker, *Appearances and Reality* (Oxford: Blackwell, 1987).
4. Hacker, *Appearances and Reality*, p. 63.
5. *Ibid.*, p. 62.
6. *Ibid.*, p. 223.

7. T. Reid, *Essays on the Intellectual Powers of Man*, vol. II (Edinburgh and London, 1785), chs 16 & 17.
8. H. H. Price, *Perception*, p. 145.
9. *Ibid.*, p. 151.
10. C. D. Broad, *Mind and its Place in Nature* (London: Routledge and Kegan Paul, 1925), pp. 141–2.
11. *Ibid.*, p. 142.
12. *Ibid.*, p. 154.
13. I am concentrating here on Broad, as he is a central figure and because it is helpful to consider a specific thinker.
14. J. McDowell, *Mind and World* (Cambridge, MA: Harvard University Press, 1994), pp. 48–54.
15. P. F. Strawson, *Analysis and Metaphysics* (Oxford: Oxford University Press, 1992), p. 62.
16. McDowell, *Mind and World*, pp. 48–9.
17. These philosophers belong to a tradition with a distinguished pedigree, one to which Kant also belongs.
18. A. Clark, *A Theory of Sentience* (Oxford: Oxford University Press, 2000).
19. *Ibid.*, p. 78.
20. This represents one account that Evans sets out. There may be more than one.

Chapter 4: Representationalism: representations as natural signs

1. A. Kenny, *Aquinas on Mind* (London: Routledge, 1993), p. 35.
2. G. Evans, *Varieties of Reference* (Oxford: Clarendon Press, 1982), pp. 122–3.
3. T. Burge, "Cartesian Error and the Objectivity of Perception", in *Subject, Thought and Content*, P. Pettit & J. McDowell (eds), pp. 117–36 (Oxford, Clarendon Press, 1986), p. 125.
4. *Ibid.*, p. 127.
5. *Ibid.*, p. 127.
6. B. Maund, "The Representative Theory of Perception", *Canadian Journal of Philosophy* 5 (1975): pp. 41–55; E. J. Lowe, "What do We See Directly?", *American Philosophical Quarterly* 23 (1986): pp. 277–85; E. Wright (1990) "New Representationalism", *Journal for the Theory of Social Behaviour* 20 (1990): pp. 65–92.
7. See Evans, *Varieties of Reference*, p. 143.
8. *Ibid.*, p. 72.
9. *Ibid.*, p. 144.
10. *Ibid.*, p. 155.
11. J. McDowell, "Singular Thought and Inner Space", in Pettit & McDowell, *Subject, Thought and Context*, pp. 137–68.
12. *Ibid.*, p. 140.
13. *Ibid.*, p. 142.
14. J. Fetzer, *Philosophy and Cognitive Science* (New York: Paragon, 1991), pp. 64–5.
15. One can never be sure.
16. One way, and perhaps the best way, of thinking of these representations is to think of them as consisting of quality-instances or tropes that are natural signs for the objects in question.
17. M. Perkins, *Sensing the World* (Indianapolis, IN: Hackett, 1983).

18. *Ibid.*, p. 5.
19. B. Maund, *Colours: Their Nature and Representation* (Cambridge: Cambridge University Press, 1995).
20. Evans, *Varieties of Reference*, p. 331.
21. I leave open the possibility that there may be some forms of perception, for example, kinaesthetic perception, that do not contain sensory components. The representative theory would not apply to such perception.
22. See H. Putnam, "Sense, Nonsense, and the Senses: An Inquiry into the Powers of the Human Mind", The Dewey Lectures, *The Journal of Philosophy* XCI (1994): pp. 445–517.

Chapter 5: Natural realism: Putnam, Austin and Heidegger

1. There have been some historical representationalists who have thought of the intermediaries as brain processes. My understanding of this position is that the brain processes are thought of as having phenomenal character. I take such a theory to be either a double aspect theory or a property-dualist theory.
2. C. W. K. Mundle, *Perception: Facts and Theories* (Oxford: Oxford University Press, 1971); J. Harrison, *Essays on Metaphysics and the Theory of Knowledge*, vol. II (Aldershot: Avebury, 1996); H. Robinson, *Perception* (London: Routledge, 1994).
3. E. J. Lowe, "Perception: A Causal Representative Thesis", in *New Representationalisms*, E. Wright (ed.), pp. 136–52 (Aldershot: Avebury, 1993) and Lowe, "What Do We See Directly?"; F. Jackson, *Perception* (Cambridge: Cambridge University Press, 1977); E. Wright, "The Irony of Perception", in Wright, *New Representationalisms*, pp. 176–201; Perkins, *Sensing the World*.
4. Putnam, "Sense, Nonsense, and the Senses".
5. *Ibid.*, p. 454.
6. *Ibid.*, p. 455.
7. Austin, *Sense and Sensibilia*, p. 4.
8. *Ibid.*, p. 2.
9. *Ibid.*, pp. 27–8, 45–8.
10. For Price, unlike Ayer, "sense-datum" is defined in such a way that it is an open question whether a physical object is a sense-datum.
11. For a critical assessment of Austin's project and its execution, see Mundle, *Perception*, esp. pp. 154–6.
12. *Ibid.*, pp. 154–6.
13. Austin, *Sense and Sensibilia*, pp. 90–92.
14. For further support, see Harrison, *Essays on Metaphysics*, pp. 31–6.
15. Austin, *Sense and Sensibilia*, p. 470.
16. See notes 2 and 3.
17. Putnam, "Sense, Nonsense, and the Senses", pp. 471–2.
18. Austin, *Sense and Sensibilia*, p. 49.
19. Putnam, "Sense, Nonsense, and the Senses", pp. 474–5.
20. Austin, *Sense and Sensibilia*, p. 29.
21. M. Burnyeat, "Conflicting Appearances".
22. N. Pastore, *Selective History of Theories of Visual Perception: 1650–1950* (Oxford: Oxford University Press, 1971), p. 12.
23. J. M. Darley, S. Gluchsberg, L. J. Kamin & R. A. Kuchla, *Psychology*

(Englewood-Cliffs, NJ: Prentice-Hall, 1984), p. 107.
24. M. Heidegger, *An Introduction to Metaphysics*, R. Manheim (trans.) (New Haven, CT: Yale University Press, 1959), pp. 98–107.

Chapter 6: Perception: the argument from illusion

1. Austin, *Sense and Sensibilia*, p. 2.
2. G. Harman, "The Intrinsic Quality of Experience", in *The Nature of Consciousness*, N. Block, O. Flanagan & G. Guzeldere (eds), pp. 663–75 (Cambridge, MA: MIT Press, 1997), p. 665.
3. *Ibid.*, p. 665.
4. C. D. Broad, *Scientific Thought*, p. 237.
5. F. Dretske, *Seeing and Knowing*, pp. 62–75.
6. *Ibid.*, p. 65.
7. Dretske, *Seeing and Knowing*, p. 62.
8. *Ibid.*
9. *Ibid.*
10. Price, *Perception*, p. 19.
11. C. D. Broad, *Scientific Thought*, pp. 239–54.
12. There is some dispute among scholars as to which philosophers held the claim, for example, there is dispute on Locke, but even so, Robinson is clearly correct.
13. Robinson, *Perception*, pp. 1–2.
14. *Ibid.*, p. 151.
15. *Ibid.*, pp. 57–8.
16. *Ibid.*, p. 32.
17. *Ibid.*, Ch. 4 and Maund, *Colours*, Ch. 9.

Chapter 7: The phenomenal and phenomenological senses of "looks"

1. Rock, *Perception*, p. 5.
2. See Rock, *Perception*, Ch. 9, p. 221.
3. Jackson, *Perception*, Ch. 2; R. M. Chisholm, *Perceiving* (Ithaca, NY: Cornell University Press, 1954), Ch. 4.
4. A. Quinton, "The Problem of Perception", in Swartz, *Perceiving, Sensing and Knowing*, p. 506.
5. *Ibid.*, p. 507.
6. Evans, *Varieties of Reference*, pp. 227–8.
7. These philosophers include Dennett, Dretske, Tye, Armstrong and Hacker.
8. J. Annas & J. Barnes, *The Modes of Scepticism* (Cambridge: Cambridge University Press, 1985), p. 24.
9. *Ibid.*, pp. 23–4.
10. Jackson, *Perception*, p. 30.
11. Jackson refers to the discussion of the epistemic use by Quinton in "The Problem of Perception", p. 504.
12. Jackson, *Perception*, p. 180.
13. Harman, "The Intrinsic Quality of Experience", p. 667.
14. Quinton, "The Problem of Perception", pp. 504–5.
15. Broad, *Scientific Thought*, pp. 236–7.

Chapter 8: Types of perceptual content

1. E. J. Lowe, *Subjects of Experience* (Cambridge: Cambridge University Press, 1996), pp. 91–139.
2. C. McGinn, "Consciousness and Content", in Block *et al.*, *The Nature of Consciousness*, pp. 295–307.
3. *Ibid.*, p. 298.
4. Lowe, *Subjects of Experience*, p. 139.
5. M. Davies, "Externalism and Experience", in Block *et al.*, *The Nature of Consciousness*, pp. 309–27.
6. *Ibid.*, p. 309.
7. *Ibid.*, p. 310.
8. Strawson, *Analysis and Metaphysics*, p. 62.
9. F. Dretske, *Naturalizing the Mind* (Cambridge, MA: MIT Press, 1995).
10. *Ibid.*, p. 11.
11. See T. Crane, *The Mechanical Mind* (Harmondsworth: Penguin, 1995), pp. 181–5, for a discussion of the claim that success is important to representation.
12. See J. Lennox, "Philosophy of Biology", in *Introduction to the Philosophy of Science: A Text,* Department of History and Philosophy of Science, University of Pittsburgh, 269–309 (Englewood Cliffs, NJ: Prentice Hall, 1992).
13. Lowe, *Subjects of Experience*, p. 101.
14. I am happy to concede that one can only do so against the background of certain conventions but it is still the case that the actual tune itself is a component of what was said.
15. N. Goodman, *Languages of Art*, 2nd edn (Indianapolis, IN: Hackett, 1976), pp. 52–67; N. Goodman & C. Z. Elgin, *Reconceptions in Philosophy and Other Arts and Sciences* (London: Routledge, 1988), pp. 19–23.

Chapter 9: The representationalist–intentionalist thesis

1. R. G. Millikan, "Perceptual Content and Fregean Myth", *Mind* 100 (1991): pp. 439–59.
2. G. Evans, "Molyneux's Question", in *Collected Papers*, 364–99 (Oxford: Clarendon Press, 1985), p. 385.
3. See Lowe, *Subjects of Experience*, p. 112.
4. Millikan, "Perceptual Content", p. 440.
5. Evans, "Molyneux's Question", p. 397.
6. Millikan, "Perceptual Content", p. 441.
7. M. Tye, *Consciousness, Color and Content* (Cambridge, MA: MIT Press, 2000).
8. I have discussed Harman's argument in more detail elsewhere. See Maund, *Colours*, pp. 182–90.
9. Tye, *Consciousness, Color and Content*, p. 45.
10. *Ibid.*, p. 47.
11. *Ibid.*, p. 48.
12. *Ibid.*, p. 46.
13. *Ibid.*, p. 47.
14. Harman, "The Intrinsic Qualities of Experience".
15. *Ibid.*, p. 667.
16. M. Tye, "Visual Qualia and Visual Content", in *The Contents of Experience*, T. Crane (ed.), pp. 158–77 (Cambridge: Cambridge University Press, 1992), p. 160.

17. *Ibid.*
18. *Ibid.*, p. 165.
19. Clark, *A Theory of Sentience*.
20. G. Strawson, "Red and 'red'", *Synthese* 78 (1989): pp. 193–232.
21. Clark, *A Theory of Sentience*, p. 2.
22. Dretske, *Naturalizing the Mind*, pp. 41–4.
23. Clark, *A Theory of Sentience*, p. 10.
24. *Ibid.*, p. 12.
25. *Ibid.*
26. For discussion of the opponent process theory, see C. L. Hardin, *Colour for Philosophers* (Indianapolis, IN: Hackett, 1988), pp. 52–8 and Thompson, *Colour Vision*, pp. 56–79.
27. Clark, *A Theory of Sentience*, p. 12.
28. Hardin, *Colour for Philosophers*, Part III; Thompson, *Colour Vision*, Chs 3 & 4; Maund, *Colours*, Chs 2 & 4.
29. Clark, *A Theory of Sentience*, p. 19.
30. D. Chalmers, *The Conscious Mind* (Oxford: Oxford University Press, 1996), p. 235.
31. Clark, *A Theory of Sentience*, p. 27.
32. *Ibid.*, p. 21.
33. *Ibid.*, p. 74.
34. *Ibid.*, p. 101.
35. See also Maund, *Colours*, especially Ch. 8.

Chapter 10: Adverbialist accounts of perceptual experience

1. T. Reid, *An Inquiry into the Human Mind*, T. Duggan (ed.) (Chicago, IL: University of Chicago Press, 1970), pp. 205–14.
2. McGinn, "Consciousness and Content", p. 298.
3. Strawson, *Analysis and Metaphysics*, p. 62.
4. Or are taken to be committed to this view. There is controversy over whether Reid gets Locke and Berkeley right.
5. See C. Ducasse, "Moore's 'The Refutation of Idealism'", in *The Philosophy of G. E. Moore*, P. Schilpp (ed.), pp. 225–51 (Chicago, IL: Northwestern University Press, 1952).
6. For a discussion of these problems, see R. Chisholm, *Theory of Knowledge* (Englewood Cliffs, NJ: Prentice-Hall, 1966), pp. 93–5.
7. See Perkins, *Sensing the World*, for greater elaboration.
8. For further development of this point see Perkins, *Sensing the World*, pp. 287–93.
9. See J. Mackie, *Problems From Locke* (Oxford: Clarendon Press, 1976), esp. pp. 62–6; Jackson, *Perception*, pp. 138–54; Maund, "The Representative Theory of Perception"; Lowe, *Locke on Human Understanding*, pp. 38–42; Broad, *Scientific Thought*, p. 268.
10. Evans, *Varieties of Reference*, pp. 157–8.
11. McDowell, *Mind and World*, pp. 48–9.
12. A. Millar, *Reasons and Experience* (Oxford: Oxford University Press, 1992), esp. pp. 106–9.
13. McDowell, *Mind and World*, p. 49, n. 6.

, p. 56; Evans, *Varieties of Reference*, p. 229.
Dowell, *Mind and World*, p. 57.
d., p. 58.
17. E. Fales, *A Defence of the Given* (Lanham, MD: Rowman and Littlefield, 1996).

References

Annas, J. & J. Barnes 1985. *The Modes of Scepticism*. Cambridge: Cambridge University Press.

Aristotle 1984. "De Anima". In *The Complete Works of Aristotle*, J. Barnes (ed.), 641–92. Princeton, NJ: Princeton University Press.

Austin, J. 1962. *Sense and Sensibilia*, reconstructed by G. J. Warnock. Oxford: Oxford University Press.

Block, I. 1961. "Truth and Error in Aristotle's Theory of Perception", *Philosophical Quarterly* 11: 1–9.

Block, N., O. Flanagan, G. Guzeldere (eds) 1997. *The Nature of Consciousness*. Cambridge, MA: MIT Press.

Broad, C. D. 1923. *Scientific Thought*. London: Kegan Paul.

Broad, C. D. 1925. *Mind and Its Place in Nature*. London: Routledge and Kegan Paul.

Burge, T. 1986. "Cartesian Error and the Objectivity of Perception". In *Subject, Thought and Context*, P. Pettit & J. McDowell (eds), 117–36. Oxford: Clarendon Press.

Burnyeat, M. 1979. "Conflicting Appearances", *Proceedings of the British Academy* 65: 69–111.

Burnyeat, M. (ed.) 1983. *The Skeptical Tradition*. Berkeley, CA: University of California Press.

Campbell, J. 1994. *Past, Space and Self*. Cambridge, MA: MIT Press.

Chalmers, D. 1996. *The Conscious Mind*. Oxford: Oxford University Press.

Chisholm, R. M. 1954. *Perceiving*. Ithaca, NY: Cornell University Press.

Chisholm, R. M. 1966. *Theory of Knowledge*. Englewood Cliffs, NJ: Prentice-Hall.

Clark, A. 2000. *A Theory of Sentience*. Oxford: Oxford University Press.

Crane, T. (ed.) 1992. *The Contents of Experience*. Cambridge: Cambridge University Press.

Crane, T. 1995. *The Mechanical Mind*. Harmondsworth: Penguin.

Crane, T. 2001. *Elements of Mind*. Oxford: Oxford University Press.

Dancy, J. 1985. *Introduction to Contemporary Epistemology*. Oxford: Blackwell.

Darley, J. M., S. Gluchsberg, L. J. Kamin, R. A. Kuchla (eds) 1984. *Psychology*. Englewood Cliffs, NJ: Prentice-Hall.

Davies, M. 1997. "Externalism and Experience". See Block *et al.* (1997), 309–27.

Dretske, F. 1969. *Seeing and Knowing*. London: Routledge.

Dretske, F. 1995. *Naturalizing the Mind*. Cambridge, MA: MIT Press.

Ducasse, C. 1952. "Moore's 'The Refutation of Idealism'". In *The Philosophy of G. E. Moore*, P. Schilpp (ed.), 225–51. Chicago, IL: Northwestern University Press.

Evans, G. 1982. *Varieties of Reference*. Oxford: Clarendon Press.

Evans, G. 1985. "Molyneux's Question". In *Collected Papers*, G. Evans, 364–99. Oxford: Clarendon Press.

Fales, E. 1996. *A Defence of the Given*. Lanham, MD: Rowman and Littlefield.

Fetzer, J. 1991. *Philosophy and Cognitive Science*. New York: Paragon.

Frede, M. 1983. "Stoics and Skeptics on Clear and Distinct Impressions". In *The Skeptical Tradition,* M. Burnyeat (ed.), 65–94. Berkeley, CA: University of California Press.

Gibson, J. J. 1979. *The Ecological Approach to Visual Perception*. Boston, MA: Houghton Mifflin.

Goodman, N. 1976. *Languages of Art*, 2nd edn. Indianapolis, IN: Hackett.

Goodman, N. & C. Z. Elgin 1988. *Reconception in Philosophy and Other Arts and Sciences*. London: Routledge.

Gordon, I. 1997. *Theories of Visual Perception*. Wiley: New York.

Hacker, P. M. S. 1987. *Appearances and Reality*. Oxford: Blackwell.

Hacking, I. 1983. *Representing and Intervening*. Cambridge: Cambridge University Press.

Hardin, C. L. 1988. *Colour for Philosophers*. Indianapolis, IN: Hackett

Harman, G. 1997. "The Intrinsic Quality of Experience". See Block *et al.* (1997), 663–75.

Harrison, J. 1996. *Essays on Metaphysics and the Theory of Knowledge*, vol. II. Aldershot: Avebury.

Haugeland, J. 1998. *Having Thought*. Cambridge, MA: Harvard University Press.

Heidegger, M. 1959. *An Introduction to Metaphysics*, R. Manheim (trans.). New Haven, CT: Yale University Press.

Jackson, F. 1977. *Perception*. Cambridge: Cambridge University Press.

Kenny, A. 1993. *Aquinas on Mind*. London: Routledge.

Kornblith, H. (ed.) 1985. *Naturalizing Epistemology*. Cambridge, MA: MIT Press.

Landesman, C. 1993. *The Eye and Mind*. Dordrecht: Kluwer.

Lennox, J. 1992. "Philosophy of Biology". In *Introduction to the Philosophy of Science: A Text,* Department of History and Philosophy of Science, University of Pittsburgh, 269–309. Englewood Cliffs, NJ: Prentice Hall.

Lowe, E. J. 1986. "What Do We See Directly?", *American Philosophical Quarterly* **23**: 273–85.

Lowe, E. J. 1993. "Perception: A Causal Representative Thesis". See Wright (1993a), 136–52.

Lowe, E. J. 1995. *Locke on Human Understanding*. London: Routledge.

Lowe, E. J. 1996. *Subjects of Experience*. Cambridge: Cambridge University Press.

Mackie, J. 1976. *Problems from Locke*. Oxford: Clarendon Press.

Marr, D. 1982. *Vision*. New York: Freeman & Co.

Maund, B. 1975. "The Representative Theory of Perception", *Canadian Journal of Philosophy* **5**: 41–55.

Maund, B. 1993. "Representations, Pictures and Resemblance". See Wright (1993a), 45–69.

Maund, B. 1995. *Colours: Their Nature and Representation*. Cambridge: Cambridge University Press.

McDowell, J. 1986. "Singular Thought and Inner Space". In *Subject, Thought and Context*, P. Pettit & J. McDowell (eds), 137–68. Oxford: Clarendon Press.

McDowell, J. 1994. *Mind and World*. Cambridge, MA: Harvard University Press.

McGinn, C. 1983. *The Subjective View*. Oxford: Oxford University Press.

McGinn, C. 1997. "Consciousness and Content". See Block *et al.* (1997), 295–307.

Millar, A. 1992. *Reasons and Experience*. Oxford: Oxford University Press.

Millikan, R. G. 1991. "Perceptual Content and Fregean Myth", *Mind* 100: 439–59.

Mulligan, K. 1995. "Perception". In *The Cambridge Companion to Husserl*, B. Smith & D. Woodruff Smith (eds), 168–238. Cambridge: Cambridge University Press.

Mundle, C. W. K. 1971. *Perception: Facts and Theories*. Oxford: Oxford University Press.

Pastore, N. 1971. *Selective History of Theories of Visual Perception: 1650–1950*. Oxford: Oxford University Press.

Perkins, M. 1983. *Sensing the World*. Indianapolis, IN: Hackett.

Pettit, P. & J. McDowell (eds) 1986. *Subject, Thought and Context*. Oxford: Clarendon Press.

Price, H. H. 1932. *Perception*. London: Methuen.

Putnam, H. 1994. "Sense, Nonsense, and the Senses: An Inquiry into the Powers of the Human Mind", The Dewey Lectures, *The Journal of Philosophy* XCI: 445–517.

Putnam, H. 1999. *The Threefold Cord: Mind, Body, and the World*. New York: Columbia University Press.

Quinton, A. 1965. "The Problem of Perception". See Swartz (1965), 497–526.

Reid, T. 1785. *Essays on the Intellectual Powers of Man*, vol. II. Edinburgh and London.

Reid, T. 1970. *An Inquiry into the Human Mind*, T. Duggan (ed.). Chicago, IL: University of Chicago Press.

Robinson, H. 1994. *Perception*. London: Routledge.

Rock, I. 1995. *Perception*. New York: Scientific American Books.

Rock, I. 1997. "The Concept of Indirect Perception". In *Indirect Perception*, I. Rock (ed.), 5–15. Cambridge, MA: MIT Press.

Ryle, G. 1965. "Sensation". See Swartz (1965), 187–203.

Schilpp, P. (ed.) 1952. *The Philosophy of G. E. Moore*. Chicago, IL: Northwestern University Press.

Smith, B. & D. Woodruff Smith (eds) 1995. *The Cambridge Companion to Husserl*. Cambridge: Cambridge University Press.

Strawson, G. 1989. "Red and 'red'", *Synthese* 78: 193–232.

Strawson, P. F. 1992. *Analysis and Metaphysics*. Oxford: Oxford University Press.

Swartz, R. J. (ed.) 1965. *Perceiving, Sensing and Knowing*. New York: Doubleday Anchor.

Thompson, E. 1995. *Colour Vision*. London: Routledge.

Tye, M. 1992. "Visual Qualia and Visual Content". In *The Contents of Experience*, T. Crane (ed.), 158–77. Cambridge: Cambridge University Press.

Tye, M. 2000. *Consciousness, Color and Content*. Cambridge, MA: MIT Press.

Warnock, G. 1965. "Seeing". See Swartz (1965), 49–67.

Wright, E. 1990. "New Representationalism", *Journal for the Theory of Social Behaviour* 20: 65–92.

Wright, E. (ed.) 1993a. *New Representationalisms*. Aldershot: Avebury.

Wright, E. 1993b. "The Irony of Perception". See Wright (1993a), 176–201.

Yolton, J. 1984. *Perceptual Acquaintance from Descartes to Reid*. Minneapolis, MN: University of Minnesota Press.

Zeki, S. & A. Bartels 1999. "Towards a Theory of Visual Consciousness", *Consciousness and Cognition* 8: 225–59.

Index